MW00654646

The Philosophy of Rabbi Shalom Ber Schneersohn

Language, Gender and Mysticism

Reuven Leigh

BLOOMSBURY ACADEMIC
LONDON • NEW YORK • OXFORD • NEW DELHI • SYDNEY

BLOOMSBURY ACADEMIC
Bloomsbury Publishing Plc
50 Bedford Square, London, WC1B 3DP, UK
1385 Broadway, New York, NY 10018, USA
29 Earlsfort Terrace, Dublin 2, Ireland

BLOOMSBURY, BLOOMSBURY ACADEMIC and the Diana logo are trademarks
of Bloomsbury Publishing Plc

First published in Great Britain, 2023

Series design by Charlotte Daniels
Cover image: Rabbi Sholom DovBer Schneersohn of Lubavitch,
photographed for a Russian passport at Rostov, 1920 (© Chabad Library /
wikimedia.org / CC BY 4.0)

A catalogue record for this book is available from the British Library.

A catalog record for this book is available from the Library of Congress.

ISBN: HB: 978-1-3503-4119-7
PB: 978-1-3503-4123-4
ePDF: 978-1-3503-4120-3
eBook: 978-1-3503-4121-0

Typeset by Deanta Global Publishing Services, Chennai, India

To find out more about our authors and books visit www.bloomsbury.com and
sign up for our newsletters.

To my wife Rochel and our children Chana, Levi,
Tzemach, Shaina and Rosie

Contents

Preface   viii
Acknowledgements   xii

Introduction   1

1   Background and context   37
2   Language   59
3   Gender   113
4   Mysticism   139

Conclusion   205

Bibliography   213
Index   234

Preface

The central themes and arguments in this book have been adapted from my doctoral research in the Faculty of Divinity at the University of Cambridge on the 1898 discourses of Rabbi Shalom Ber Schneersohn; however, their real genesis goes back considerably further. At a young age I made a life-altering decision to prematurely move away from the typical educational trajectory that was expected of me and entered the seemingly other-worldly system of the *yeshivah*. In addition to extensive and intensive study of the Talmud and its commentaries, my main preoccupation was trying to gain a foothold in the vast and demanding realm of *Habad hasidic* thought. My first encounter with the discourses of 1898 was as a seventeen-year-old student, and while I was intrigued by both their style and content, I lacked the maturity and experience to fully appreciate their importance. However, that would change a couple of years later when I had the privilege of studying under the tutelage of Reb Volf Greenglass at Yeshivat Tomchei Tmimim of Montreal. One day I was invited to his home, and he showed me a small notebook containing his handwritten copy of the discourses of 1898. When the Nazis invaded Poland, Reb Volf was himself a student at the Central Yeshivat Tomchei Tmimim in Otwoczk, a suburb of Warsaw. Together with a group of his fellow students he managed to escape, first to Vilna, then to Shanghai and, eventually, to Montreal. On the night before their escape, he realized that it might be a long time before they reach safety and have access to books from which to study and learn. He thereupon stayed up the whole night copying the discourses of 1898, completing nearly half of them. This notion of a spiritual 'provision for the way' (*tseidah la-derekh*) affected me deeply and inspired me to re-engage with the 1898 discourses, probing them with greater attention and care.

After eight years of *yeshivah* study, which included rabbinic ordination, my wife of less than eight months and I were charged with the task of establishing a Chabad House at the University of Cambridge. I considered it central to my mission to find ways to convey the depth and integrity of *Habad* thought. It became obvious to me that a greater working knowledge of familiar Western philosophical conventions would enable me to communicate more effectively with my audience. This approach was initially tactical; however, over time I developed a greater curiosity as to how these thought traditions could more meaningfully engage with one another. A significant influence in this regard were the works of Emmanuel Levinas. Starting with his *Talmudic Readings* and then moving on to his major works, I discovered for the first time a contemporary philosophy with an orientation and a vocabulary capable of articulating some of the novel insights of *Habad* teachings.

Having abandoned a traditional academic path all those years ago, I now decided that it provided the best platform to explore in greater depth the possible confluences of contemporary philosophy and *Habad* thought. Quickly realizing there were several hurdles to this project, I set about developing a conceptual framework within which my desired discourse could flourish. Concerned how *Habad* thought was too easily pigeonholed as mysticism and rarely if ever considered pertinent even to scholars of Jewish philosophy, I began to write on the relationship of Rabbi Shneur Zalman of Liady, the founding thinker of the *Habad* school, with Jewish philosophy, with a particular emphasis on Maimonides. I also recognized how there were social and academic conventions, some spoken some not, which acted as barriers to the type of uninhibited and unconstrained dialogue I was attempting. This led me to consider more fundamentally the assumed tensions of tradition and modernity, asking pointedly in one essay whether traditional Jewish thinkers of the modern period can be considered modern. While my ultimate goal was to construct the possibility of a new direction in philosophical dialogue, to help assuage some of the scepticism to my research I also felt it necessary to present an example of a thinker in whom *Habad* thought and contemporary philosophy had already converged, not simply as a synthesis but as a confluence of concerns. Such an example would serve as my 'legitimate exception' in the Kierkegaardian sense and make the type of doctoral work I would later undertake much easier. This led me to explore and examine the life and thought of Rabbi Avraham Yehudah Chein (1877–1957) who embodied the type of thinking that transcended the conventional boundaries and binaries of modern thought. As well versed in Habad thought as in Russian literature and existentialist philosophy, Chein's rare, blended thinking did not come at the expense of one for the other. The fruit of much of this earlier research can be found in this book's introduction and provides the framework for the main chapters.

While my entry into the academy has been slightly unconventional, I would like to think that it also provides me with certain critical advantages. My lack of ideological attachment to certain academic conventions, such as disciplinary boundaries, has enabled me to think more freely than is maybe common. By contrast, my extensive exposure to *Habad* thought has helped me appreciate its intellectual rigour and served as a catalyst to probe its relevance to other philosophical systems. I am aware of how my personal and professional situatedness as a *Habad* adherent and representative might affect the sort of research questions I pursue. However, I have benefited immensely from and am extremely grateful for the diverse academic community I am part of in Cambridge, where my ideas are regularly challenged and thereby improved. In truth, none of us are free from a range of natural and nurtured dispositions that can create academic blind spots, and all I can say in response is that my allegiances are open for all to see, and I am always happy to be challenged on the substance of my work. My hope is that this book will inaugurate a new type of philosophical conversation, providing the opening for others to examine further the intellectual contribution and philosophical relevance of Schneersohn in particular, and contemporary rabbinic thought more generally.

Acknowledgements

I would like to acknowledge the team at Bloomsbury Academic who have guided this book project from start to finish, with special thanks to my editor Liza Thompson and her team for all their guidance and advice. Parts of the current book rework material which were originally published in *Tsimtsum and Modernity: Lurianic Heritage in Modern Philosophy and Theology* (Berlin: De Gruyter, 2020) and I gratefully acknowledge the editors and publishers for their permission to include that material here.

My doctoral research, which heavily informs this book, was made possible by a generous studentship from the Polonsky-Coexist Fund in the Faculty of Divinity at the University of Cambridge, and for which I am immensely grateful. I have been fortunate to call Daniel Weiss both a friend and an academic supervisor. Daniel emulates the academic traits of open-mindedness and curiosity that I try to advocate for in this book, and he has gently encouraged me all the way with patience and tolerance, teaching me to both think creatively and write conventionally. I would also like to express my thanks to Robbie Duschinsky, Simon Goldhill, Ed Kessler, Catherine Pickstock and Liba Taub for always being generous with their time and advice. Over the years I have been lucky to draw from their wisdom and benefit from their friendship.

At our Chabad House, we have always strived to cultivate a stimulating and challenging setting for ideas and lives to flourish. I am thankful to George and Pamela Rohr and David and Lara Slager for believing in our project and for generously enabling our activities to flourish. While too many to mention individually, I am thankful for all the students and academics who have graced our unique *Shabbat* dinner table over the years. You tested the limits of my thinking and helped shape many of the contours of the arguments in this book.

I am indebted to my parents for their support and encouragement at critical stages of my life and wish them many more years of good health, to Rabbi Zali and Mrs Deborah Unsdorfer for so expertly facilitating my entry into the world of *Habad* and to Rabbi Yitzchak and Mrs Rivkah Tenenbaum for their extraordinary hospitality and care before, during and after my years as a student in the Central Yeshivat Tomchei Tmimim. I am also forever thankful to Reb Volf Greenglass, of blessed memory, and Reb Itche Meir Gurary for impressing upon me the importance and relevance of *Habad* thought and guiding me in its application. I am eternally grateful for the blessings, support and encouragement I received from the Lubavitcher Rebbe, Rabbi Menachem Mendel Schneerson, which continue to impact my daily life.

This book is dedicated to my wife Rochel and our children Chana, Levi, Tzemach, Shaina and Rosie who are my whole world.

Introduction

It is enthroned in the hearts of kings,
It is an attribute to God himself;
And earthly power doth then show likest God's
When mercy seasons justice

(*The Merchant of Venice*, Act 4, Scene 1)

At first, God thought to create the world with the attribute of
justice. . . . But God saw that the world could not endure, so God
combined the attribute of mercy with it.

(*Genesis Rabbah*, 12:15)

This book will examine some of the philosophical ideas of Rabbi
Shalom Ber Schneersohn (1860–1920)[1] on language, gender and
mysticism in his discourses of 1898, and bring them into discussion
with the postmodern philosophy of Emmanuel Levinas (1905–95),
Jacques Derrida (1930–2004) and Julia Kristeva (1941–).[2] One may
initially wonder why such a discussion would be useful or interesting.
Schneersohn is a relatively unknown and under-researched rabbinic

---

[1] Rabbi Shalom [Dov]Ber Schneersohn is often referred to with an acronym as 'The Rebbe
RaShaB' and within *Habad* circles he is often referred to as 'The Rebbe *Nishmato Eden*
(his soul is in Eden)'. Throughout this book he will be referred to as Schneersohn. For
clarity, references to other members of the Schneersohn family will include first names
or initials.

[2] I am conscious how the term 'postmodern' may be an unsuitable collective term for the
ideas of Levinas, Derrida and Kristeva; however, the term will be used here primarily as
a convenience to outline an argument more succinctly. In the course of the book, it will
become clearer where I see their respective projects merging and diverging from each
other, and ultimately, the usefulness of the term 'postmodern' in this context will be
brought into question.

figure, and outside of the *Habad-Lubavitch* movement that he led, he has so far eluded the attention of most scholars of modern Jewish thought, not to mention scholars of theology and philosophy more generally.[3] However, notwithstanding this initial scepticism, this book will argue that Schneersohn is deserving of scholarly consideration, not merely as an interesting contributor to the field of modern Jewish thought but also as a relevant interlocutor with some of the central concerns of contemporary philosophy, and someone who surprisingly anticipates many prominent dynamics of twentieth-century thought.

Schneersohn was a prolific writer and communicator. He delivered and wrote over 1,000 discourses, developing ideas within the context of the Jewish philosophical and mystical traditions as they had been configured in the thought of his predecessors in the *Habad* school. However, notwithstanding this genealogy of thought, Schneersohn reimagines the broad corpus of *Habad* philosophy and emerges as an original and distinctive thinker in his own right.[4] My primary focus will be on a series of discourses that were written and delivered in the autumn of 1898.[5] A central and dominant theme of these discourses is the disruption of traditional hierarchical binary structures, with a sustained focus on the role of speech in knowledge production and the role of women in reproduction. More broadly, Schneersohn

---

[3]   For example, see companion editions and readers such as Morgan and Gordon (eds.) (2007) and Frank, Leaman and Manekin (eds.) (2000) where there is no mention of Schneersohn or, for that matter, any other traditional and kabbalistically orientated rabbinic thinkers.

[4]   I will discuss later in the book how this reimagining is so thorough that he becomes indispensable to the understanding of the *Habad* movement in the twentieth century and beyond. For example, the series of discourses of 1898 that will be explored in this book should be seen as foundational to the later development of *Habad* thought, especially in the later discourses of Rabbi Menachem Mendel Schneerson (1902–94). It could be argued that the philosophy of outreach and the controversial messianic direction of M. M. Schneerson's thought finds its conceptual origins in the 1898 discourses, such that any attempt at understanding the philosophical underpinnings of the contemporary *Habad* movement requires an investigation of the key elements of the discourses of 1898. See Wolfson (2009b, 210–13) where he makes a similar observation.

[5]   Schneersohn (2011), 1–110.

considers the role of the physical body *vis-à-vis* the soul, and the materiality of existence *vis-à-vis* the spiritual realm. The structure of these pairings is described in terms of provision and reception. In all these instances, he challenges a conventional approach that privileges the role of what he calls the provider (*mashpia*), while at the same time undermining and denigrating the recipient (*mekabel*). Binary pairs of *masphia* and *mekabel*, as instantiated in consciousness and speech, men and women, souls and bodies, are examined, and in each case, Schneersohn points out how the first of the pair (as *mashpia*) is commonly privileged and the second (as *mekabel*) is maligned. To counter this perception, the discourses develop an appreciation of a profundity inherent in receptivity, which aims to undo the historic subordination of the recipient (*mekabel*).

What presents itself as especially significant is the way in which Schneersohn both seeks to disrupt established attitudes to oppositional binaries, by contesting the primacy and privileging of the provider, and still maintains and preserves the positional integrity of the recipient. This new-found appreciation of the recipient in these discourses is not intended to invert the existing hierarchies, thereby recreating the same relationship simply in an inverted pattern, but, rather, to entirely reconsider the dynamic of hierarchical structures. This approach places Schneersohn in contrast to some of the critical reappraisals of hierarchies that have become emblematic of the modern period, which at times in their attempt to reassert the importance of a previously maligned feature, such as speech or women, have sought to afford the underdog the status of the previously dominant feature, thereby resulting in speech assuming the role of giving meaning, or advocating for women to achieve dominance over men. For Schneersohn, the problem does not lie in the notion of hierarchical structures *per se*, but, rather, in the under-appreciated and misunderstood quality of passivity and absence to be found in the recipient. Distinctive to Schneersohn's approach is his attempt to locate in the often-maligned role of the passive recipient, be it in the form of speech, the female or the body, a significance that is not in spite of, or in conflict with, its recipient status, but precisely because of it. Through stressing a profundity in the recipient *qua* recipient, the dynamics between provider and receiver become fundamentally reconfigured, but within the same structure, something I will describe as a reconstruction of binary and dualistic structures. The provider (*mashpia*) is no longer considered to be the primary component; instead, it serves as a means by which to reveal the otherwise hidden qualities of the recipient (*mekabel*). This approach seeks to preserve the recipient role in any given hierarchy, since it is specifically those qualities of passivity and inactivity that indicate its primacy. Consequently, Schneersohn reconstructs the various hierarchical systems in a manner that appreciates the ontological primacy of the recipient (*mekabel*), as well as the indispensable role of the provider (*mashpia*).

Schneersohn's reconsideration of the significance of speech, women and the body will be shown to anticipate some of the significant shifts in the philosophy of language and gender in the twentieth century. The challenging of oppositional binaries, with particular emphasis on language and gender, became a central concern of postmodern philosophy in the second half of the twentieth century. The scholarly literature of this method of analysis often emphasizes its negative and dismantling aspect, while overlooking or ignoring more positive, reconstructive facets that are present, even if less obvious, in postmodern writings.[6] Similarly, the perception of this field of enquiry in popular culture predominately stresses its antagonism towards historically favoured qualities such as meaning and sense.[7]

---

[6] For examples of this trend, see Taylor (1993); Belmonte (2002).
[7] For examples of how this perception is sometimes presented unquestioningly in popular media, see Lodge (1985); Smith (1998).

Consequently, much of the criticism of postmodern thought has been premised on an evaluation which concludes that 'deconstruction' is ultimately unconstructive. This book will argue that when juxtaposing prominent postmodern thinkers with Schneersohn's reconstructive approach, similar reconstructive tendencies become more discernible in their writings, thereby posing a challenge to criticisms of postmodernism as being merely negative and unconstructive. Perhaps surprisingly then, this book will argue that a traditional nineteenth-century rabbinic figure is both a prescient precursor to twentieth-century postmodern ideas and a thinker who offers a valuable framework to better appreciate those ideas. Additionally, this argument will bring into question the pertinence of labels such as 'traditional' and 'postmodern'.

As mentioned, Schneersohn's ideas will be brought into conversation with three central figures of postmodern thought: Emmanuel Levinas, Jacques Derrida and Julia Kristeva. Each of these three thinkers engages in challenging perceptions of an inner meaning that metaphysically precedes outer expression or indication, whether in the context of the said and the saying in Levinas, sense and writing in Derrida or the symbolic and semiotic in Kristeva. In the main chapters of the book I will attempt to show how Levinas's project is broadly aligned with the objectives of Schneersohn in the 1898 discourses, and how these discourses may be viewed as a much earlier iteration of key Levinasian themes such as 'the trace' and 'the saying'. More specifically, I will show how, with the help of Schneersohn, it may be possible to link Levinas's evocation of the kabbalistic idea of *tsimtsum* with his more developed theory of the trace in the saying. Moreover, with the help of Schneersohn, I will contextualize Levinas's controversial ideas on the feminine and the maternal body, and thereby propose a defence from, as well as a challenge to, some of the sustained feminist critique of his work. I will also explore how Derridean deconstruction involves an often overlooked second phase that posits a more positive approach to presence, which is already anticipated in the 1898 discourses. Benefiting from Schneersohn's more explicitly positive approach, which similarly reconstructs an alternative relationship between sense and expression, I will highlight a more constructive aspect of Derrida's work. Additionally, I will consider the similarities between Schneersohn's critique of the privileged provider and Derrida's critique of a phallogocentrism, and how the resultant ideal is the figure of the mother. Furthermore, I will emphasize how Schneersohn foreshadows several of Kristeva's central philosophical contributions. I will explain how Kristeva, in a manner similar to both Levinas and Derrida, seeks to disrupt the traditional hierarchy of signification where meaning and consciousness suppress the semiotic quality of language. Additionally, again in a manner akin to, but possibly in a manner more thorough than Levinas and Derrida, I will show how Kristeva attempts to restore a semblance of continuity in the signification process that retains the objectifying impulse of operating consciousness. As will be explained, Kristeva's more thorough reconstruction of the signifying process than we find in Levinas or Derrida may offer a more meaningful discourse with Schneersohn, and reciprocally provide helpful enhancements to his ideas. Importantly for our present discussion, Kristeva makes explicit the connection between the semiotic aspect of language and the maternal body,[8] which situates her work unambiguously within the same concerns as Schneersohn.

While the primary focus of this work is to establish a purposeful cross-cultural philosophical dialogue between previously isolated systems of thought, I also want to question the assumptions which have enabled that isolation to persist until now. It is to be expected that scholars who operate within the traditional disciplinary

---

[8]   See Kristeva (1986), 163. See also Kristeva (1980), 238.

boundaries of both Jewish studies and philosophy, which have historically excluded traditional rabbinic thinkers from the academic field of philosophy, may find the claim of this book both surprising and disruptive. However, since there is no evidence to suggest that Schneersohn read any of the canonical texts of Western philosophy, he presents an opportunity to question the validity of these disciplinary borders, and how they limit the exploration of philosophically rich rabbinic thinkers of the modern period – that is, to question why it should be surprising that a hasidic rabbinic thinker would share, and even anticipate, later twentieth-century philosophical orientations. To be clear, I am not proposing a new genealogy of ideas in which Schneersohn's thought was drawn upon or appropriated by Jewish philosophers. There is no evidence to suggest that even Emmanuel Levinas, who was familiar with some modern rabbinic texts, was acquainted with Schneersohn's writings.[9] Rather, my claim is that Schneersohn, operating from within an alternative, but not entirely foreign, intellectual tradition than these philosophers, developed a comparable critique of oppositional binary systems.

I will soon argue at greater length that there are several scholarly assumptions, in the fields of both philosophy and Jewish studies, that have operated to exclude traditional rabbinic thinkers from contemporary philosophical discourse. Firstly, the historic exclusion of Jews and Jewish thought from the practice and study of philosophy;

---

[9] On Levinas's familiarity with Rabbi Hayyim of Volozhyn's *Nefesh ha-Hayyim* see Meskin (2000), 98–9. See also Meskin (2007, 220, fn. 13) where he recounts how Levinas requested recommendations of appropriate Jewish texts to study from Gershom Scholem. In addition to *Nefesh ha-Hayyim*, Scholem recommended one of the foundational works of Habad thought, the *Tanya*. While Levinas possessed a *Tanya* in his library and wrote notes in its margins and underlined sections, there is no indication from any of his published works that Levinas wished to directly engage with hasidic thought. In correspondence with the head archivist of the Levinas archive, which remains closed for public viewing, I was informed that the search terms '*Tanya*' and 'Habad' produced no results. Moreover, the 1898 series of discourses was only formally published and widely disseminated in 1976, a number of years after the writings of Levinas under consideration here.

secondly, the exclusion from modern Jewish philosophy of thinkers who live culturally traditional lifestyles; and thirdly, the exclusion from even Jewish philosophy of *kabbalistically* orientated thinkers. Consequently, Schneersohn's Jewishness and preoccupation with Jewish themes, his traditional lifestyle and the *kabbalistic* orientation of his work help explain why until now there may have been a presumption of his irrelevance. To a certain extent, all these assumptions have been individually challenged, such that, for example, the historic exclusion of Jews from academic posts in philosophy departments has to a large degree been overcome. Nevertheless, the legacy of these assumptions remains strongly embedded even in our contemporary intellectual culture, to the extent that it remains surprising to many that there could be a relevant discourse between a thinker such as Schneersohn and philosophical thinkers such as Levinas, Derrida and Kristeva. Although studies of medieval rabbinic figures such as Maimonides and Crescas emphasize and accentuate the philosophical dimension of their works, modern rabbinic thinkers have been predominantly appraised from a historical or sociological perspective. Whereas in recent decades there has been considerable effort to address the exclusion from mainstream philosophical discourse of thinkers on grounds of race or gender, with the publication and promotion of previously ignored black and female philosophers,[10] ignored and overlooked traditional rabbinic philosophers of the modern period have yet to be acknowledged in contemporary philosophical discourse as an excluded category. This book will be among the first to consider and address this lack and encourage further research into Schneersohn as well as other philosophically astute rabbinic thinkers. Hopefully, Schneersohn's disruption of the entrenched binaries of meaning/speech, male/female and body/soul can also aid in the

---

[10] See Tuana (2007) and Outlaw (2007) for overviews on the emergence of new gender- and race-based philosophical trends.

disruption of the often-assumed binary between traditional Judaism and modernity, which stymies the potentially rich intellectual encounter of diverse and creative thinkers.

The structure of the book will be as follows: this introduction will proceed to give an outline of what I consider to be important preparatory information to better appreciate the main chapters of the book. I initially give an overview of my methodological approach and review some alternative approaches in comparable works. I then take a closer look at the historical biases towards thinkers such as Schneersohn, which I mentioned briefly earlier, and suggest ways in which those prejudices might be overcome. At that stage I use the opportunity to review some of the existing literature on *Habad* thought and lay out the different approach in this book. The introduction is followed by a chapter that provides background and context including some personal and intellectual biographical information about Schneersohn. After presenting a general overview of Schneersohn's themes in the discourses of 1898 and their importance, I provide some bibliographical information about the discourses of 1898. Hopefully, these introductory comments will help orient the readers and allow them to proceed to the main chapters unencumbered by certain dominant conventions that have until now facilitated Schneersohn's exclusion. The book's main chapters focus on the three themes that constitute the book's title: language, gender and mysticism. Chapters 2 and 3 on language and gender present Schneersohn's philosophy as presented in the discourses of 1898, after which they are brought into dialogue with Levinas, Derrida and Kristeva. The manner in which the discourses explain the catalytic impact of speech on consciousness and women on men is juxtaposed with similar movements in Levinas, Derrida and Kristeva enabling us to discern areas of convergence as well as divergence. Chapter 4 then draws from these earlier dialogues to present Schneersohn's mystical thought on creation and the purpose of existence. The philosophical discussions on language and gender in the earlier chapters should provide a useful context in which the philosophically trained scholar can more readily access the mystical material. For the conclusion, I will summarize the main themes in the book and discuss their implications for further research.

Methodology

To a certain degree, this book will be an exercise in comparative philosophy, so let me highlight some major approaches commonly employed in comparative philosophy and indicate how I intend to deploy these approaches here most effectively. There is both an *interpretative* and *evaluative* (constructive) component to this book. Terms and concepts from one philosophical tradition will help us understand and interpret another philosophical tradition (interpretive), while at the same time seeking to advance and develop philosophy itself through cross-tradition engagement (evaluative).[11] To date, the potentially beneficial categories and techniques that emerge out of comparative philosophy have yet to be applied to an analysis of modern rabbinic philosophy and its Western European counterpart. The field of comparative philosophy is, in the main, preoccupied with the comparison of Western philosophy with traditions from Asia and Africa. In fact, when choosing which philosophies to compare, there is a stated preference among the theorists of methodologies of comparative philosophy for traditions that have emerged in developmental isolation from each other.[12] Consequently, philosophical traditions that have emerged in relative

---

[11] For helpful definitions of these terms and approaches, see Cline (2013); Garfield (2015); Connolly (2015), 28–45.

[12] See Yu and Bunnin (2001, 296) where they argue for the benefits of such an approach.

geographical proximity with each other, such as Eastern European Jewish thought and Western European philosophy, are not usually considered fruitful territory for the application of a comparative approach.[13] Hence, Schneersohn, as well as many other modern rabbinic figures, might be thought of as too similar to Western thought due to their relative geographical proximity to the West.

Moreover, Schneersohn might be viewed as being included in a so-called Judeo-Christian tradition. The intertwined histories of Judaism and Christianity have at times led to a presumption of similarity, epitomized in the idea of a Judeo-Christian tradition,[14] between Jewish thought and the Christian West. As a result, it is uncommon for traditions of Jewish thought to be considered a relevant subject of enquiry in comparative studies in philosophy. Additionally, the integration to varying degrees of several philosophers of Jewish descent into European philosophy, such as Barukh Spinoza, Moses Mendelssohn, Hermann Cohen and Emmanuel Levinas, has further contributed to a sense that certain Jewish philosophical traditions can be appreciated as naturally compatible variants of the Western tradition. Ordinarily, these features of geographical proximity, historical affinity and cultural integration that pertain to modern Jewish thought might bring into question the applicability of employing a comparative approach to Schneersohn and Western philosophy.

Accordingly, to develop a meaningful dialogue between Schneersohn and modern philosophical thought rests on two contrasting premises: Firstly, that Schneersohn is sufficiently different and distinct from modern European philosophy to render meaningful the observation of his anticipation of its ideas, and

---

[13] There is a similar lack of interest in a comparative approach to Western thought and Russian thought more generally.

[14] For an early critique of the idea of a Judeo-Christian tradition, see Cohen (1969).

secondly, that Schneersohn is sufficiently similar to Levinas, Derrida and Kristeva to validate the importance of his acceptance as a relevant philosophical interlocutor with them. As in all attempts to compare two thought traditions, there will be a tension in managing these two distinctive perspectives. For example, there persists an intellectual and cultural distinctiveness to Schneersohn's thought that I do not intend to subsume within postmodern categories of thought. In fact, the culturally distinctive character of Schneersohn's thought could make him more, not less, suited as a point of encounter with modern Western thought. Consequently, while developing a discourse between Schneersohn and modern philosophy, I will emphasize the ways in which traditional rabbinic thought is a distinctive genre with its own intellectual contribution. Moreover, one of the reasons given by scholars of comparative philosophy for comparing philosophies that are geographically distinct from each other is in order to enhance our awareness of the degree of separateness and initial disconnectedness.[15] In this way, the two thought traditions can more purposefully interact with each other. Similarly, recognizing the distinctiveness of Schneersohn's thought from other European philosophical traditions, notwithstanding his relatively close geographical proximity to those traditions, will enhance the subsequent discourse between them. In a general sense, which I will elaborate on shortly, I will attempt a *fusion of horizons* in the Gadamerian sense, which respects the particularism and otherness of culturally specific traditions, while seeking out the mutually beneficial outcome of their encounter with each other.

In addition to drawing from other more familiar streams of Jewish thought such as *kabbalah* and Jewish philosophy, the discourses of 1898, in common with other *Habad* texts, have their own specific idiomatic structure. As such, the material in its original form is

---

[15] See Yu and Bunim (2001), 296; Connolly (2015), 59–62.

not immediately accessible to the philosophically trained scholar. Therefore, when considering how to present the ideas in the discourses of 1898 in an accessible and relevant fashion, I have considered a number of challenges. In the instances when the task of comparative philosophy is undertaken, examples abound of ways in which Western hermeneutical and philosophical methods are imported into the study of non-Western texts that privilege a distinctively Western interpretive lens. In this piece of research, I hope to avoid the trap of simply comparing Schneersohn's work to an assumed standard that originates in Western texts; likewise, I do not aspire to conclude patronisingly that his ideas merely approximate to Western views and arguments.[16]

In general, the task of conceptual translation, in the sense of transferring a text into a new context, is fraught with danger. The translation is an intermediary between the original and the recipient, and as Schneersohn himself once explained, an intermediary must be neither entirely of the original nor of the recipient in order to be an effective transmitter, but in some way combine them both.[17] Franz Rosenzweig, who undertook together with Martin Buber a new translation of the Bible into German, explained how every act of communication is an act of translation, 'When we speak, we translate from our intention into the understanding we expect in the other . . . . When we hear, we translate words that sound in our ears into our understanding.'[18] In this continuous act of translation it is imperative that neither the 'other possesses our ears or our mouth – in that case translation would be of course unnecessary', and so too it is 'not asked that the translation be either the old original – in which case the hearing people would be superfluous – or a new original – in which case the

[16] For an analysis of such dangers in comparative philosophy, see Garfield (2002), 152.
[17] See Schneersohn (1991), 3.
[18] Buber and Rosenzweig (1994), 47.

speaking people would be annihilated'. It is required to preserve the independence of the translation from the overwhelming presence of the original as well as the reductive demands of the recipient. This challenge is sharply depicted by Friedrich Schleiermacher, (quoted by Rosenzweig), who divided translations into two groups: 'those that leave the writer in peace and move the reader in his direction, and those that leave the reader in peace and move the writer.'[19] Whereas Rosenzweig and Schleiermacher were more specifically referring to linguistic translations, their insights could aptly be applied to cross-cultural conceptual translations as well. Thus, my goal will be to retain a version of the source material that would be familiar and recognizable to 'native' readers of *Habad* thought, while at the same time opening out into the thought categories of the academic field of philosophy.

In certain ways, this work builds upon other attempts at cross-cultural dialogue between rabbinic and modern thought. For example, the approach of literary theorist Susan Handelman follows what comparative philosophy might call a more universalist, rather than a differentialist, method. A universalist approach attempts to identify a common theme across distinct thought traditions, which can sometimes blur the areas of difference. By contrast, a differentialist approach seeks to highlight ways in which thought traditions are distinctive from each other. I would argue that Handelman's attempt to converge and assimilate rabbinic thought and modern literary theory can sometimes result in a partial understanding of each tradition, instead of allowing them to speak to each other in a mutual dialogue. As Handelman readily admits, she has 'extended the term Rabbinic into realms where it is usually not applied' in order to defend her central thesis that 'these [Rabbinic] thought patterns and structures

---

[19] Buber and Rosenzweig (1994), 48.

have been displaced and re-emerge in secular thought'.[20] I contend that this approach can at times overlook important differences between rabbinic thought and the modern non-rabbinic thinkers that Handelman speaks of, such as Freud, Lacan and Derrida. Handelman herself notes that she by no means intends to imply that 'Freud, Lacan, and Derrida are rabbinic simply because some of the same principles resurface in their work'; she does, however, wish to say they are rabbinic because of a general 'understanding of texts, meaning, language, and interpretation'.[21] While Handelman's pioneering work has been a strong influence in the formation of this book, in the dialogical approach I will propose, there will be a greater emphasis on the preservation of distinctive interlocutors.

More specifically in relation to scholarship on *Habad* thought, I have considered two approaches. The first approach tends to describe and define *Habad* thought within the categories of Classical Western and Enlightenment thought categories. In the works of Gershom Scholem and Louis Jacobs, for example, there appears to be a desire to lay out and systemize the *Habad* texts in a manner that ensures they conform with a linear logic natural to Western thought.[22] This approach can, indeed, be helpful when presenting often-obscure texts and ideas to an audience schooled in Western thought; however, instead of being a window into the distinctiveness of *Habad* thought, more often than not it becomes a dominating colonial discourse that strips the original texts of their unique style and presentation.

The second approach employs what could be described as an analogical logic, which draws inspiration from postmodern thought. In general, this approach, most notably employed by Elliot Wolfson,

---

[20] Handelman (1982), xvi.
[21] Handelman (1982), xvii.
[22] See Scholem (1954), 340–1; Jacobs (2006), 64–76. Roman Foxbrunner, as well as Immanuel Schochet and Nissan Mindel, follows this approach. See Foxbrunner (1993); Mindel (1973); Schochet (1995).

tends to pay closer attention to textual elements and significant wordings. In my view, this approach more successfully conveys *Habad* thought in a manner that is readily understood in twentieth-century philosophical categories. Wolfson's approach generally preserves the distinctive terminology and structure of *Habad* thought; however, at times he leaves unexplored the ways in which the *Habad* texts can develop a meaningful dialogue with non-rabbinic thought. For example, his analysis of Schneersohn's conceptualization of the *kabbalistic* concept of the *reshimu* (lit. trace) is entirely without reference to non-rabbinic philosophical thought except for some final undeveloped comments on 'some interesting parallels to contemporary representations of the trace, especially the Levinasian idea of the trace of illeity and the Derridean idea of the arch-trace'.[23] To an extent, I intend to expand upon and develop Wolfson's approach and ensure Schneersohn is able to usefully engage in a dialogue with non-rabbinic thought.

Common to both approaches, however, is an assumption that *Habad* thought is an evolved form of *kabbalistic* mysticism. This assumption, which I will discuss at greater length soon, has meant that studies on *Habad* have been strongly influenced, and have emerged out of, the academic field of Jewish mysticism. It is my contention that this heavy reliance on mystical categories to understand *Habad* works has developed only a partial view of the texts under discussion. I will argue that treating *Habad* thought as a variation of *kabbalah* inhibits our attempts to grasp its ideas and the manner in which they were communicated.

In an attempt to present these discourses so they can serve as both distinctive and relevant interlocutors with modern philosophy, and to

---

[23] Wolfson (2013), 117. In more recent publications, Wolfson has developed an approach that engages *Habad* thought with modern philosophy in a more sustained manner akin to what I am proposing here. See, for example, Wolfson (2016).

overcome some of the methodological shortcomings identified earlier, I have chosen to undertake a systematic reading of the discourses that may be best described as a guided tour. Instead of extracting only what may more obviously appear to be the philosophically relevant material and discussing it within the categories of philosophical thought, I wish to present to the reader the manner in which these ideas are contextually situated and to recommend an approach to reading.[24] Ultimately, if we are to appreciate the complexity of Schneersohn's thought, I contend that it deserves to be read not only in the service of or as an adjunct to other systems of thought, but also as a mode of thinking in its own right. Coming to grips as much as possible with Schneersohn's thought on its own terms will then enable us to more effectively bring it into dialogue with modern philosophy.

This dialogical approach is strongly influenced by the ideas of Russian thinker Mikhail Bakhtin.[25] Bakhtin stresses the need to recognize the diversity and uniqueness of 'languages' while appreciating that there exists a common plane which 'methodologically justifies our juxtaposing them'.[26] That juxtaposition allows for them 'to mutually supplement one another, contradict one another and be interrelated dialogically'.[27] Extending Bakhtin's idea to our present concern, instead of trying to assimilate, contrast or parallel rabbinic thought with other thought traditions as is sometimes practised, this work will endeavour to preserve, to borrow an anthropological term, the 'emic' meaning of Schneersohn's categories, while presenting etic terminology to allow for a meaningful juxtaposition with non-rabbinic

---

[24] Examples of a similar approach to this methodology on *Habad* thought include Steinsaltz (1988) and (2016). I have been particularly influenced by the approach of Morgan (2007) where he takes a body of material that is renowned for its complexity (the works of Emmanuel Levinas) and gradually works his way through the major texts, guiding and advising the reader how best to read the material.

[25] For a helpful presentation of Bakhtin's dialogism, see Holquist (1990).

[26] Bakhtin (1981), 291.

[27] Bakhtin (1981), 292.

thought.[28] This approach will attempt to closely reflect Gadamer's idea of a *fusion of horizons*.[29] That is to say, an important premise of this book is that Schneersohn and his proposed postmodern interlocutors inhabit their own distinctive horizons with all that it entails. It will be specifically through acknowledging the otherness of the other, as Gadamer suggests, that a new horizon borne out of the dialogue between Schneersohn and the postmodernists might emerge.[30] This comparative approach will demonstrate the effectiveness of appreciating modern rabbinic thought as a distinct tradition. Unlike other approaches that I highlighted earlier, in which rabbinic thought is appreciated as either an iteration or, conversely, as the underlying influence of another prominent philosophical school, Schneersohn will be presented here as a distinct and alternative thought tradition. Similarly, I will avoid presenting Levinas, Derrida and Kristeva as quasi-*kabbalists* and allow them to retain their own distinctive voices.[31] Consequently, by not erasing the otherness of Schneersohn, Levinas, Derrida or Kristeva, a purposeful dialogical encounter will hopefully become possible.

Historical biases: The exclusion of Jewishness from philosophy

Let us now consider the historical bias towards Jews and Jewish thought in the study of philosophy mentioned earlier. The self-

---

[28] This approach itself could be identified as rabbinic in the way it expects and respects layers of meaning without the urge to assimilate them in a restrictive way. See Boyarin (2003), 95.

[29] See Gadamer (1975), 302–7.

[30] For an understanding of the implications of this idea in Gadamer, see Taylor (2011).

[31] At the beginning of Chapter 4, I will explain in more detail why I have chosen to not overly emphasize the supposed mystical elements in Levinas's, Derrida's and Kristeva's work and why I think to do so would undermine the objectives in this book.

perception of the field of philosophy has historically maintained its own impartial and universal quest for knowledge. Consequently, the perceived parochial and particularistic nature of Jewish thought has often been presumed as outside the concerns of philosophy. Moreover, this tradition has at times maintained that only European men are capable of arriving at universal truths, and has argued for the specific exclusion of non-whites, Jews and women, as well as many others, on the grounds of inferior intellect.[32] In fact, many of the most influential philosophers of the modern period already theorized the irrelevance of Judaism to philosophical discourse. Kant, for example, regarded Judaism as a form of legalism limited to a particular group of people. This particularistic obedience to laws and statutes based largely on revelation did not accord with Kant's notion of morality, and in his view lacked the ambition to establish universal rational laws to improve moral dispositions.[33] Similarly, Hegel viewed Judaism as primitive. Judaism, as understood by Hegel, insists on God's transcendence and the impossibility of reconciling humanity with God. In his view, Judaism is therefore the antithesis of his development of history as a movement of self-consciousness, since Judaism is unable to offer a dialectical relationship with transcendence.[34] Consequently, the academic field of philosophy has been constituted within a context that excludes Jews and Judaism from participating in the understanding of philosophical problems. This philosophical disposition towards Judaism contributed to the exclusion of Jews from prominent roles in the academy. For example, except for Hermann Cohen, there were no tenured or non-tenured Jewish professors of philosophy anywhere in Germany at the beginning of the twentieth century.[35]

---

[32] On the exclusion of people of colour and women from philosophical discourse, see Yancy (2007), 3–5.
[33] See Kant (1998), 130–4; Rotenstreich (1963), 23–47; Leaman and Nyman (1998), 311–12.
[34] See Hegel (1931), 366–7; Rotenstreich (1963), 48–75; Leaman and Nyman (1998), 312.
[35] See Zank (2000), 79.

More recently, there has been increasing awareness and acceptance that the discipline of philosophy is not necessarily the neutral pursuit of truth as some of its practitioners would have us think. As American philosopher George Yancy has forcefully argued, the philosophical gatekeeper who determines the purity of philosophical borders, 'speaks from an identity that is narrow and fixed, unreceptive to different philosophical voices/identities that merge from different ways of engaging with the world, understanding the world, and being-in-the-world'.[36] This supposedly authoritative voice of philosophy assumes the right to define and delineate alternative, and sometimes contesting, thought traditions within a hierarchy. As Yancy describes, this 'voice is presumed self-grounded and unconditioned . . . it is deemed outside the flux of history, context, multiplicity, and heteroglossia'.[37] Whereas other thought traditions are always qualified by their particularity, the canonical voice of philosophy resists seeing itself as different and particularistic, thereby denying any relation between its philosophical assumptions and its identity as raced, gendered, sexed and classed.[38] While a more accurate description of the academic field of philosophy might acknowledge its origins in Plato and Aristotle, and its development as the specific intellectual tradition of European Christian men, the exclusion of Jewish thought, as well as many other thought traditions, from modern philosophical discourse is a reminder of the persistence of philosophy's status quo.[39]

While I would argue that the persistent exclusion of any thought tradition from the academic study of philosophy is problematic, there is a particular prejudice in the exclusion of Jewish thought that should

---

[36] Yancy (2007), 7.
[37] Yancy (2007), 8.
[38] See Yancy (2007), 6.
[39] This exclusionary practice can lead to a lack of resources in Western philosophy to apprehend certain philosophical concepts that attract greater attention in other thought traditions. See Boyarin (1993), 80; Weiss (2013), 804.

be addressed. For whereas it could be argued that thought traditions that emerged in both historical and geographical isolation from Western philosophy might have only limited points of convergence with the latter, Jewish thought can be situated both geographically and historically within the Western tradition itself. Moreover, the preoccupation in Jewish thought on the contents of the Hebrew Bible, a foundational text in Western culture, offers a valuable alternative model to the particularities of Western traditions.[40] Similarly, the wide-ranging impact of Western philosophy on the development of Jewish thought has resulted in some cases in a convergence of concerns, and offers the possibility of developing an entirely natural discourse between these distinct, yet comparable, thought traditions.

This historical bias and discrimination against Jews has, to a great extent, been overcome in the second half of the twentieth century, where we find many prominent philosophers of Jewish descent and many academic chairs held by Jewish professors. However, this improvement is specifically on ethnic grounds, where Jews are no longer discriminated against in the field of philosophy for their ethnicity. Yet, the practice of a form of philosophy linked to particularly Jewish texts and concepts remains, even to this day, largely outside the parameters of normative philosophical discourse and finds expression mainly in departments of Jewish studies. As is evident in the wide range of guide, companion, reader and introduction volumes to modern philosophy including philosophers of Jewish descent, while rarely if ever including philosophy which is characterized as Jewish. For example, Edmund Husserl, Emmanuel Levinas and Jacques Derrida might be included, while Martin Buber, Joseph Soloveitchik and Emil Fackenheim will typically be excluded.[41] Bearing in mind this

---

[40] See Weiss (2013), 789–90.
[41] For example, see the list of titles in the Cambridge Companions to Philosophy Series in Cherniss and Smith (2018), ii; Jackson and Smith (2008).

exclusionary practice, it becomes clearer why Schneersohn, who as I will soon show is even excluded from the study of Jewish philosophy in Jewish studies scholarship, would be considered irrelevant to, and outside the concerns of, the study of contemporary philosophy.

In addition to the exclusion of Jewish thought from both the academic study of philosophy and philosophy proper, there are further scholarly assumptions about the relationship of tradition with modernity that operate to exclude traditional rabbinic thinkers such as Schneersohn from the study of Jewish philosophy. As we enter the early modern period, Spinoza in his *Theologico-Political Treatise* placed the traditional practice of Judaism in direct opposition with the developments of modernity. He argued that Jewish ritual observances were relevant only in the ancient Israelite kingdom and 'therefore could have relevance only so long as that state survived'.[42] Spinoza's rejection of the relevance of traditional Jewish practice absent Jewish sovereignty challenged the plausibility of the continued existence of a traditional Judaism that included obedience to the laws and rituals in the early modern period. With the advancement of Enlightenment thought, many other thinkers further challenged the purpose of traditional Jewish practice,[43] and in the nineteenth century, with the acquisition of citizenship rights for Jews and all the opportunities that entailed, the challenge to understand the relevance of traditional Judaism became more urgent. The possibility of being equal citizens who were allowed full participation in national affairs supposedly brought with it a crisis of identity:[44] What is the need for Judaism when Jews are no longer required by the state to be defined as Jews?[45]

This perceived crisis of identity, which separated tradition from modernity, brought about a further separation of traditional Jewish

---

[42] Spinoza (2007), 68.
[43] See Mendes-Flohr (1995), 93; Kant (1998), 115; Schleiermacher (1996), 113–14.
[44] See Katz (1986), 94.
[45] See Hertzberg (1968), 360.

thought from the study of modern Jewish thought. These tensions can be better understood in the context of the influential theories of Max Weber, who defined traditional societies as pre-modern societies whose acceptance of tradition as a source of authority is unquestioned.[46] Moreover, for Weber, 'the threshold of modernity may be marked precisely at the moment when the unquestioned legitimacy of a divinely preordained social order began its decline.'[47] Karl Mannheim, who sought to contrast the static nature of traditional societies with modernity's dynamism, defined traditionalism as 'a general psychological attitude which expresses itself in different individuals as a tendency to cling to the past and a fear of innovation.'[48] This model, which views modernization as a transition from traditional societies to modern ones, has been a strong influence on the study of Judaism in the modern period.[49] Thus, the academic field of modern Jewish philosophy, which is broadly excluded from the academic field of philosophy as discussed earlier, in turn excludes traditional rabbinic thinkers. Subsequently, the portrayal of traditional Jews, like Schneersohn, as either remnants of a pre-modern past or as reactionaries to the advances of modernity, has led to their presumed irrelevance to modern Jewish thought.

These influential theories of modernization, however, have been extensively challenged and critiqued. Even within the specific empirical example of modernization in Western Europe, it would be inaccurate to suggest that there was a uniform process of secularization resulting in the decline of tradition. Swedish social scientist Bjorn Wittrock argues that as in all periods of fundamental cultural and institutional crystallization, one of the foci of the modern period was

[46] See Weber (1964), 341.
[47] Faubion (1993), 113.
[48] Mannheim (1971), 157.
[49] See Katz (1986), 3–17; Silber (1992), 24–5; Halbertal (2002). For notable exceptions, see Ravitzky (2007) and Sagi (2006).

a reflection of the limits of personal finite existence, which brought a discourse on ways to 'bridge the chasm between the mundane and the transcendental order'.[50] In some instances, this reflection involved a rejection of that chasm and the secularization of a society; however, in many other instances, there was not a determined anti-traditional stance and it would be misleading 'to describe the formation of modernity as involving a uniform process of secularization'.[51] Defining modernity as the condition of a critical reflection on the relationship between the mundane and the transcendental does not assume an inherent binary between tradition and modernity as the sole conclusion of that reflection, and acknowledges the possibility of 'multiple modernities'. This suggests that a 'deep seated epistemic transformation'[52] is the underlying cause of the various forms of modernization, and that transformation also finds expression *within* traditions. As the Israeli sociologist Shmuel Noah Eisenstadt points out, 'one of the most important implications of the term "multiple modernities" is that modernity and Westernization are not identical: Western patterns of modernity are not the only "authentic" modernities'.[53] Rejecting attempts to monopolize the process of modernization as a Western and Central European phenomenon allows room for an enquiry into multiple authentic articulations of modernity, many of which will not depend on the decline of tradition. Eisenstadt's observation provides an alternative framework from which to understand the modernization of traditional Judaism, a process no longer restricted to a focus on a binary between tradition and modernity and on the degree to which a thinker explicitly engages with the concerns of Enlightenment thought. Through recognizing broader categories and markers of modernization such

---

[50] Wittrock (2000), 56.
[51] Wittrock (2000), 57.
[52] Wittrock (2000), 41.
[53] Eisenstadt (2000), 1.

as autonomy, subjectivity and experience, it becomes possible to discern shifts in some traditional thought systems and recognize them as modernizing tendencies.[54] Consequently, recognizing the traditional lifestyle of Schneersohn, which appeared to eschew the typical outward signs of modernization, need not inherently be seen as a case for his exclusion from a scholarly philosophical discourse. To be clear, the positive argument for Schneersohn's relevance will be made and demonstrated in the later analysis; in the meantime, the present argument is to remove the scholarly obstacles that presume his irrelevance, and thereby allow the positive argument in the later chapters to proceed unencumbered.

Another pertinent feature of Eisenstadt's analysis of modernity is his outline of the dialectics of transcendence and immanence, which gradually replaces static dualisms and paves the way towards modernity which is seen as 'the bridging of the tension between the transcendental and the mundane order'.[55] According to Eisenstadt, the combination of the transcendent and the mundane will sometimes develop as an opposition to the simple dimension of everyday life, putting a pressure on the mundane this-worldly reality, by demanding that it conforms to the transcendental ideal. Another option, and this is where a potential modernity actualizes itself, is when this demand takes a dialectical form, that is, when it does not content itself with condemnation of the fallen world, but sees in the material reality a chance to develop according to the transcendental ideal. Eisenstadt's elaboration delivers a metaphysical definition of modernity as an attempt to decrease the tension between transcendence and immanence by lifting the latter to the status of the former, but in such a manner that it does not eliminate itself. According to this

---

[54] See Rosati and Stoeckl (2012) for a range of examples of how religious traditions can effectively mobilize, from within their own semantic universe, comparably modern ideas.
[55] Eisenstadt (2003), 252.

metaphysical definition, which does not restrict modernization to Western culture alone, modernity occurs whenever there appears an attempt to transform the immanent reality in accordance with a transcendent ideal. Accordingly, this theoretical model could help explain why all these thinkers (Schneersohn, Levinas, Kristeva, and Derrida), while participating in their different, yet overlapping, variants of modernity would question the statism of binary oppositions and develop, instead, more dialectical and dynamic solutions. When the tension between transcendence and immanence is presented in a less dualistic and more dialectical manner, modernity, in whichever form it takes, aims at a thorough working-through of the worldly ontological status quo.[56]

A further scholarly obstacle to the development of a philosophical discourse between traditional and non-traditional thinkers is the delineation of philosophy and *kabbalah* as two divergent strands of Jewish thought. Together with the perception of modernity as the antithesis of traditionalism, this delineation has created a scholarly environment that is surprised at the possibility of philosophical relevance among *kabbalistically* orientated thinkers. To better understand why a traditional *kabbalistically* orientated thinker like Schneersohn might be excluded from a modern philosophical discourse, it will be helpful to briefly consider the prevailing academic narrative regarding the development of *kabbalah* and Jewish philosophy.

The portrayal of the intellectual encounter of Judaism and classic philosophical thought stemming from Plato and Aristotle, as reflected in both the sources within Jewish tradition and contemporary scholarship on Judaism and philosophy, places considerable emphasis on a presumed tension that is axiomatic to that encounter.[57] During

---

[56] Eisenstadt (2003), 249–64.
[57] For a good overview of scholarship on Judaism and its encounter with Hellenism in antiquity, see Levine (1998), 3–33.

the initial Jewish encounter with non-Jewish philosophy during the Greek reign in the Second Temple period, Jews began acquiring Greek names and the Bible was translated into Greek. This form of cultural assimilation led to a number of attempts by the rabbis to restrict and control the dominance of Greek language and culture among Jews; however, these attempts displayed a large degree of uncertainty and inconsistency. For example, a Talmudic opinion forbade the teaching of Greek wisdom to one's children, yet it remained permissible to teach oneself, while a more stringent opinion prohibited the learning of Greek language unless it was needed for diplomacy. These early rabbinic sources from late antiquity seem to give credence to a narrative of separateness and difference that would influence later scholarship. At the same time, we can learn from these attempts at restricting Greek influence a tacit recognition that a blanket ban was probably unachievable, due to the already successful expansion of Greek culture into Jewish culture. Although there was a degree of consensus among the later medieval rabbinic authorities that elements of the Greek cultural inheritance required legislation, there was disagreement regarding which aspects of that inheritance should be avoided. The plurality of views already evident in late antiquity served the needs of later medieval rabbinic leaders, who found precedents for their own attitudes towards Greek culture and thought.[58]

One key theological challenge that Greek philosophy posed to medieval Jewish thinkers was the method of attaining truth.[59] Jewish thinkers in the medieval period understood Greek philosophy to be arguing that truth could be attained through the unaided exercise of human reason, as opposed to prophetic revelation.[60] Among the Jewish thinkers who engaged positively with philosophy, there

---

[58] See Zevin (1997, 67–8) for a useful compilation of the plurality of views.
[59] See Tirosh-Samuelson (2003), 221.
[60] See Davidson (1974), 53.

developed a wide spectrum of opinions on how to balance and manage this challenge; however, the common denominator among these medieval thinkers would be their acceptance, to some degree, of the ability to attain truth through rational thought.[61] At the same time, there were other thinkers who rejected the power of unaided rational thought as a means of attaining truth and, instead, affirmed the primacy of revelation to understand scripture and Jewish life.[62] While these thinkers insisted on the importance and necessity of a revelatory tradition, they also drew heavily upon philosophical ideas. Consequently, there emerged two main categories of Jewish medieval thought: Jewish rationalist philosophy that accepted truths were accessible by reason without tradition, and *kabbalistic* thought, which while drawing heavily upon Neoplatonic philosophical ideas,[63] maintained an insistence on the necessity of revelatory prophetic tradition.

The *kabbalistic* thinkers developed their own solutions to many of the same questions that were preoccupying the rationalist philosophers. The area of starkest contrast between the schools was in the interpretation of scripture. Both groups perceived the scriptures as containing an esoteric as well as an exoteric explanation; according to the rationalist philosophers, this hidden, secretive level was the truths of philosophy, the truths of the metaphysics or ethics of Aristotle, or Alfarabi or Avicenna – truths, in other words, that were capable of being discovered outside the sphere of religion.[64] Gershom Scholem explains, however, that according to the *kabbalistic* thinkers, the scriptures are not allegories of philosophical truths but, rather, symbols that are an expressible representation of something which

---

[61] See Davidson (1974), 54; Kellner (1986), 207.
[62] See Zevin (1997), 68.
[63] See Idel (1988), 5; 42; 136.
[64] See Scholem (1954), 26.

lies beyond the sphere of expression and communication.[65] Although there were many strands within *kabbalah*, it represented a method of engagement with some of the same questions troubling the rationalist philosophers that did not place a primacy on reason or intellect, but on the authenticity and holiness of revelation. Throughout this period there were also many proponents of both traditions who did not perceive the two traditions as being in conflict, and who developed ideas that attempted to harmonize them; these included *kabbalists* such as Abraham Abulafia and philosophers such as Moses Narboni.[66] However, there remained a large gulf between many of the main exponents of these two camps, which led to considerable conflict, involving book burnings and excommunications by those opposed to rationalist philosophy, creating a hostile environment for philosophical study in many Jewish communities.[67] Subsequently, with the approach of the early modern period the prevailing intellectual culture of Eastern European traditional Jewry was the tradition of the *kabbalah*, and the tradition of Jewish rationalist philosophy was no longer the dominant mode of thought.[68]

Academic interest and scholarly research of *kabbalah* emerged in the nineteenth-century school of *Wissenschaft des Judentums*.

---

[65] See Scholem (1954), 27.

[66] On these two philosophers, see Wolfson (2000); Altmann (2016).

[67] See Silver (1965), 16. For an explicit example of medieval hostility towards philosophical thought, see Ibn Aderet (1657), 150.

[68] See Scholem (1954), 341; Tirosh-Samuelson (2003), 219. The attitude of traditional Jews towards Jewish philosophy in eighteenth-century Eastern Europe is complex. Dinstag (1964, 307) argues that the *hasidim*, in contrast to the earlier *kabbalists*, considered Maimonides a useful ally in the dissemination of their ideas. He identifies a number of examples where early hasidic leaders quoted Maimonides's *The Guide for the Perplexed* and concludes that there was a rather benign attitude towards Maimonideanism. Although such quotes do suggest a familiarity with *The Guide*, the relatively few examples imply a rather more limited relationship. More significantly, the majority of his examples are cases where the authors conceal their source and do not openly identify with Maimonides. This might suggest, in fact, a more hostile environment towards *The Guide*, which precluded an open acceptance of Maimonidean thought. A definitely hostile stance was adopted by the Vilna Gaon, who expressed extreme opposition to the philosophical thinking of Maimonides, and even suggests that he erred in his legal codes due to the corruption of philosophy. See Eliach (2002); Nadler (2007), 231–56.

While there was not the universally negative evaluation of *kabbalah* as suggested by Scholem,[69] there were nevertheless plenty of anti-*kabbalistic* critiques. As Moshe Idel notes, these negative critiques were not merely academic, but were also prompted by religious and cultural motivations. He suggests how recent developments in Jewish mysticism in the form of *Sabbateanism*, as well as Eastern European *Hasidism*, may well have aroused these sharp reactions.[70] By contrast, Gershom Scholem, the towering figure of twentieth-century academic scholarship on Jewish mysticism, presented a determinedly positive evaluation of *kabbalah*, and regarded it as a vital part of Judaism. The predominantly rationalistic bias of the nineteenth-century *Wissenschaft* scholars inspired a largely negative evaluation of *kabbalah*, and the 'religious anarchism' of Scholem appears to have inspired the opposite.[71] However, while Scholem and his *Wissenschaft* predecessors may have disagreed on the value of *kabbalah*, there was a general consensus concerning the distinctiveness of *kabbalah* from a rationalistic mode of Jewish thought.[72]

As I have argued elsewhere, the persistence of this perceived incongruity between philosophy and *kabbalah* is problematic when considering the considerable influence of *kabbalistic* thought on the development of Western European philosophy.[73] Jewish *kabbalistic* thought entered into the consciousness of European philosophers primarily through the works of renaissance Christian kabbalists, who collated and translated a variety of *kabbalistic* texts into Latin. Many of these *kabbalists* were indebted to the writings of Abraham

---

[69] See Scholem (1974), 307–9.

[70] See Idel (1998), 9–10.

[71] See Meyer (1967), 167; Biale (1979), 2–3.

[72] See Idel (1988), 11; 284 fn. 80, where he highlights how Scholem would overemphasize the differences between *kabbalah* and philosophy.

[73] Leigh (2021), 86. For one example, see Schulte (2014) and Bielik-Robson and Weiss (2021) where the influence of the *kabbalistic* idea of the *tsimtsum* is identified in a wide range of modern philosophical works.

Cohen de Herrera, which offered an important bridge between the world of *kabbalah* and European philosophy.[74] Christian Knorr von Rosenroth's *Kabbalah Denudata*, first printed in 1677, provided a collection and translation of the largest number of *kabbalistic* texts available to the Latin-reading public until the nineteenth century and included Herrera's *Sha'ar ha-Shamayim*. Von Rosenroth's close friend and collaborator Francis Mercury van Helmont travelled extensively, and with evangelical zeal introduced the *kabbalah* to influential figures such as Gottfried Leibniz[75] as well as the Cambridge Platonists Henry More and Anne Conway.[76] In the eighteenth and nineteenth centuries, works by Friedrich Oetinger[77] and Franz Molitor[78] provided further access to *kabbalistic* texts and ideas, and are believed to have had a significant influence on Friedrich Schelling.[79] This brief sampling of *kabbalistic* interaction with Western philosophy serves to weaken the assumption that *kabbalistic* thought should be viewed as being inherently incommensurable with Western philosophy.

The impact of segregating the study of philosophy and *kabbalah* poses a particular difficulty in relation to the *Habad* school of hasidic thought, which may be seen as sitting awkwardly between the two fields. Chroniclers of *Hasidism* have always seen *Habad* as an 'unusual' or 'aberrant' school within *Hasidism*, primarily due to its rationalistic approach.[80] While clearly conceiving of *Habad* as a variation of the *kabbalah*, Scholem nevertheless hints at the tension to be found in *Habad* thought. He writes: 'What gives the writings of the Habad school their distinctive feature is that striking mixture of enthusiastic worship of God and pantheistic, or rather acosmistic,

---

See Cohen de Hererra; Krabbenhoft (trans.) (2002). See also, Beltran (2016).

[75] On Leibniz and his awareness of *kabbalah*, see Coudert (1995).

[76] On the *kabbalistic* influences on More and Conway, see Hutton (1999).

[77] See Oetinger; Ohly (ed.) (1979).

[78] See Molitor (1834). See also, Koch (2006).

[79] See Goodman-Thau, Mattenklott and Schulte (1994).

[80] See Schatz-Uffenheimer (1993), 263.

interpretation of the universe on the one hand, and intense preoccupation with the human mind and its impulses on the other.'[81] This 'intense preoccupation' on the psychological make-up of human beings, placed *Habad*, at least for Scholem, on the margins between the mystically orientated *kabbalah* and the then emerging fixation on the self in European Enlightenment thought. Following Scholem, scholars of Jewish mysticism who have studied *Habad*, while noting the alternative nature of *Habad* thought, maintain a primary focus on its historical and sociological importance, and often underplay its potential philosophical relevance.

While many of the studies on *Habad* have focused either on the movement's founder and its early formation or on its contemporary iteration, with minimal interest shown to the intervening years which cover Schneersohn's lifetime, they still highlight the intellectual conventions that have shaped *Habad* scholarship. For example, Rivkah Schatz-Uffenheimer explains how the *Habad* founder, Rabbi Shneur Zalman of Liady, deviated sharply from the views of his teacher, Rabbi Dovber of Mezherich. She argues that 'there is no more thoroughly anti-hasidic document than the *Tanya*' and points out how the *Habad* interpretation of the *tsimtsum* and the *sefirot* was 'a quasi-Maimonidean system of attributes.'[82] Nevertheless, she fails to fully explore what that may imply, instead focusing on its deviation from earlier *Hasidism*. She demonstrates the tendency to leave unexplored the potentially philosophical nature of *Habad* writings, even while identifying its presence. Similarly, in the more comprehensive studies of Habad in the works of Rachel Elior, there is no attempt to consider and compare *Habad* thought within a philosophical discourse. Elior gives a thorough analysis of what she sees as the basic

---

[81] Scholem (1954), 260. This view has been criticized in Weiss (1985), 44; Loewenthal (1990), 48.
[82] Schatz-Uffenheimer (1993), 263.

principles of *Habad* thought, and a basic axiom of her work is 'the assumption that Habad literature reflects a mystical and theosophical manner of thinking'[83] Naftali Loewenthal notes that Rabbi Shneur Zalman had 'an interest in the medieval Jewish philosophers and this is consistent with the philosophic, discursive style of R. Shneur Zalman's later hasidic teachings, and with his harmonizing attitude to apparent conflicts between Maimonides' philosophic ideas and kabbalistic thought'[84] However, he avoids an investigation into the philosophical dimension of Rabbi Shneur Zalman's teachings and, instead, emphasizes the historical and sociological aspect.[85]

This tendency is particularly prominent in the research of Moshe Hallamish,[86] where there is little attempt to explore the relationship of Rabbi Shneur Zalman to philosophy. In the instances where a possible relationship may be detected, it is roundly dismissed. For example, when considering the issue of change and multiplicity in God, he notes that Rabbi Shneur Zalman recalls 'early philosophers' who had difficulty understanding how 'it could emerge multiplicity from the simple oneness'[87] Yet, he immediately notes that Rabbi Shneur Zalman would ridicule the philosophers and quotes a disparaging comment about philosophers from one of the discourses. While Hallamish is clearly aware of a relationship between Rabbi Shneur Zalman and philosophy in general and Maimonides in particular, there is also a clear attempt to negate the extent of that relationship. Hallamish eventually confronts the argument that Rabbi Shneur Zalman could

---

[83] Elior (1993), 219.
[84] Loewenthal (1990), 43.
[85] Yaakov Gottlieb (2009) provides a significant addition to the field. Gottlieb analyses the *Habad* approach to Maimonides and provides a valuable collation of the material dispersed throughout the texts. The bulk of his work focuses on the third and the seventh generation of *Habad* leadership. In general, he tends to consider *Habad* thought as one continuum and does not take enough care to consider the leaders of the movement as independent and separate thinkers.
[86] See Hallamish (1980).
[87] Hallamish (1980), 42.

be perceived as a philosopher in his section on human intellect.[88] He suggests that 'there are those who would label Rabbi Shneur Zalman as a philosopher', without mentioning who those people may be, and presents their reasons as based on Rabbi Shneur Zalman's special stress on the purpose of intellect in his ideology. He responds that in truth, Rabbi Shneur Zalman sees intellectual activity as a lower rung in the order of divine service and, similar to the *kabbalists*, he considers the attainment of the soul more important than the attainment of the intellect. It appears from Hallamish's answer that he thinks that Rabbi Shneur Zalman must be *either* a *kabbalist or* a philosopher, and he does not consider the possibility of a relationship with both disciplines. He ultimately defines *Habad* thought as 'kabbalah in hasidic garb'[89] and rejects the possibility of a substantial relationship with philosophy.

Beyond these critical academic studies, the *Habad* movement itself, as one would imagine, has produced a considerable amount of research into the thought of its founder. The most comparably critical contribution is by Nissan Mindel,[90] who provides a summary and explanation of the first section of the *Tanya*. There is regular reference to Maimonides and other philosophers throughout the book, yet at the same time an insistence that Rabbi Schneur Zalman's ethical system basically rests on *kabbalistic* foundations. This is a further demonstration of the tendency to see an axiomatic dichotomy between philosophy and *kabbalah*, which requires *Habad* thought to be defined as one or the other.

This portrayal of *Habad* literature as exclusively a form of mysticism is, I argue, overly simplistic.[91] While it is undeniable that all *Habad*

---

[88] See Hallamish (1980), 220.
[89] Hallamish (1980), 400.
[90] See Mindel (1973).
[91] Schneersohn himself expressed his frustration at this misunderstanding. He is quoted as saying, 'the world thinks that *hasidut* is an explanation of kabbalah, this is a mistake' and goes further to declare that in fact 'kabbalah is an explanation of *hasidut*'. See Schneersohn (2003b), 172. See also Schneerson, M. M. (2003b).

texts are deeply engaged with explicating *kabbalistic* themes, and to the casual observer they may appear to be of the same genre, a more thorough appraisal of the material reveals a system of thought that pursues its own specific agenda. This observation will be more fully addressed later in the book when reading Schneersohn's discourses. In the meantime, we can note how it should not be surprising that traditional thinkers would ground their ideas in earlier thought, as the nature of traditional societies requires at least the veneer of fidelity to its authoritative canonical texts. Nevertheless, it is vitally important for the reader to remain aware of the potentially creative innovations of these thinkers, regardless of how concealed and embedded they are within a normative traditional discourse. I concur with Saba Mahmoud who invokes the Foucaldian idea of 'discursive formation', claiming that tradition need not be seen as symbols that justify present practices, nor as dogmatic prescriptions in opposition to the contemporary and the modern. Rather, 'the past is the very ground through which the subjectivity and self-understanding of a tradition's adherents are constituted'. Comparatively, the seemingly traditional discourse of Schneersohn should not preclude his discursive formation as an innovative thinker in the present.[92] This observation, in my opinion, holds true for a large portion of *Habad* material, but especially so with regards to the discourses of 1898, which include whole sections on topics such as language and gender that do not resort to *kabbalistic* phraseology or conceptual framing. Earlier approaches in *Habad* texts to language and gender generally frame their discussions in the context of the holiness of the Hebrew language or specifically Jewish maternity, thereby making it initially harder to discern any broader and more universal philosophical relevance. By contrast, Schneersohn's observations on language are

---

footnote[92] See Mahmoud (2012), 113–17.

presented in the broadest possible terms and make no reference to Hebrew, and his portrayal of conception and gestation makes no distinction between Jewish and non-Jewish mothers. Consequently, the discourses of 1898 are ideally placed to challenge prevailing assumptions, which place a limitation on the examination of *Habad* thought from a philosophical perspective.

Let us now summarize some of the points made thus far. I have presented three types of exclusionary practices that, when taken together, have operated to isolate traditional and *kabbalistically* orientated Jewish thinkers of the modern period from contemporary philosophical discourse. I have argued how the scholarly assumptions that undergird the exclusion of Jewish thought in general, and traditional and *kabbalistically* orientated thinkers more specifically, do not stand up well to scrutiny. Therefore, notwithstanding the absence of an overt interaction between many traditional rabbinic thinkers and modern philosophical discourse, I argue that rabbinic texts, such as Schneersohn's, should not automatically be presumed to be devoid of philosophical relevance, and need not be of interest solely to religious adherents or scholars of Jewish mysticism. Moreover, this book will argue that once historic prejudices are put aside, Schneersohn's 1898 discourses provide a valuable case study of reading modern rabbinic thought as philosophically relevant. As a result, the recognition of the philosophical relevance of at least one rabbinic thinker may encourage those interested in Western philosophical thought to investigate and explore other traditional thinkers, thereby drawing upon an additional source of modern thinking that could enrich understanding of key philosophical issues.

1

Background and context

Having considered several scholarly hurdles that may impede the
development of a meaningful dialogue between Schneersohn and
Levinas, Derrida and Kristeva, it is worth reflecting on the intellectual
circumstances that inspired a traditional rabbi in a small village in
Russia to develop ideas that would later find resonance in *avant-garde*
thinkers of 1960s and 1970s Paris. Rabbi Shalom Ber Schneersohn
was born on 5 November 1860 in the small town of Lubavitch, which
sits on the Russian and Belorussian border, where his grandfather –
Rabbi Menahem Mendel (1789–1866) – sat as the grand rabbi (*rebbe*)
of the Habad-Lubavitch branch of *Hasidism*. Schneersohn was the
second son of Rabbi Shmuel (1834–82),[1] himself the seventh and
youngest son of Rabbi Menachem Mendel, and as such, a distant
heir to the throne, and making him an unlikely candidate to be the
ultimate successor of his grandfather. However, upon the death of his
grandfather when he was five years old, an intense dispute broke out
between his father and a number of his uncles, which resulted in his
father assuming the position of *rebbe* in Lubavitch, while a number
of his uncles established rival centres in nearby towns. The *hasidim*
split between the candidates, and the once thriving and dominant
centre of *Habad Hasidism* in Lubavitch under the leadership of Rabbi

---

[1] Rabbi Shmuel had three sons and two daughters. There was a further son – Avraham
Sender – who died in infancy. See Schneerson, M. M. (1997) for biographical information
on Rabbi Shmuel.

Menahem Mendel was significantly diminished during the reign of Rabbi Shmuel. Schneersohn's childhood was thus an experience of intense familial conflict, a conflict he would personally take up against his cousins during his own time as *rebbe*.[2]

Another notable feature of Schneersohn's childhood was his father's ill health. Rabbi Shmuel suffered from a range of ailments that in part contributed to many periods of prolonged absence from Lubavitch for visits to European treatment centres. This conduct of the father would later be mirrored in the conduct of the son, with Schneersohn experiencing a number of physical and psychological problems that would see him spend extensive periods away from Lubavitch visiting doctors and recuperating in popular European sanatoriums. Notwithstanding all these distractions, the dominant image of Schneersohn's childhood is that of disciple to his father. Like his predecessors, Rabbi Shmuel would deliver regular discourses on *Habad* thought, many of which would be transcribed by Schneersohn. The large quantity of transcripts, many written in his young teens, indicates an impressive grasp of complex ideas, as well as an outstanding memory.[3] Already from the age of eight he would be present at the delivery of a discourse, and by the age of fourteen was already suited to repeat and review his father's talks.[4] During this period of apprenticeship, he wrote over 350 transcripts of his father's discourses with additional notes and explanations of his own. Furthermore, his overall expertise in the broad corpus of Jewish thought including *midrash*, the *Talmud*, *halakha*, Jewish philosophy and kabbalah indicates a childhood immersed in extensive study.[5]

---

[2] For further background on the conceptual aspect of these disputes, see Roth (2013).
[3] Discourses would invariably be delivered on a Sabbath or festival when according to Jewish law, notes could not be taken, requiring Schneersohn to remember, at times, over an hour of oration for a lengthy period of time.
[4] See Schneersohn (2000), 9–10.
[5] See Schneersohn (2000, 9–10) for details of his daily study schedule and accomplishments in his studies.

On 11 September 1875, Schneersohn married his first cousin, Shterna Sarah Schneersohn (1860–1942). Their grandfather had arranged the match when he and his bride were young children,[6] which may explain how Rabbi Shmuel and his feuding brother were able to agree to the betrothal; however, Rabbi Shmuel did not attend the wedding, which took place at the court of his brother. Five years later, on 21 June 1880, Shterna Sarah gave birth to Yosef Yitshak, their first and, ultimately, only child.

The death of Rabbi Shmuel on 26 September 1882 at the relatively young age of forty-eight left the still fragile Lubavitch branch of *Habad* in the hands of Schneersohn, who was only twenty-one years old, and his older brother Rabbi Zalman Aharon (1858–1908) who was twenty-four. For approximately ten years Schneersohn shared the leadership with his older brother, with each of them delivering discourses and advising the hasidim. Very few of Rabbi Zalman Aharon's discourses have been preserved; however, it is evident from the extant manuscripts that he was not as fluent and erudite as his younger brother.[7] By contrast, already in the collection of discourses from 1882, which immediately followed the death of his father, Schneersohn demonstrates a skilful mastery of *Habad* thought and an organized and systematic pedagogical style. This style would ultimately become the hallmark of his discourses and would earn him the title of 'the Maimonides of *hasidut*'.[8] Just as Maimonides codified Jewish law from the Talmud and its commentaries, so too Schnnersohn managed to weave together a coherent narrative of hasidic thought from a large range of seemingly disconnected material. However, it was not until 1893 with the departure of his brother to the nearby town of Vitebsk that Schneersohn fully assumed the title of *rebbe* and

---

[6] See Schneersohn (2000), 8–9.
[7] See Schneersohn, S. Z. A. (2008) for an example of an early discourse delivered by Rabbi Zalman Aharon.
[8] Schneersohn, Y. Y. (1992), 196a.

the position of sole leadership of Habad-Lubavitch. He began to sit in his father's place in the synagogue, established fixed times for private audiences (*yehidut*), answered written correspondence and allowed for the manuscripts of his discourses to be copied and distributed, all symbolic markers of a Habad *rebbe*.[9] The formidable reputation of his rival uncles and older cousins would have suggested the likely demise of the Lubavitch line; however, at the conclusion of his near forty-year period of leadership, Schneersohn would have eclipsed all his relatives, and would be the head of the sole surviving branch of *Habad Hasidism*.

Arguably the most significant moment of Schneersohn's leadership came in 1897 during the wedding celebrations of his only son, when he announced the establishment of a *yeshivah* (rabbinical school). The *Yeshivat Tomkhei Temimim* would grow to become the central institution of *Habad Hasidism*, and through its students significantly influence Jewish life on a global scale. The present-day phenomenon of a *Habad* presence in nearly every Jewish community around the world originates in the original ethos and guidance of *Tomkhei Temimim*. Schneersohn invested immense energy in procuring elite students for his *yeshivah*, whom he personally interviewed and gave detailed instructions for their academic and personal advancement. While many of the administrative responsibilities of the *yeshivah*, including student enrolment, fundraising and discipline, were entrusted to his son Rabbi Yosef Yitshak, Schneersohn kept a vigilant eye on every aspect of the project.[10]

The *yeshivah* was initially based in Zembin, a small town approximately 250km south-west of Lubavitch; however, by the following year a portion of the students were educated in Lubavitch itself. The presence of the *yeshivah* students in Lubavitch seems to

---

[9]   See Schneersohn (2000), 12; Schneerson M. M. (2003a), 1:94.
[10]   See Schneersohn, Y. Y. (1992), 30a.

have been the catalyst for significant developments in Schneersohn's teaching of *Habad* thought. From the autumn of 1898 until his passing, Schneersohn would deliver numerous discourses many of which would constitute a *hemshekh*. A *hemshekh* is a longer series of discourses that tackles complex ideas more systematically and stands in contrast to his earlier discourses, which stood in relative isolation from each other. Although Schneersohn had previously delivered *hemshekhim*, they were all relatively short and infrequent, whereas from 1898 onwards the *hemshekhim* were presented regularly. Schneersohn's father was the first *rebbe* to present *Habad* thought in extensive serial form, yet it was the son who fully evolved the format. These *hemshekhim* from 1898 until his passing in 1920 constitute a thorough analysis on nearly the entirety of *Habad* thought and are considered to be indispensable to its understanding.[11]

Schneersohn considered himself in the vanguard against what he saw as the corrupting influences of the *Haskalah* and Zionism. He described the students of his *yeshivah* as 'soldiers from the House of David'[12] that were entrusted to figuratively fight against these ideologies, by promoting Judaism throughout their surroundings. They were expected to be 'lamps to shine' and fight against the destructive forces of secularizing Enlightenment thought and nationalistic politics that were competing for the minds and hearts of Jewish youth.[13] Schneersohn's successors as *rebbe* developed an international outreach movement that relied heavily on the concepts that he innovated and expounded.[14] The intellectual calibre of his

---

[11] See Schneersohn, Y. Y. (1992, 298a), which identifies the summer of 1898 as the beginning of a new and more in-depth style to Schneersohn's delivery of discourses.

[12] In Hebrew: *hayalei beit David*, a new and alternative interpretation of the acronym *Habad*.

[13] See Schneersohn, Y. Y. (1992), 787b–95b.

[14] The atmosphere of *Tomkhei Temimim*, which cultivated a sense of utter devotion to the cause of outreach – 'lamps to shine' – prepared the qualities necessary for the students to act as *shluhim* (emissaries) for the movement. The numerous studies on the *Habad* movement in the second half of the twentieth century mainly fail in appreciating the significance of Schneersohn as the initiator of this trend and prefer to emphasize the

discourses coupled with a novel emphasis on outreach would bring about a renaissance of Habad-Lubavitch, and provide the foundation for the emergence of one of the most influential Jewish movements of the twentieth century.

Schneersohn's emphasis on an outreach ethos for the *yeshivah* was not seemingly premised on an outward and open approach to wider society. The students of the *yeshivah* were highly regulated and were forbidden from reading non-religious texts or even from dressing in non-hasidic garb.[15] Schneersohn was strongly opposed to the use of Russian language in his educational institutions and publicly ridiculed the study of even the classics of Jewish philosophy such as Maimonides's *Guide for the Perplexed*.[16] It remains confusing that Schneersohn claimed to have not read the classics of Jewish philosophy when he had written extensive notes and commentary on a number of them.[17] His apparent social conservatism and insular approach to Jewish life are problematized further when we read the accounts of his numerous trips abroad. Ostensibly, the foreign trips were for health purposes, and Schneersohn did visit many doctors

originality of Schneersohn's successor-but-one Rabbi Menahem Mendel Schneerson (1902–94) and his supposed divergence from earlier *Habad* norms, see Fishkoff (2003); Heilman and Freedman (2010); Telushkin (2014). These studies focus primarily on the institution of *shlihut*, which was invigorated by Rabbi Menahem Mendel during his tenure; however, they fail to grasp the importance of the *yeshivah* system, where the ideals of the movement are inculcated into the prospective emissaries. The present-day *yeshivah* system of *Tomkhei Temimim* remains structured in broadly the same way since its founding, and the curriculum continues to focus on Schneersohn's discourses. For a historical account of the *yeshivah*, see Mondshine (1987). For over 100 years, a *yeshivah* student's initiation into *Habad* thought has begun with the discourses of 1898, and I would argue that the novel approach in these discourses is a significant contributor to the embodied approach to Jewish practice that is emblematic of *Habad* outreach. Encouraging people to perform Jewish rituals, with an emphasis on the primacy of performance over intention, is a central tenet of *Habad* outreach, which finds its conceptual origin in the discourses of 1898. Thus, these discourses and their author have had a noticeable impact on the orientation of a prominent contemporary Jewish movement, further underlying their sociocultural significance.

[15] See Glizenstein (1969); Mondshine (1987).
[16] See Schneersohn, S. B. (2003b), 1.
[17] See, for example, Schneersohn (1986a), 269 for his analysis of the *Sefer ha-Ikkarim*.

and sanatoriums; however, it seems clear that these trips were also a form of escapism.[18] Schneersohn, in fact, seriously considered leaving Lubavitch for good, to live in seclusion away from the pressures of leadership.[19]

From the various accounts of these trips, one gains a definite sense of Schneersohn's appreciation for the anonymity they afforded him, and that he enjoyed the opportunity to engage with others and the world, free from the demands and expectations of his hasidim. In contrast to the insular approach he publicly advocated in Lubavitch, Schneersohn went to Vienna to be analysed by Freud, enjoyed the beauty of the French Riviera and explored the magnificent treasures of the Louvre in Paris. I plan to explore this tension more fully, for if we hope to draw a biographical picture that will inform our understanding of his thought, it is important to consider the broad spectrum of Schneersohn's experiences.[20] The 1903 visit to Vienna, for example, provides a far more complex picture of a traditional Jew than may be readily discernible from studies of traditional Eastern European Jewry. Schneersohn's encounter with Viennese psychoanalysis, beyond demonstrating that he suffered bouts of

[18] See Schneersohn, Y. Y. (2004, 42), where he describes the 1903 trip to Vienna as a form of self-imposed exile, a practice that was common among mystics and scholars to evade public recognition.
[19] See Schneersohn (2000), 13. See Schneerson, M. M. (2003a, 1:94), where Schneersohn is described as being naturally depressive, although he managed to hide it from most people. See also, Schneerson, M. M. (2003a), 5:346.
[20] The reliability of sources when trying to accurately piece together episodes in Schneersohn's life has already been questioned. His son Rabbi Yosef Yitshak, who has been described by prominent historian of *Hasidism* Ada Rapoport (1988) as an unreliable source, is often the sole recorder of the historical account of Schneersohn's life. She claims Rabbi Yosef Yitshak purposely constructed a falsified narrative for the purpose of establishing the centrality of *Habad* to the broader hasidic mission. The purpose of the present historical enquiry is not to establish an objective historical truth, if that was even possible, but, rather, to understand how Schneersohn and those around him perceived events, and specifically how those perceptions can contribute to a broader intellectual history. Therefore, I will specifically make use of the testimony of Rabbi Yosef Yitshak as it provides, at the very least, a significant voice and inside perspective of events. See Wolfson (2009b, 13), where he makes some pertinent remarks with regards to historical research on *Habad*.

depression, can point to ways in which Schneersohn engaged with a contrasting world to his own. Consequently, describing Schneersohn's encounter with Freudian analysis can suggest ways and strategies in which his own thought can become discursive with new interlocutors.

The autumn of 1902 marked the twentieth anniversary since the passing of Schneersohn's father, Rabbi Shmuel, and it proved to be a very emotional and difficult period for Schneersohn. He had prepared a complex theme for the discourses of that year dwelling on the meaning of inheritance after twenty years, which he planned to begin delivering on the Jewish New Year; however, at the last minute he opted for an alternative theme. Nevertheless, the discourses were considered a success and he was praised by Rabbi Shmuel Betsalel, a prominent hasid and close confidant of Schneersohn's father, who said that for the first time in twenty years he was able to sense the level of *rebbe* in the discourses.[21] Similarly, that year's nineteenth Kislev festivities, a central day in the *Habad* calendar marking the release from prison of the movement's founder, were celebrated with especial exuberance, and ostensibly it would seem that Schneersohn's projects and activities were successful and achieving their goals. Notwithstanding the positive feedback, Schneersohn expressed deep feelings of insufficiency to his wife, insisting that he had yet to refine his character and was unable to think clearly.[22] In addition to his persistent melancholy, Schneersohn suffered from a paralysis in his hand, and under the pretence of a necessary medical trip, arranged to travel to Vienna. He instructed his son to prepare for himself a passport, as he wanted him to accompany him together with one of the household staff.[23] They arrived on 11 February 1903 and stayed

---

[21] See Schneersohn, Y. Y. (2004), 42; Schneerson, M. M. (2003a), 5:402.
[22] See Schneerson, M. M. (2003a), 3:262.
[23] See Schneersohn, Y. Y. (2004), 42.

at a hotel for ten days before renting a three-room private apartment and staying in Vienna until 5 April.[24]

The Vienna trip of 1903, as I will presently show, provides an example of the pain and burden experienced by Schneersohn. He suffered from an intense intellectualism, which, in his own estimation, he was unable to fully ground and convey in everyday life. *Habad* thought demands that the intellect must find expression in the emotions and ultimately have an effect on daily life, but Schneersohn, in his own estimation and to an extent confirmed by Freud, struggled to live up to these demands satisfactorily. Schneersohn's preoccupation in the discourses of 1898 with the dynamics of hierarchical structures, especially as they are experienced internally in the self, could point to his own personal concerns of disharmony between his inner and outer life.[25]

Upon arrival, Schneersohn had an appointment with Freud to discuss the paralysis in his hand; Freud brought in Hermann Nothnagel (1841–1905) to discuss the case, and they both advised a course of electrotherapy.[26] It is unclear whether Schneersohn underwent a formal session of psychoanalysis; however, his son records a particular conversation where Freud enquires about Schneersohn's schedule and asks about the nature of hasidic thought. I will quote here the entire record:

> My father replied: 'The discipline of hasidism requires that the head explain to the heart what the person should want, and that the heart implement in the person's life that which the head understands.'
>
> 'How can that be done?' asked the professor. 'Are head and heart not two continents separated by a vast ocean?'

---

[24] See Schneersohn (1986b), 379.

[25] The feelings of depression were not isolated to 1903 and can therefore still be informative for our concerns with the writings of 1898, see Schneerson, M. M. (2003a, 5:346) regarding bouts of depression both before 1903 and afterwards.

[26] See Levine (2010).

To this my father answered: 'The task is to build a bridge that will span these two continents, or at least to connect them with telephone lines and electric wires so that the light of the head should reach the heart.'[27]

In another recollection of this encounter, Rabbi Yosef Yitshak adds a further detail, where Freud diagnosed Schneersohn by saying that 'the heart desires more than the head can handle, and the head understands more than the heart can handle.'[28] In a different record Freud is quoted as saying, 'the head grasps what the heart cannot handle, and the heart cannot handle what the head grasps.'[29] Notwithstanding the seeming repetition in the latter version, it appears to capture more consistently the problem Schneersohn was experiencing, namely an inability to convey the full profundity of his mind into his lived and shared experience.

Freud recommended that Schneersohn should maintain a pleasant environment and rest, and the hasidim should study his works and follow his directives, making sure to let him know they are being impacted by him. These instructions were conveyed to the faculty of the *yeshivah* and they began to send reports of the achievements of the students. Rabbi Yosef Yitshak described the impact of these reports as being transformative. For example, on the Purim festival, which fell in mid-March, several hasidim and relatives from Russia visited Schneersohn in Vienna, but he declined to interact with them and secluded himself in his room. When a letter arrived with a very positive report about the *yeshivah* students and their studies, Schneersohn was deeply impressed and agreed to engage with the guests, talking with them late into the night with confidence and assurance.[30]

---

[27] Schneersohn, Y. Y. (1992), 82a.
[28] Schneersohn, Y. Y. (1986d), 28.
[29] Schneerson, M. M. (2003a), 3:262.
[30] See Schneersohn, Y. Y. (1986d), 37.

Freud also advised daily walks, during which Schneersohn used to visit the numerous synagogues in Vienna, all the time guarding his anonymity. On one occasion, he was confronted by an elderly congregant who reproached him saying, 'everything in the head, everything in the head, there also needs to be the heart'. Schneersohn asked the old man how one goes about learning how to use the heart, to which he responded, 'we have a precious little book called *Likutei Amarim [Tanya]*'. Schneersohn kept a straight face and fingered through the urtext of *Habad* thought written by his great-great-grandfather, replying, 'it looks like a good book.'[31] The intellectual and non-emotional demeanour of Schneersohn was evident even to the casual observer and further underlines the nature of his problem.

During the early days of the trip, Schneersohn confided in his son his deep sadness at his inability to relate to the hasidim and broke down in tears;[32] however, by the end of their stay Schneersohn was in very high spirits and reinvigorated.[33] The electrotherapy had improved the feeling in his hand, and the advice of Freud was clearly helping. The intensity of his intellectual experience would remain a constant personal problem but would inspire volumes of creative thought that would ultimately reconfigure the entire corpus of *Habad* writings. Schneersohn's travels in general, and the Vienna trip in particular, present us with a reluctant leader who cherished the opportunity for anonymity. He appears to have been open to worlds outside of his own, and on some occasions reflected on how positively affected he was by these experiences.[34]

With the advance of German forces into the interior of Russia in 1915, Schneersohn reluctantly left the quiet rural setting of Lubavitch that had been home to the movement for over 100 years, moving to

---

[31] Schneersohn, Y. Y. (2004), 23.
[32] See Schneersohn, Y. Y. (2004), 42.
[33] See Schneersohn, Y. Y. (1986d), 87.
[34] See Schneersohn, Y. Y. (1985), 293.

the large industrial city of Rostov. The move was extremely disruptive, not least with it coming in the middle of Schneersohn's most ambitious intellectual project, the discourses, which spanned the years between 1912 and 1916. This *hemshekh,* which includes 144 instalments, as well as further material that was never delivered orally, is venerated among hasidim for its depth and orderliness.[35] Yet, notwithstanding this upheaval, as well as the destabilization caused by the Russian revolution, which saw heavy fighting in Rostov, Schneersohn's intellectual productivity continued apace, such that in 1918 and 1919, he would deliver discourses more frequently than at any other time of his leadership.

On 20 March 1920, Rabbi Shalom Ber Schneersohn passed away at the age of fifty-nine. On his deathbed he is reported to have said, 'I am going to the heavens, but the manuscripts I am leaving with you.'[36] These manuscripts of his prodigious intellectual output became a guarded treasure for his son, remaining intact notwithstanding both Soviet and Nazi persecution. The original handwritten manuscripts of Schneersohn's discourses are now housed in the central Habad-Lubavitch library in New York and have been typeset and published in twenty-nine volumes.

This brief biographical sketch highlights how Schneersohn, at times, resists some of the stereotypical assumptions that may persist in both academic and popular discourse concerning traditional Eastern European Jews. While promoting an insular approach to Jewish life in his *yeshivah,* Schneersohn himself was comfortable exploring major European capital cities and spending extended periods of time in locations such as Menton on the French Riviera, a destination popular with the Russian nobility at the time. The complexity of Schneersohn's persona is presented here to unsettle

---

[35] See Schneersohn (1991).
[36] Schneersohn, Y. Y. (1982), 113.

prior assumptions of what traditional thinkers might look like and how they might behave, and hopefully to create a larger opening for the reception and consideration of his thought. Schneersohn is arguably one of the most prodigious theological rabbinic thinkers of his period,[37] yet his complex writings remain largely untouched by academic scholars of Jewish thought. Beyond his fierce opposition to Zionism and the sparse record of his visit to Freud,[38] Schneersohn has yet to attract significant scholarly attention. In the course of this book, the assumed absence of philosophically astute traditional rabbinic thinkers in the modern period will be directly challenged through a careful examination of Schneersohn's discourses of 1898. It will become clear that Schneersohn is not only a rigorous and methodical thinker on matters of shared concern with contemporary philosophy, but also someone who anticipates many crucial twentieth-century developments in the philosophy of language and gender.

Overview of Schneersohn's main themes

Before we begin reading through the discourses and seeing the way Schneersohn develops his ideas, let me set out the main structure of his argument in broad strokes. The series of discourses of 1898 are an extensive interpretation of three *midrashim* in *Genesis Rabbah*[39] on the creation narrative.[40] These *midrashim* identify the two names of God

---

[37] Schneersohn deferred to other *Habad* rabbinic figures such as Rabbi Menahem Mendel Chein (1879–1917) and Rabbi Yaakov Landau (1893–1986) on *halakhic* issues. However, they consulted with him closely and he influenced their rulings. A single volume of Schneersohn's *halakhic* writings have been published, see Schneersohn (2013).

[38] See Katz (2011) for a speculative analysis of Schneersohn's experience of psychoanalysis, and Brawer (2000) for insight into Schneersohn's leadership style.

[39] On *Genesis Rabbah*, see Gribetz et al (2016).

[40] On the structure of *Habad* discourses, see Golomb (1994), 43–9.

found in *Gen.* 1:1 and *Gen.* 2:4 – *Elokim and YHVH*[41] – as representing the divine attributes of justice and mercy, whose combination in the act of creation establishes the orientation and structure of existence. The terse and cryptic *midrashic* material undergoes a thorough analysis in the discourses, where the relationship of justice and mercy is more fully considered. These divine forces are initially portrayed as adversarial and oppositional to each other, but ultimately are found to contain a complementary dimension to their interplay. This analysis of an initially assumed oppositional binary in the divine forces of justice and mercy is further expanded upon to think more broadly about the dynamics of several other binary relationships. Many societally embedded dualisms such as intellect and speech, male and female, and soul and body are challenged, resulting in an alternative perception of orality, gender and physicality than was previously common both in rabbinic thought, and in philosophical thought more generally. Schneersohn identifies societally embedded structural dynamics across a range of conditions, whereby elements that exhibit qualities of expression and presence are privileged over elements that appear passive. Significantly, he highlights the binary structure of consciousness and speech, pointing out the historic privileging of intellectual cognition and the denigration of language in general and speech production in particular. This observation is already significant, in that a structural dynamic that had ordinarily been taken for granted was now being noticed and critiqued. Perhaps more surprisingly, Schneersohn highlights the oppositional binary of gender in the erotic encounter and notes the assumed inferior value of women in relation to men. In addition to a number of other binary pairs, Schneersohn establishes throughout the discourses the

---

[41] On the names of God in *Habad* thought, see Shneur Zalman of Liady (1978), 80a–b; Wolfson (2009b), 82–4.

significance of speech and women, thereby placing himself as an early pioneer of new philosophical concerns.

The discourses offer a thorough exploration of the dynamics at play in hierarchical relationships where one element ostensibly provides and the other receives. For example, Schneersohn explores how in the relationship between intellectual consciousness and speech, consciousness is commonly perceived as providing meaning to speech. As a consequence, in a cultural system that values providing over receiving, intellectual consciousness is privileged and favoured, whereas the receptive role of speech is denigrated. To counter this perception, the discourses develop an appreciation of a profundity inherent in receptivity, which aims to undo the historic subordination of the recipient. Significantly, this new-found appreciation of the recipient does not simply re-appropriate the former hierarchical structure in an inverted form. Turning the tables and bestowing the revered quality of provision on the previously passive recipient would still retain the original binary logic. Instead, the discourses challenge the presumed superiority of providing and the presumed inferiority of receiving, and develop a theory where the passive, static and, in some sense, stable nature of the recipient conveys a core, primal and essential ontological state. This state is exemplified in its role as a recipient, hence not in spite of its receptivity, but because of it.

The disrupting of these relationships allows for an appreciation of the previously subordinated recipients, not in a manner that further subordinates these recipients by 'elevating' them to the status of their providers, but one that acknowledges and values their identities as recipients. Whereas receptivity might be construed to imply a dependency on a provider, Schneersohn emphasizes that a recipient, unlike a provider, exemplifies a state of independent and stable being that is not compelled to be expressive. This state of being, which is self-contained and non-expressive, is portrayed in the discourses as originating, and subsequently expressing, a fundamental and core quality of God. While it may appear that the recipient is dependent on the provider, the discourses emphasize, instead, that it is the provider who can, in fact, be viewed as being dependent on the recipient. The provider in the act of giving displays a need to convey and be expressive, which itself reflects an instability and dependency. Furthermore, the giving of the provider demonstrates an urge and compulsion to engage with the recipient, which the discourses interpret as a desire to achieve proximity and engagement with the recipient's ontological primacy. The recipient, however, is defined by its lack of content in contrast to the provider, and it is this emptiness and absence that identifies the recipient with an essential quality. The independence and non-contingency of God is thus imitated in the neutral and non-aligned realm of the recipient. Consequently, this ontological primacy of the recipient helps explain how recipients, such as speech and women, are not merely containers or even conduits for their providers, but, rather, act as catalysts, capable of an impact far above and beyond the potential of the original gift of the provider.

Schneersohn thus portrays a range of supposedly oppositional binary relationships, and how there, in fact, inheres a primary significance to the supposedly secondary and inferior component in these relationships. He argues that speech, women, the body, the people of Israel and *malkhut*, while functioning as recipients of intellect, men, the soul, the Torah and the *sephirot*, respectively, are actually the condition for, and initiators of, all the beneficence that they receive. Moreover, through the act and function of receiving they make possible the manifestation and disclosure of what is ordinarily concealed and inexpressible. Schneersohn explains how this transformative quality of the recipients is due to their innate originality and primacy in God. The passive and non-expressive qualities of the recipients and their apparent independence and separateness mirror the very same qualities in the essence of God and thus indicate their primordial origin in the divine essence.

Unlike some other attempts to disrupt binary relationships, where structural systems are overturned, these discourses retain the original structural dynamics between the provider and the recipient. I will argue that it is this specific feature of the discourses that makes them not only a prescient precursor to philosophical developments in the twentieth century but also a potentially innovative contributor to the field. In addition to arguing that Schneersohn foreshadows several developments in postmodernism, I will argue that this reconstruction by Schneersohn can also significantly inform our reading of Levinas, Derrida and Kristeva, and help us reconsider the dynamics at play between the saying and the said, language and meaning and the semiotic and the signified, respectively. For these discourses, the problem is not located in the structure of supposedly hierarchical relationships, but in our understanding of the dynamics of providing and receiving. Through stressing a profundity in the recipient *qua* recipient, the 'power' dynamics between provider and receiver become fundamentally reconfigured within the same structure and present as a reconstructive element alongside an otherwise deconstructive method of challenging binary and dualistic structures. Ultimately, the discourses will also re-evaluate the character of the provider and present a mutually dependent and beneficial relationship between the provider and the recipient. According to this re-evaluation, the innate and seemingly inexpressible essential characteristic of the recipient can become expressed only through the expressive characteristic of the provider.

A key insight of the discourses is the recognition of receptivity, passivity, absence and otherness as crucial characteristics of the oft-maligned and denigrated binary elements. In this way, Schneersohn enables his critique of the constitution of these binaries to avoid the obvious pitfall of renouncing the very defining characteristics of these elements. Meaning to say, the objective of the discourses is not a rejection of our perception of speech as performed, or women as mothers but, rather, a reconsideration of how we understand their significance in the roles that they play. Therefore, the active and expressive qualities of consciousness and men are not rejected or even denigrated; instead, they are employed in the service of realizing the value and significance of speech and women. Some might think that Schneersohn's preserving of the reciprocal relations between the binary elements merely maintains the status quo and does not substantially alter or affect the potentially corrosive social impact of the binary structures. However, Schneersohn might argue that the problem does not lie in binary structures *per se*, but, rather, in the perceived values that society constructs and assigns to the binary elements.

Admittedly, Schneersohn does not seem overly concerned with the social implications of these oppositional binary structures, and in that way is noticeably different from the postmodern philosophers we will be considering. However, possibly because of this emotional detachment, he is able to confer greater legitimacy to the arguments that disrupt these socially embedded hierarchies. The social and political agenda of many postmodern philosophers might bring into question their objectivity when analysing these historical social structures, and thereby raises an issue as to the philosophical credibility of their work. Schneersohn, by contrast, would appear to be advancing ideas that run contrary to his ostensibly conservative and traditional lifestyle and outlook. Consequently, the similarity in approach between the seemingly socially conservative Schneersohn and these *avant-garde* postmodern thinkers enables the ideas being discussed to disrupt the stereotypical assumptions, which affect each of them. Even those who do not identify with the social activism that has become synonymous with postmodern thought may come to appreciate the conceptual framework that postmodernism provides. Similarly, those who had previously assumed an absence of philosophically rich insights from a traditional nineteenth-century

Eastern European rabbi writing in rabbinic Hebrew might begin to look beyond these social characteristics and markers.

At its core, Schneersohn is embracing a fundamental value inherent to those elements that most ostensibly lack universally appreciated qualities. Moreover, by transforming the self-perception of the hitherto superior and dominating element, it can effectively convey the infinite qualities of the previously inferior element. Consciousness can configure the spoken word in such a way that it will articulate the primacy of the other and otherness, men can arouse in women their maternity and divine-like creative power, and most importantly for Schneersohn, the Torah can reveal the divinity of the Jewish people in particular and in creation more generally.

The overarching objective of Schneersohn in the delivery of these discourses was to encourage and inspire his followers to follow a more intensive and committed approach to the study of the Torah and the fulfilment of its commandments. This objective is perhaps what we might expect from a late-nineteenth-century rabbinic figure such as Schneersohn. However, what may have been less anticipated was the philosophical orientation that he develops as a means to achieving this objective. Prior to its popularization in twentieth-century philosophy, Schneersohn brought into question the privileging of certain elements in oppositional binary structures. The presumed primary importance of the soul, of intellectual consciousness and of men were challenged, allowing for the emergence of an alternative perception of the significance of the body, speech and women. In this way, Schneersohn unexpectedly heralds some of the major concerns and developments in twentieth-century philosophy.[42]

---

[42] I consider the claim of this book, namely, Schneersohn's anticipation of and importance to postmodernism, to have significant implications for our understanding and appreciation of modern rabbinic thought. The hitherto overlooked thought of the otherwise white, male, European Schneersohn in both Jewish and general philosophical discourse suggests a specific prejudice against modern rabbinic thinkers who eschewed some of the norms of the European Enlightenment.

The text

Let me conclude this chapter with some bibliographical notes regarding the 1898 series of discourses. Schneersohn, like his predecessors, would deliver discourses (*maʾamar* [sing.], *maʾamarim* [pl.]) on a regular basis. On such occasions, usually Friday nights, he would talk while in a trance-like state and all present would stand and listen.[43] In the days following an address he would edit an earlier draft of the discourse, which would be copied and distributed both locally and further afield to followers who lived outside of his hometown of Lubavitch.[44] Until the establishment of the *yeshivah* (rabbinical academy) in Lubavitch in 1898[45] most of these talks were stand-alone pieces that were not necessarily thematically connected.[46] Starting from 1898, Schneersohn began delivering series of discourses on a regular basis that provided a structured curriculum in hasidic thought for the students of his newly established *yeshivah*.

---

[43] The manner of delivery reflected the status afforded the *maʾamar* as representing a form of revelation. In *Habad* circles *maʾamarim* are also called *divrei Elokim hayyim* (words of the living God). See Jacobson (1996), 12, where he describes the first time he heard a *maʾamar* from Schneersohn.

[44] On the importance and value of handwritten copies and their distribution, see Lieberman (1980), 27. On the town of Lubavitch, see Levine (2001).

[45] More accurately, the *yeshivah* was established in 1897 outside of Lubavitch, and in 1898 the bulk of the student body moved to Lubavitch, as described earlier. For a comprehensive review of the *yeshivah*, see Mondshine (1987).

[46] Each of the *Habad* leaders would have their own method of preparing, delivering and recording their discourses. Schneersohn's father Rabbi Shmuel (1834–82) would write a draft of the discourse prior to delivery and then edit it afterwards. When the draft would become too long to be delivered in one sitting, Rabbi Shmuel would divide the draft into sections and then add short introductions and conclusions to each section on a subject relating to the time of its delivery. In this manner, Rabbi Shmuel developed the concept of the *hemshekh*, and over the course of his seventeen-year tenure he delivered a number of *hemshekhim*. The advantage of the *hemshekhim* was the possibility of expounding on a concept in far more depth than was possible in a single discourse. Schneersohn emulated his father's practice, and from the beginning of his leadership he delivered a mix of single discourses as well as a few *hemshekhim*. As noted earlier, these earlier *hemshekhim* were sporadic and relatively short in comparison with the *hemshekhim* between the years 1898 and 1920. On the development of the *hemshekh*, see Schneersohn, S. (2004), 389–90; Golomb (1994), 43–9.

Additionally, they provided arguably the most organized, thorough and analytical approach to hasidic thought that had been attempted up to that point, and as mentioned earlier this led to Schneersohn acquiring the honorific 'The Maimonides of Hasidism' among some of his followers.[47] These discourses (1898–1920) remain to this day part of the core curriculum in hasidic thought in the *yeshivah* network that he founded.[48] In light of this, the series of discourses of 1898 is significant in marking the beginning of a deliberate and sustained attempt by Schneersohn to educate and inform a young generation of hasidic students on the intricacies of hasidic thought.[49]

In the summer of 1898, Schneersohn travelled to his summer *datsche*, where he spent many hours preparing the discourses that he would begin delivering at the beginning of autumn.[50] The discourses were broadly based on a single discourse of Schneersohn's grandfather, Rabbi Menachem Mendel (1789–1866).[51] As was his style, he composed the entire series of discourses as one long transcript prior to its delivery, and then at the time of delivery he divided the material into individual discourses and supplemented opening and closing remarks suited to the occasion on which it was delivered. Moreover, after delivering each discourse, Schneersohn would write additional notes on each discourse, some of which were intended to be inserted into the final transcript, while others were clearly marked to not be copied in.[52] The manuscripts were then given to Schneersohn's

---

[47] See Schneersohn, Y. Y. (1992), 296a; Schneerson, M. M. (1991), 281. Schneersohn's well-organized discourses were reminiscent of Maimonides's codification of Jewish law in his *Mishneh Torah*.

[48] On the curriculum of the *yeshivah*, see Mondshine (1987), 167–74.

[49] The extent to which these discourses were markedly different and more advanced than from previous years is highlighted by Schneersohn's son's description of how an older and venerated *Hasid* needed the young *yeshivah* students to explain to him the seventh discourse in the 1898 discourses due to its difficulty. See Schneersohn, Y. Y. (1992), 216a.

[50] See Schneersohn (2011), 293.

[51] See Schneersohn, M. M. (1985), 2452–76.

[52] The original handwritten manuscript (ms. 2970) can be viewed on the website of the *Habad* central library.

transcriber Shmuel Sofer, who copied the original manuscript with the additional notes. Sofer's copy would then be widely distributed for everyone to study.

In 1976, Schneersohn's successor, Rabbi Menachem Mendel Schneerson, instructed the *Habad* publishing house to prepare and print this 1898 series of discourses, as well as the other discourses from that year. The editors of this first edition were given access to a photocopy of Schneersohn's original manuscript, who used it to correct any discrepancies in Sofer's copy. For the third edition, printed in 1984, the editors included, as an appendix, the additional notes that Schneersohn had originally marked not to copy. In 2011, marking 150 years since Schneersohn's birth, the discourses of 1898/9 were completely re-typeset with extensive footnotes and references. Throughout this book I have used the 2011 edition, and all page numbers refer to that edition. All translations are mine unless stated otherwise.

2

Language

As previewed earlier in our discussion on methodology, this chapter will aim to faithfully present Schneersohn's philosophy as it is presented in the 1898 discourses, while at the same time seeking to make it intelligible to the philosophically trained scholar. The focus on language is threaded throughout the discourses, with the most sustained analysis appearing in the first discourse. Once we have gained a sufficient grounding in Schneersohn's linguistic thought, I will begin the dialogue with Levinas, Derrida and Kristeva and draw out how I think these thinkers can be mutually beneficial. To better appreciate how language is incorporated into the wider concerns of the discourses I will also outline how the first discourse opens and develops; this will provide important framing for all the themes in the discourses and clarify the affinity between language, gender and mysticism, which will be developed over the course of the book.

The Festival of *Rosh Hashana* . . .[1]

On 17 September 1898, marking the beginning of the Jewish New Year, and following some preparatory remarks, Schneersohn paraphrased a *midrash* in the following way:

---

[1] The discourse begins with an analysis of a Mishnah that discusses the rules of the Jewish New Year when it coincides with the Sabbath as it did in 1898 (Mishnah, *Rosh Hashanah*, 4:1. This Mishnah has been extensively analysed in *Habad* New Year discourses.) After

At first, God thought to create the world with the attribute of justice. Hence the verse, 'In the beginning *Elokim* [God] created . . .',[2] *Elokim* being the name of God associated with justice. But God saw that the world could not endure, so God combined the attribute of mercy with it. Hence the verse, 'These are the histories of heaven and earth on the day *YHVH-Elokim*[3] [Lord, God] created earth and heaven'[4] – mentioning also the name *YHVH*, which is the name associated with the attribute of mercy.[5]

The *midrash* depicts two contrasting forces within God, which God combined for the sake of creating a viable world. However, God initially desired to create the world solely with the attribute of justice. In this context, the definition of justice is the administration of the law and the authority to enact punishment. For Schneersohn,

posing a series of questions, which ultimately remain unanswered in these discourses, Schneersohn begins a new line of enquiry on the nature of the Jewish New Year, specifically why it coincides with the sixth day of creation, when humans were created, and not the first day of creation, which marks the beginning of existence. In these opening remarks, Schneersohn repeats questions from earlier *Habad* texts that serve to connect the discourse to the time of the year but will have little if any bearing on the theme of the discourses. See Schneersohn, S. (2004), 389, on the relationship between the title and content of a discourse.

2   Genesis 1:1.
3   The discourse uses a colloquial form (*Havayah*) of the Tetragrammaton YHVH, which is a reconfiguration of the letters and indicates existence. See Shneur Zalman of Liady (1978), 79a.
4   Genesis 2:4.
5   Schneersohn (2011), 2. See *Genesis Rabbah* 12:15; ibid. 14:1; *Rashi* on Gen. 1:1. The present formulation of this *midrash* appears to be compiled from a variety of sources. It most closely resembles the way the *midrash* is quoted by the eleventh-century exegete Rabbi Shlomo Yitshaki on Gen. 1:1 ('God's creation of the heavens and the earth: But it does not say 'of the Lord's creation of' (i.e., it should say 'of the Lord God's creation of' as below 2:4 'on the day that the Lord God made earth and heaven') for in the beginning it was God's intention to create it with the divine attribute of justice, but God perceived that the world would not endure; so God preceded it with the divine attribute of mercy, allying it with the divine attribute of justice, and that is the reason it is written: 'on the day the Lord God made earth and heaven'. However, note how Rashi says that God *preceded* mercy to justice, in contrast to justice preceding mercy in the present discourse. See Schneerson, M. M. (1999, 30–7); see other versions in *Pesikta Rabati* 40:2. See also, *Pesikta Rabati de-Rav Kahana* 41:2. However, although the content of the *midrash* is represented in the earlier sources, the specific formulation in this discourse is a direct quotation from the discourse of Schneersohn's grandfather upon which the entire series of discourses is based (Schneersohn, M. M. (1985, 2453.)) The earliest presentation of the *midrash* in this form is in Shneur Zalman of Liady (1978), 79b.

the idea that God would wish to create the world with justice seems incompatible with the notion of a benevolent creator, for surely if 'the nature of the good is to be good then the creation of the world should have been with the attribute of mercy'.[6] Furthermore, quoting the sixteenth-century *kabbalist* Rabbi Hayyim Vital (1542–1620), Schneersohn describes how the purpose of creation was for God to 'show kindness to his creations',[7] and questions how to reconcile the benevolence of God, with the *midrashic* description of an intention to create the world with the attribute of justice.

Schneersohn continues his enquiry with a second *midrash* that attempts to explain the first by means of a parable:

> There was once a king who possessed fragile cups.[8] The king said, 'If I fill them with hot [fluids] they will crack. But if I fill them with cold, they will congeal.' What did the king do? He mixed the hot with the cold, poured it into the cups, and they remained intact. So, said the Holy One Blessed be He: 'If I create the world with the attribute of mercy, sinners will abound. But if I create the world with the attribute of justice, how will the world endure? Rather, I will create it with both the attribute of justice and the attribute of mercy and would that it may endure!'[9]

---

[6] Schneersohn (2011), 2. In classical rabbinic literature it would also seem that mercy was considered preferable to justice, see *Tosefta, Sotah*, 4:1.

[7] Schneersohn (2011), 2.

[8] The version of the *midrash* as represented in this discourse refers to the cups as *kosot dakim* (thin/fragile cups) on the authority of the eleventh-century *Sefer Haʾarukh* (see there the entry for *keres*). Interestingly, whereas the printed versions of this book do attest to this reading, in the manuscript version in the British Library (Add MS 26881) it is written clearly as *kosot raykim* (empty cups). There is yet another version in printed editions that say *kosot rakim* (fragile/thin cups). See the Venice editions of 1531 and 1552.

[9] Schneersohn (2011), 3. See *Genesis Rabbah* 12:15. In this parable, the hot and cold fluids refer to justice and mercy, respectively; however, when the parable is explained the order is reversed and God is paraphrased as considering creating with mercy before justice. The fact that Schneersohn does not note this change of order even though it could have implications for his earlier question of why God would prefer to create with justice is possibly because he read the reversed order in the *midrash* as merely stylistic and not altering the intention of the parable. The discourse's quotation of the second *midrash* is a much more faithful rendition than the first as it appears in the standard versions of *Genesis Rabbah*.

Since the discourses will, in some sense, be a commentary on a *midrash*, let me say a few words on the genre of rabbinic *midrash* in general, especially the use of the parable as a literary tool,[10] and their relevance to these discourses. The *midrashic* approach to Scripture has been described as interpretive and viewing the text as intentionally obscure and ambiguous. Robert Alter describes it as 'a certain indeterminacy of meaning' that requires 'continual revision';[11] the text does not represent a specific or particular meaning, but, rather, demands a continuous process of subtle interpretation. Classical rabbinic thought will often view the text as polysemous, and therefore does not seek to reduce the text to a particular and exclusive meaning, preferring, instead, to expand and extend its scope and application.[12] A distinctive way in which the *midrash* expands and extends Biblical narratives is through the pervasive use of the *mashal* (the parable).[13] This method of exemplarity does not try to exhaust the meaning of the subject of comparison; instead, through the parable the polysemic nature of the text is expressed. By creating examples that are slightly different, the *midrash* extends the possibility of the original text. As the Talmudic scholar Daniel Boyarin notes, the *mashal* is the 'placing of a concrete entity beside another concrete entity in such a way that characteristics that are obscure in one are revealed by association with those same characteristics in the other, where they are obvious or explicit'.[14] This expansion of the text by means of associations and examples is reflected in the *midrash* quoted earlier, whereby the parable of a king with fragile cups opens up the original *midrash* concerning the divine attributes and, as we will see, allows for more subtle interpretations

---

[10] On the use of parable in midrashic sources, see Boyarin (1990); (2003), 89–163; Stern (1981).
[11] Alter (1981), 12.
[12] See Boyarin (2003), 95; Handelman (1982), 34.
[13] See Stern (1981), 261–91; Boyarin (1990).
[14] Boyarin (2003), 99.

of the process of creation. Schneersohn's analysis can also be seen as continuous with this rabbinic mode of interpretation, for as we will see, he proposes further parallels and similitudes to the original text, thereby expanding the parameters of the original subject.[15] These two cited *midrashim* will form the basis for the entire series of discourses with a focus on the following four themes: the meaning of cups as an analogy for creation, an understanding of the attributes of justice and mercy, why God initially wanted to create the world with judgement, and the implication of combining justice with mercy.

Seemingly, the most obvious meaning of the parable is that cups refer to the created world. However, Schneersohn suggests that the cups refer more specifically to the *kabbalistic* category of *malkhut* (sovereignty):[16]

> *malkhut* in general is called a cup. For just as a cup serves as a vessel to receive wine or water, so too *malkhut* receives all the revelation and radiance of the levels above it.[17]

The early rabbinic idea of God having attributes (justice and mercy)[18] developed into a more complex and structured theory for the *kabbalists*, especially in the book of the *Zohar* that included ten attributes called *sephirot* that emanated from God.[19] For the *kabbalists*, these *sephirot* bridge the gap between a simple God and a

---

[15] See Loewenthal (2013) and Rubin (2015) for a general discussion on the role of *midrash* in *Habad* thought. It is said that Schneersohn would study the whole *Midrash Rabbah* every year (Schneerson, M. M. (1995), 42).

[16] Lit. Royalty or Kingship; the tenth and last of the *sephirot. Malkhut* is referred to in the *Tikkunei Zohar* (intr., 17a) as the 'Mouth of God' – the word or speech of God by which the world comes into actual being. The *Zohar* (I:249b; 251b) compares *malkhut* to 'the moon that has no light of its own save that which is given to it from the sun'. See Schneersohn (2000b), 24.

[17] Schneersohn (2011), 3.

[18] See also, Mishnah *Berachot* 5:3; Ibid., 9:3; *Megillah*, 4:9; *Sanhedrin*, 7:1. This notion of one God and multiple attributes is also attested to in Greek philosophy, see Dahl and Segal (1978), 28; Liebes (2000), 51. The origin of the idea of the attributes and their relevance to the discourses will be discussed more fully in the chapter on mysticism.

[19] See *Tikkunei Zohar* (2nd Introduction); *Zohar* I:22b; I:15a; I:65a; II:239a. See Scholem (1954), 205–43; Jacobs (2006), 27–48.

complex creation, and *malkhut* serves as the last of these emanations. *Malkhut* is distinguished in the *kabbalistic* texts from the other *sephirot* for being primarily a container for the previous *sephirot,* in order to facilitate the creation of a finite world. Since the *sephirot* are emanations from God they also reflect God's infinity, and *malkhut* acts to contain and conceal that infinity which enables the creation of a finite world. Therefore, even though the analogy in the *midrash* refers more generally to the created world, Schneersohn relates the cups more specifically to the *sephirah* that enables that creation, namely *malkhut.*[20]

In order to understand the conceptual link between cups and *malkhut,* Schneersohn draws a further comparison of cups with the human faculty of speech. These layers of similitude are a common feature of *Habad* texts and are not simply used to provide a parallel phenomenon in the physical realm, but, rather, they serve to identify continuous themes between these different realms.[21] This perspective allows for the comparison to work both ways, where our understanding of human speech can inform our understanding of *malkhut,* and *malkhut* can similarly inform our understanding of human speech. The purpose of presenting the comparison is not merely to gain a deeper understanding of the target but equally to introduce the concept of the correlate.[22] Until this point, Schneersohn was closely following the flow of ideas as they are arranged in his grandfather's text that are the source material for his discourses, albeit with additional explanation and interpretation. However, whereas

---

[20] Using the concept of cups to refer to *malkhut* is found (albeit not in the context of the *midrash*) in *Zohar,* Intr. 1a; Ibid., Gen. 250a, and in earlier *Habad* texts in Shneur Zalman of Liady (2001), Ex. 79a; (2002a), Deut. 80c.

[21] See Schneerson, M. M. (2006), 475–6; Wolfson (2013), 79.

[22] To support this point it is worth noting how Schneersohn's son added short title summaries to his father's discourses and described this first discourse as 'the superiority of speech over intellect and emotions', even though it might seem that the sections dealing with speech are just a means to understand *malkhut.*

the earlier text now proceeds to focus on the attributes of justice and mercy and their mystical implications, Schneersohn now begins an original and elaborate exploration of language and gender. The discourses will eventually return to the discussion of *malkhut*, justice and mercy and will be addressed in Chapter 4.

In the meantime, the comparison of *malkhut* and speech is expressed as follows:

> Just as speech is the vessel into which the powers of the soul, intellect and emotions, are drawn and contained,[23] so too the level of *malkhut*, which is called supernal speech, is the vessel into which the flow of all the ten *sephirot* is drawn.[24]

The comparison of *malkhut* with human speech suggests that *malkhut* is not only a container, as might be implied by the parable of cups, but also a conduit. Just like speech, which in addition to containing ideas acts as a communicator of those ideas, so too *malkhut* communicates the ten *sephirot* to the creation as well as containing them. Although *malkhut* is responsible for the entire creation and the cup analogy in the *midrash* refers to creation in general,[25] Schneersohn says that the 'main intention [of the analogy of the cups] refers to the souls of

---

[23] In *Habad* thought the soul is conceived as emanating from the very inner essence of God and therefore possesses ten powers that parallel the ten *sephirot* that emanate from God. These ten powers are divided into two groups, namely, the intellect and the emotions, and are expressed through thought, speech and deed that are called 'garments of the soul'. See Shneur Zalman of Liady (1978), 8a. A person's clothes are entirely foreign to the person themselves and have no intrinsic connection to the person wearing them; just like they can be worn they can be taken off. So too is the relationship between the garments of the soul and the soul itself: thought, speech and deed are not a part of the soul itself, and therefore it is possible to take them off – when a person does not wish to do or say something they can refrain from doing or saying it, and even not to think it – for even though a person is always thinking they can easily switch from one thought to another. This is in contrast to the powers of the soul, which are extremely difficult, and in some cases impossible, to change. See Shneur Zalman of Liady (2001), Gen. 13c; Schneerson, M. M. (1991), 291–2.

[24] Schneersohn (2011), 3.

[25] See Schneersohn, M. M. (1985), 2474.

Israel'.[26] Meaning to say, that of all the creations created by *malkhut*, the creation of the souls of Israel is the function most aptly analogized with cups, as will be explained later in the discourse.

The next section of the discourse expounds in more detail on the role and the impact of speech on the development of ideas. To more fully understand the developments in the next section of the discourse I will present a brief introduction to the key terms employed by Schneersohn. The psychological make-up of the human being is presented as expressions of a soul that manifest in a body. The human psyche, consisting of drives and impulses that are categorized as desire (*ta'anug*) and will (*ratson*), are treated as intimate reflections of the soul and that remain somewhat aloof from the body. That is to say, these drives and impulses are experienced in a manner that is less obviously associated with a particular area of the body. For example, when a person says, 'I desire' or 'I want', it suggests a more encompassing notion of the self.[27] By way of contrast, the psyche also contains intellectual and emotional abilities that become invested and expressed through the body's receptors, such as 'I understand' in the mind or 'I feel' in the heart. However, these abilities are expressions of the soul that do not readily express themselves in the physical body, and they require a mediating force that can facilitate what we would describe as human cognition. The mediating forces of thought (*mahshavah*), speech (*dibbur*), and action (*maaseh*) are called garments (*levushim*) that enable the soul's intellectual and emotional abilities to become expressed in the relevant parts of the body.[28] Although our awareness of human cognition is always at the stage when the soul's abilities and its garments are combined, to the extent that they seem indistinguishable from each other, an understanding and appreciation

---

[26] Schneersohn (2011), 3.
[27] See Shneur Zalman of Liady (1978), 148b; Schneersohn (2010), 78–102.
[28] See Shneur Zalman of Liady (1978), 8a; Schneersohn (2010), 52.

of the next section of the discourse is dependent on recognizing this key distinction between the soul's abilities of intellectual and emotional expression and the garments that facilitate that expression.

Schneersohn initially classifies speech as a recipient from, and a container of, something else: 'all that is articulated by speech stems from the intellect and emotions, since on its own, speech has nothing more than what it receives from the higher faculties.'[29] Furthermore, speech does not receive intellect and emotions directly but only after they have been received in thought, the effect of which is that 'the idea is far more revealed in thought than it is in speech, since thought precedes speech in the line of reception from the intellect and emotions.'[30] Additionally, he asserts that not only the content of speech but also the form of articulation of the specific idea is determined by the faculty of intellect and not by speech itself.[31] Since the same intellectual concept can be expressed in multiple ways, the decision to express the idea in any specific way is said to originate in the intellect. It should therefore follow that no additional 'insight and enlightenment could be attained through speech that is not already present in the idea as it is in the mind, since the mind is the source of all that speech reveals.'[32] Schneersohn has tried to show that speech would seem to be only a container and receptacle for the intellect, in which the intellectual ideas are more restricted and diminished than they were in thought. It would therefore stand to reason that speech would have no beneficial impact or effect on the ideas that it conveys.[33]

---

[29] Schneersohn (2011), 4.
[30] Schneersohn (2011), 4.
[31] More specifically, he says that power to form the words stems from *hokhmah* (lit. wisdom), which refers to the highest level of the thinking process: the initial, unstructured flash of insight. See Schneersohn (2000b), 29.
[32] Schneersohn (2011), 5.
[33] This idea of speech as a reduced representation of ideas would be consistent with dominant strands of Western thought, and as Reddy (1979) points out, is the basic

It is noteworthy how Schneersohn initially constructs a hierarchical relationship between meaning and speech that is reminiscent of dominant strands in Western thought, where meaning and signification dominate and dictate verbal expression, before he sets about critically reconsidering the dynamics at play in oral communication. This means that fifteen years prior to the publication of Saussure's *Course in General Linguistics*, which has been credited as the beginning of the 'linguistic turn' in twentieth-century philosophy,[34] a modern rabbinic thinker was already challenging the prevailing linguistic orthodoxy and arguing for a greater appreciation of orality.

Schneersohn proceeds to describe how, notwithstanding the points made earlier, we observe how an idea is developed and expanded upon specifically through its articulation in speech. Schneersohn notes how 'every intellectual idea that emerges from the source of intellect appears in a measured and limited form: in its length, width, depth'.[35] The 'length' of an idea signifies the extent to which its thinker manages to communicate it to another person of lesser conceptual abilities. The lower he can bring the idea, the 'longer' the thought is said to be. The 'width' of a thought is the extent to which it gives rise to deductions and links with other ideas.[36] The 'depth' of a thought is the extent to which it is connected to a more profound or more encompassing thought. However, 'when it takes the form of speech, we see clearly that the idea expands immensely . . . with many details and ramifications, incomparably surpassing its initial stage in the words of thought'.[37] The 'length' of the idea, that is, the extent to which it can be conveyed to people with different degrees of intellectual ability, is

framework in which language is conceived. Reddy labels this framework 'the conduit metaphor' that is strikingly similar to the cup parable here.
[34] See Walton (2012), 25.
[35] See Schneersohn; Marcus and Miller (2000b), 30.
[36] This is referred to in the Talmud (*BT Shabbat* 31a) as 'understanding one thing from another'.
[37] Schneersohn (2011), 5.

enhanced. Specifically, 'when a person verbalises an idea, he discovers several subjects to which the idea can be applied', thereby enabling the idea to become 'accessible even to one of limited understanding'.[38] Similarly, the idea when verbalized can extend its 'width' and be conceived in a wider range of ways. Additionally, through speech the depth of a concept becomes apparent, eliciting 'a new insight from the source of the intellect that is not revealed when the concept initially emerges from its source. Even deep pondering of the concept will not reveal the depth of the concept . . . only speech can accomplish this'.[39] Thus, even though, *a priori*, one would not expect any enhancement of an intellectual concept once articulated in speech, we notice from empirical experience that the concept is, indeed, enhanced.

Schneersohn's argument rests primarily on his belief in a common shared experience where the articulation of ideas in speech enhances the quality of those ideas. Even though a certain logic would dictate that speech should be unable to have this effect, experience would suggest otherwise.[40] Although this may not be the universal experience for all his listeners and readers, the recognition that such an experience is common to some people should be sufficient for the purpose of his argument. Schneersohn contends that from experience one observes that speech has a superiority over thought in the way it can affect intellect, even though speech has no content of its own except that which it receives from the intellect. The assumption of an inferiority of spoken language would seem understandable since the intellect is initially expressed in thought-language and only then does it express itself in speech-language, suggesting that in thought-language the

---

[38] Schneersohn (2011), 5.
[39] Schneersohn (2011), 6. This idea is attested to in the Talmud (BT *Eiruvin* 54a), which states that Torah study should be vocal for through vocal study one can gain deeper insight.
[40] This reliance on experience as a significant source of understanding is noteworthy.

intellect is in some sense closer to the original intellectual idea.[41] It should therefore stand to reason that there would be no access to greater insight of the intellect in speech than in thought, and yet, nevertheless, 'we see that there is an increase in light in intellect when it expresses itself in the letters of speech than there was prior to its expression.'[42] Specifically through speech, a person is able to expand and elaborate the original concept.

After demonstrating the effectiveness of speech in influencing the intellect, Schneersohn asserts that the reason for this effectiveness is due to the primacy of 'speech in its root which transcends even the source and origin of intellect'. This ontological primacy of language in general, and more specifically the physically vocalized letters of speech, enables speech to 'force' the faculty of intellect to express itself to a greater extent than it could do so out of its own urgency. Here is the key passage in full:

> The reason for all this is the lofty stature of speech in its source, which transcends even the source and origin of intellect. Indeed, the letters stem from *keter* (crown),[43] which transcends *hokhmah* (wisdom). And as far as its position in the soul, it is at the level of the essence of the soul, which transcends the soul's power of *hokhmah*. Therefore, the letters of speech compel the intellect (*koah hamaskil*)[44] to be revealed, so that even that which it is unable to reveal on its own is revealed by force of the letters of speech.[45]

Schneersohn adduces that the letters of speech originate in the very essence of the soul and are ontologically prior to the intellect, and

---

[41] This is further reflected in the nature of thought to be continuous, that it remains internal and that the language of thought is not physical, unlike speech, which is not continuous, is external and physical. See Schneersohn (2011), 5.

[42] Schneersohn (2011), 5.

[43] Lit. Crown. *Keter* is the *kabbalistic* emanation that transcends the ten *sephirot*.

[44] Lit. 'power of intellectualism'. The soul's ability to intellectualize.

[45] Schneersohn (2011), 8.

therefore these letters have the ability to influence the effluence of intellect.

To explain this seemingly inverse hierarchy whereby the secondary and recipient element is in truth more primary, Schneersohn expands the field of enquiry from speech in relation to intellect to the broader subject of the relationship between the body and the soul. Schneersohn, following his pattern of analysis of speech, describes the body/soul relationship in a manner that initially assumes a hierarchy whereby the soul is superior to the body, prompting the question why the superior soul ever wishes to be in relation with the inferior body. The soul is described as having a natural yearning towards God that would become stymied when invested in a body. Schneersohn asserts that, similar to speech, the superior originality of the body attracts the soul:

> Now the soul is compelled to descend, contrary to its nature. . . .
> For the soul lives inside the body against its will, contrary to its
> nature and essential desire. And what, indeed, coerces it? The body.
> For the source and origin of the body transcends the soul.[46]

It is because of the ontological primacy of the body that it is able to force the soul, against its nature, to enliven the body. And as was the case with regards to speech and its effect on the intellect, the soul is enhanced through its engagement with the body. The soul is able to know Godliness from the superior perspective of the body, as well as benefit from the performance of the divine commandments that can be performed only through the body.

This broader analysis that the body is the cause of the soul's descent proposes that in addition to enhancing the intellect, speech is also the initial cause of intellectual expression:

---

[46] Schneersohn (2011), 8.

> In a general sense, the letters stem from the essence of the soul, which transcends the faculty of intellect. On account of their primordial root, the letters cause the light of the intellect to clothe itself in words of speech . . . . In other words, the letters compel even the depth and essence of the light that transcends revelation to be drawn forth and revealed. Hence, through speech one apprehends the depth of the intellect, which cannot be grasped through the mind's exploration alone.[47]

Schneersohn thus proposes an entirely inverse relationship between speech and language and the perceived higher faculties of intellect and emotions than may have been understood from the parable of the cups. Not only do speech and language enhance the intellectual faculties, but the former are also the very cause of the latter's expression and development in the first place. These expressions of the soul would otherwise remain contained, and thus dormant, within the soul, and would feel no compulsion to express themselves in the body. It is the profundity of the body that initially stimulates the soul to become invested in the body more generally, and then the garment of speech more specifically can elicit the expression of the intellectual and emotional abilities of the soul. Schneersohn thus argues for not just an ontological and chronological primacy for the somatic and the semiotic, but also a functional primacy that catalyses and dictates the effusion of the soul and its functions.

To more fully appreciate the novelty in Schneersohn's approach to the themes of language, gender and the body, it is worth noting the dominant philosophical attitudes that would have been prevalent at the end of the nineteenth century. Admittedly, there is a chequered history of these ideas, with notable pockets of resistance to what we might call an otherwise logocentric and phallocentric world view. For example, classical rabbinic thought, when freed from its medieval

---

layers of interpretation, can often appear to transcend dualistic constraints.[48] Similarly, the counter-Enlightenment ideas of Johann Georg Hamann can be viewed as an early attempt at disrupting binaries that becomes more fully developed in the writings of Nietzsche.[49] Moreover, a number of scholars have begun to challenge the historical representation of seminal thinkers of Western thought such as Plato and Aristotle. These new readings of early Greek thought seek to overcome the many dualistic assumptions that have impacted the reception of their thought. Notwithstanding these complexities, it nevertheless remains consistent to claim that both the Western and rabbinic philosophical traditions, as interpreted and inherited up until the late nineteenth century, can be described as operating on broadly logocentric and phallocentric lines.[50] As such, Schneersohn's disruption of a binary analysis of language, gender and the body is an innovative, if not original, approach, and is arguably one of the earliest and most thorough explorations of the subject in the modern period.

A central concern of twentieth-century developments in the philosophy of language is the relationship between logic and spoken language, and their relative priority. The dominant viewpoint throughout the history of Western philosophy, has prioritized logic as the basis for meaning over spoken language. As Newton Garver noted, the priority of logic holds for 'Plato's theory of forms, of Aristotle's doctrine of predication, of the medieval controversy over universals, of Leibniz' grand project for a universal symbolism, and

---

[48] See Weiss (2013) on non-dualistic tendencies in classical rabbinic thought.

[49] On Hamann's opposition to dualistic thought, see Berlin (2000), 291–2, and on his influence on Nietzsche, see Berlin (2000), 283; 295. On non-dualism in Nietzsche, see Brown (2006).

[50] It could be argued that the continued study of earlier classical rabbinic texts that resist, to a certain extent, the imposition of typical binary categories, could explain why a specifically rabbinic thinker might be among the earliest developers of an alternative perspective to historically constituted binary pairs.

of rationalism and idealism in general. It is also true . . . of empiricist philosophy from Hobbes and Locke to Brentano and James and Russell'.[51] While there were a few exceptions to this consensus, such as can be found in the works of Jean-Jacques Rousseau (1712–78), Etienne Bonnot de Condillac (1714–80) and Johann Georg Hamann (1730–88),[52] the dominant perspective of Western philosophy regarded spoken language to be secondary and inferior to the realm of thought and logic.

In Plato's *Cratlyus* and Aristotle's *De Interpretatione*, language in general and the spoken word in particular are depicted as failing to convey the truth of the forms or the categories. As Socrates asks in the Platonic dialogue, 'He who follows names in the search after things, and analyses their meaning, is in great danger of being deceived'[53] since '. . . the knowledge of things is not to be derived from the names'.[54] As Gadamer has noted, this understanding of words as holding no innate truth banishes knowledge to the realm of intellect and thought.[55] Similarly, Aristotle considers words to be unable to denote truth, and knowing requires a person to go beyond the spoken word. Names for Aristotle are spoken sounds 'significant by convention'.[56] This understanding of language, as merely conventional, leads to a privileging of thought, and places thought as the arena where knowing truth becomes possible. These ideas also played an important role in the emergence of a prominent strand of Christian theology, especially as articulated by Augustine, who places a primacy and importance on silence and spirit as opposed to the vocal and the word.[57] Although

---

[51] Derrida (1973), xi.
[52] See Rousseau (1998); Philip (2014); Hamann (2007).
[53] Plato (1997), 152 (*Cratylus,* 436a).
[54] Plato (1997), 154 (*Cratylus,* 439b).
[55] See Gadamer (1975), 405–18.
[56] Aristotle (1984), 25 (*De Interpretatione,* 16a19).
[57] See Mazzeo (1962, 196), who concludes that Augustine's thought 'led him to look more and more to the intelligible, the eternal, and the silent'.

there have been recent readings of Classical Greek and early Christian thought that contest this characterization,[58] it is widely agreed that the Platonic and Aristotelian inheritance, which helped shape and fashion the Western philosophy of speech and language, perceived spoken language to be inferior to the realm of cognition and thought.

The developments towards the end of the nineteenth and beginning of the twentieth century in the works of Frege, Husserl, Russell and the early Wittgenstein further entrenched the submission of the philosophy of language to the primacy of logic. Language was understood to be founded upon 'signs that represent ideas' and that 'the primary purpose of language is epistemological'.[59] In other words, in these works the philosophy of language becomes subsumed into a philosophy of mind that privileges ideas and knowledge over signs and articulation.

However, these common logical presuppositions about language have, in the second half of the twentieth century, been subjected to a thorough critique. In this critique, speech or writing is posited as the very condition for language and meaning, resulting in logic being treated as secondary and derivative in relation to speech or writing. In a manner not dissimilar to Schneersohn, these critiques set about dismantling the assumptions that dismissed the relevance and importance of language and speech. More broadly, they also identify in multiple structures the operation of oppositional binaries, which, as in the case of thought and speech, uphold undue privileging of the component of the polarity that most resembles thought. This emphasis on ostensibly restoring the binary elements, albeit with an

---

[58] See, for example, Pickstock (2011), where she develops an alternative reading of Plato – an onomatopoeic theory of language – which is remarkably similar to Schneersohn's approach, while at the same time acknowledging the more pervasive approach to reading Plato, namely, as the initiator of a rationalist metaphysics that eschewed bodily and emotional mediations.

[59] Garver (1973), xiii.

entirely different power dynamic, is sometimes overlooked or simply unnoticed in Levinas, Derrida and Kristeva. With the help of the more explicit and developed constructive thought of Schneersohn, I will highlight and emphasize what can similarly be found in their works. Admittedly, the reconstructive side of these thinkers is less accentuated and deliberated upon in their writings; however, it is an important and arguably necessary corrective to other aspects of their systems of thought.

Let us now consider how these ideas can engage and inform our understanding of some of the central themes in the writings of Emmanuel Levinas. Levinas was a pivotal thinker in the development of a postmodern critique of entrenched oppositional binaries. Central to Levinas's project was a challenge to an all-dominating and totalizing consciousness, and its embodiment in a subject, which always seeks to assimilate the other in the self. Throughout his works, he attempts to expose the primacy and importance of the Other, and subsequently reconstitute the conscious self in the service of the Other. The primacy of the Other, and what he calls Alterity, enables him to argue for a notion of ethics that precedes, and subsequently constitutes, philosophy and thematized thought. Drawing primarily from his two major works, *Totality and Infinity* and *Otherwise than Being*, I will consider how Levinas critiques, and then seeks to overcome, the operation of hierarchical assumptions in the encounter of the Same with the Other. Levinas's 'idea of infinity' and the way in which it manifests within experience will be compared with Schneersohn's articulation of an essential revelation in the 'letters of speech,' highlighting how these themes were anticipated by Schneersohn in the discourses of 1898.

In his preface to *Totality and Infinity*, Levinas refers to a 'traditional opposition between theory and practice', which he says was hitherto 'not conceivable other than as a solidarity or a hierarchy'. This tradition, he claims, then leads to an assumption where 'activity rests on cognitions that illuminate it.'[60] In this way, Levinas situates his book as an attempt to undo what he describes as the violence of cognition, which operates as a totalizing force in relation to both the otherness of the self, exemplified by action, and of others more generally. Whether it is with regards to the more general categories of the Same and the Other, or the more specific example of theory and action, Levinas identifies the traditional hierarchical dualisms that have historically privileged the cognitive component of these relationships. In a challenge to these historical traditions, Levinas, instead, locates in the exteriority of the other a transcendence that withstands 'the theoretical exercise of thought, which would monopolise transcendence.'[61] That is to say, notwithstanding the totalizing impulse of thought, or of the Same, as Levinas prefers to say, there remains a transcendence, or infinity, in the Other, which resists being dominated by the Same.

While for Levinas, the development of his philosophical ideas as instantiated in speech are fully realized only in *Otherwise than Being*, for Schneersohn, speech and its relationship with consciousness are the primary site of consideration. Whereas Schneersohn does not specifically refer to a binary of theory and action in these discourses, and, instead, focuses on cognition and speech, the notable feature of speech for Schneersohn, is its exteriority and orientation towards the other. 'The entire purpose of speech is specifically for the sake of the other, since for oneself there is no need for speech at all.'[62] Although Schneersohn locates transcendence in the discernibility of speech, where the previously imperceptible patterns of thought are expressed, he similarly recognizes in the initial stage of exteriority, especially in his treatment of the significance of the performance of *mitsvot*, the broader category of action and its significance as an idea of the

---

[60] Levinas (2008a), 29.
[61] Levinas (2008a), 29.
[62] Schneersohn (2011), 47.

infinite. What is of primary significance is how both for Levinas and for Schneersohn, it is the exteriority of action and speech that marks them out as instantiations of the idea of infinity. The reason that Schneersohn may have focused on speech rather than action could be due to his desire to identify an incarnated otherness specifically within the self, which is satisfied by the externalization of breath and sound in speech. By contrast, in action, the material and inanimate otherness is found in the separate physicality of an object. From his other examples, though, it is clear how Schneersohn recognizes the Levinasian idea of infinity in action, such as in the performance of the commandments, but considers speech to be a more appropriate example of otherness in the self.[63]

Schneersohn emphasizes, in a manner akin to Levinas, that consciousness entirely dominates the production of knowledge and its expression in speech. 'All expressions in speech come from consciousness, since speech has nothing of its own, only that which it receives from the faculties which transcend it.'[64] Moreover, not only the content of speech, but even the manner of articulation and 'the configuration of the letters'[65] is ordained and dictated by consciousness. Therefore, surmises Schneersohn, it appears that consciousness entirely dominates and controls the process of exteriorization in speech. Yet, notwithstanding this monopolizing and totalizing impulse of consciousness, speech resists the initial limits of the consciousness it receives. In the act of speaking, 'speech elicits a new insight from beyond consciousness, that is not revealed when the concept initially emerges.'[66] For Schneersohn, this capacity of the

---

[63] It is not until *Otherwise than Being* that Levinas will similarly engage with speech and language as valuable tools in the development of his ideas. See Levinas (2008a, 98), where he intimates why speech might be preferred to action as a more useful binary correlate to theory. See also, Schneersohn (2011), 108–9, on the primacy of action and practice.

[64] Schneersohn (2011), 4.

[65] Schneersohn (2011), 5. See also Schneersohn (1988), 487.

[66] Schneersohn (2011), 6. See also Schneersohn (1984b), 345.

supposedly passive and entirely determined speech to provoke and stimulate greater insight than the original exercise of thought points towards a profundity in the exteriority of speech that exceeds and originates beyond consciousness. As he notes, 'the reason for all this is the lofty stature of speech in its source, which transcends even the source and origin of consciousness.'[67] In Schneersohn's terminology, this source is referred to as *atsmut,* which is commonly translated as essence. For the purpose of the current comparison with Levinas, it should be noted that *atsmut,* in fact more closely resembles Levinas's *beyond essence,* since it is similarly not meant to connote any concrete and fixed notion of being. Schneersohn presents in the exteriority of speech his own version of transcendence and the idea of infinity, namely, the rootedness of speech in *atsmut.* Since Schneersohn defines speech as necessary only for communication with an other, as such, speech represents otherness. Moreover, a person's true essence and their infinity can be expressed only through speech and its interaction with others. For insofar as a person remains concerned only with the interiority of consciousness, before exteriorizing through speech, he/she remains limited to the constraints of thought. Through interaction with the other, through speech, the infinite essence of the person becomes manifest.

Levinas is careful to note how his affirmation of 'the philosophical primacy of the idea of infinity'[68] and his move beyond totality should not be described 'in a purely negative fashion', but, rather, should be understood '*within* the totality and history, *within* experience'.[69] Levinas realizes how in his attempt to designate something as outside totality, the terms and names he defines become restored to the exercise of thought they were supposed to exceed.[70] In that context,

[67] Schneersohn (2011), 8.
[68] Levinas (2008a), 26.
[69] Levinas (2008a), 23.
[70] See Davis (2007), 35.

however, Levinas makes clear how he wants to overcome the impulse of reversing the hierarchy between theory and practice, and, instead, 'deal with both as modes of metaphysical transcendence'.[71] Levinas's solution to the problem, where the transcendence of the Other is subsumed into the totality of the Same, is to fundamentally disrupt the assumed boundaries and organizing tendencies of the Same. As the title of his book suggests, Levinas is not engaging in an either/ or approach, and infinity does not exist separately from the way it is posited in the totality of the self; rather, 'it is produced in the improbable feat whereby a separated being fixed in its identity, the same, the I, nonetheless contains in itself what it can neither contain nor receive solely by virtue of its own identity'.[72] Levinas is trying to explain how a person, within the fixed parameters of the self, nevertheless possesses an infinity that is not produced by the consciousness of the self, and which cannot ordinarily be contained by it.

For Levinas, it is specifically in the realm of action that the domination of thought is violently shattered. The incarnation of thought and its descent into the real brings it into confrontation with a surplus and plurality of being, which was lacking in the theoretical exercise of thought. The variability and unpredictability of the realm of practice confronts and disrupts the certainty and control of thought. In this disruption, Levinas immediately seeks to rehabilitate the unsettled category of thought and locates the fundamental origin of thought in the very same idea of infinity that disturbed it in the first place. 'Theoretical thought, knowledge, and critique, to which activity has been opposed, have the same foundation. The idea of infinity, which is not in its turn a representation of infinity, is the common source of activity and theory'.[73] This common grounding

---

[71] Levinas (2008a), 29.
[72] Levinas (2008a), 26–7.
[73] Levinas (2008a), 27.

of activity and theory in the idea of the infinite leads to a new conceptualization of theory and knowledge, which 'does not consist in equalling being with representation', and the 'welcoming of the face' is not 'interpretable in terms of disclosure'.[74] Levinas wants to say that through activity one can come to realize how both activity and theory are rooted in the idea of the infinite, and then subsequently, the prior role of the signifying and designating consciousness is no longer dominant. That is to say, the signification of consciousness – 'the comprehension effected through a bringing to light – does not constitute the ultimate event of being itself'.[75] Rather, through the encounter of consciousness with activity, the Same with the Other, their common source in the idea of the infinite becomes apparent. Consequently, consciousness overcomes an impulse towards a totalizing objectivity, and opens up to a subjectivity that welcomes and contains the infinity and transcendence of the Other.

As with Levinas, who notes the apparent confusion of the encounter between the Same and the Other, but nonetheless insists on the necessity of it being understood within totality and within experience, Schneersohn similarly goes to great lengths to understand how the idea of the recipient's infinity can be conveyed through the strictures and limitations of the provider. Firstly, Schneersohn notes how the infinity of *atsmut,* as found in the otherness of speech, for example, remains dormant and unproductive unless it comes into relation with the organizing and expressive qualities of the provider.[76] That is to say, without the coherence and sense of consciousness, the profundity of speech would be imperceptible.[77] On this basis, Schneersohn queries

---

[74] Levinas (2008a), 27–8.
[75] Levinas (2008a), 28.
[76] See Schneersohn (2011), 17; 99. See also, Schneersohn (1980), 66.
[77] In contrast to the claims of Isidore Isou and the Letterist approach, which advocates the primacy of letters, especially in their incoherent combination. Schneersohn rejects the capacity of non-sensical speech to elicit and disclose the infinite source of speech on its own.

how the infinite and transcendent qualities of speech are able to be expressed and made sensible through the categories of conscious thought, which it exceeds. In other words, how the fixedness of consciousness can 'contain more that it is possible to contain'.[78]

Schneersohn explains with an example from within consciousness itself. He describes how ordinarily a person does not at first comprehend the essential principle of a concept. Rather, 'when a person has already considered and understood an idea in an orderly fashion, and then afterwards through questioning which they ask regarding the idea . . . through this they arrive at the essential principle of a concept'.[79] The process of comprehension will normally involve a thorough process of study and analysis, which when successful, will lead to the grasping of the fundamental nature of the concept under consideration. For if at the outset a person would be aware of the essential idea, without previously processing all the pertinent details that emerge from the concept, then 'in truth, the expression [of the idea] would be merely general, and it would not be grasped in a thorough manner at all'.[80] That is to say, the previously transcendent and ungraspable conceptual point is made manifest through the detailed exposition, which augmented its discovery. Moreover, once the essential point of the concept is grasped, each of the manifold considerations of the earlier analysis becomes an articulation of the essential point of the concept, to the extent that 'in the limiting details of the provisional analysis, radiates the infinite essence of the concept', and consequently, 'these details also have a heightened sense of their lack of division and of their unity'.[81] Once the fundamental principle and essence of a concept is grasped, each and every component and detail of the intellectual enquiry becomes a consistent and coherent articulation of the same point. With this

---

[78] Levinas (2008a), 27.
[79] Schneersohn (2011), 104–5.
[80] Schneersohn (2011), 104.
[81] Schneersohn (2011), 105.

example, Schneersohn wants to similarly explain how the essential and transcendent origin of speech might be articulated and conveyed through the details and categories of thought.

With this example, Schneersohn expresses how, notwithstanding the ontological primacy he places on speech, the previously limiting and constraining dimensions of consciousness are required to fully communicate that primacy. Accordingly, through the engagement of consciousness with speech, a person's consciousness is exposed to the origin of speech and becomes a vehicle for the infinite essence of the self.[82] Just as Levinas wished to 'affirm the philosophical primacy of the idea of infinity',[83] and at the same time show how it is 'reflected *within* the totality and history, *within* experience'.[84] Similarly, Schneersohn wants to assert the primacy of speech, as well as all the other instantiations of the *mekabel* (recipient), while maintaining the importance of and the necessity for consciousness, and all the other examples of the *mashpia* (provider).

For whereas Schneersohn had previously stated how the component letters of speech are not considered to be generated by the intellect or emotions and ontologically precede any state of intellectual or emotional consciousness, he proceeds to emphasize that the emergence of these letters in a tangible and discernible form, and not just as mere sounds, occurs by way of that consciousness. Schneersohn observes that while the letters of speech (*otiyot ha-dibbur*) may originate from a primordial source within the self, they lack, on their own, the capacity to articulate and convey that sublime source. It is worth noting, that the characteristics that identify something as essential (*atsmi*) in *Habad* thought are self-containment and a lack of dependency on anything else, in contrast to what is classified as expressive (*giluy*) that displays

---

[82] See Schneersohn (2011), 8–11.
[83] Levinas (2008a), 26.
[84] Levinas (2008a), 23.

its reliance on an original luminary. Consequently, were these letters (as essential and primordial) to become isolated from the coherence of intellectual or emotional consciousness, they would fail to communicate the profundity of their source since they lack the quality of expression.

Schneersohn's appreciation for the superior origin of the letters, does not lead him towards a reification of a nonsense. Such a position would merely invert the traditional Platonic and Aristotelian hierarchical relationship between consciousness and speech and would result in the degradation of consciousness. Instead, he recasts intellectual and emotional consciousness from being the true inner meaning of speech as conceived in much of Western and rabbinic thought, to becoming the necessary tools to convey the sublime qualities that are here assigned to speech. The expressive character of the intellect serves to provide the framework in which the essential quality of speech can be voiced.

Let us now turn our attention to the way in which Schneersohn's understanding of human speech and its parallel in the dynamics of creation with divine speech can help inform our understanding of Levinas's idea of 'the saying' in *Otherwise than Being*. The perspective of language, which emphasizes the significance of the oft-maligned spoken word, and which accentuates the importance of articulated speech, finds expression in the concept of the saying (*le dire*). Levinas distinguishes between the said (*le dit*), which historically has been the primary concern of philosophy, and the saying, which is the underlying condition of every representation of the said. The said is the coherent thematization of consciousness discussed earlier, and the saying is the idea of infinity, which is described as *otherwise than being*. While the said may precede the saying chronologically, it nevertheless presupposes the saying, and thus the saying constitutes the condition whereby the said becomes possible.[85] Levinas notes that

---

[85] See Davis (2007), 75.

the emphasis on the said by philosophy overlooks the importance of
the saying, which is made possible by an encounter with the other.
However, as outlined in our earlier discussion on thought and action,
any attempt to designate or define the idea of the infinite in the saying
runs the risk of incorporating it within the domain of the said. As
Levinas notes, 'a methodological problem arises here, whether the
pre-original element of saying (the anarchical, the non-original,
as we designate it) can be led to betray itself by showing itself in a
theme'.[86] In this way, Levinas sets himself the task of reconsidering the
possibilities of the thematic, and while the saying may never be fully
present in the said, it leaves what he describes as a *trace*. To clarify,
Levinas explains how, far from cognition and thematization standing
in conflict with signification or saying, in fact, within the saying
is 'the latent birth of cognition and essence, of the said'.[87] The said
then serves as the explanation of the saying and not vice versa since
'the saying is fixed in the said'.[88] Yet, this beyond-essence of saying
does not become dominated by the said, but, rather, 'overflows both
cognition and the enigma through which the Infinite leaves a trace
in cognition'.[89] This trace of the Infinite, is both the 'breaking point
where essence is exceeded by the infinite', and also 'the binding place'
that allows for the said to convey the beyond-essence of the saying.

Levinas recognizes, as does Schneersohn, how a focus on the
saying could lead to 'the possibility of pure non-sense invading and
threatening signification',[90] and clarifies how his project will not
'fail to recognize being or treat it, ridiculously and pretentiously,
with disdain'.[91] Levinas recognizes the importance of the said as the
means by which to communicate the infinite and transcendent trace

[86] Levinas (2008b), 7.
[87] Levinas (2008b), 157.
[88] Levinas (2008b), 159.
[89] Levinas (2008b), 162.
[90] Levinas (2008b), 50.
[91] Levinas (2008b), 16.

of the saying. Similarly, Schneersohn devotes a significant part of
the discourses to explain the underlying importance of 'combining
the attribute of justice with the attribute of mercy', which in the
present context refers to the letters of speech (*otiyot ha-dibbur*) and
consciousness.

In *Otherwise than Being: Or Beyond Essence*, Levinas explains the
relationship between the saying and the said and confronts many
of the same concerns about language and speech as Schneersohn
does in his discourses. Even though communication involves the
'subordination of the saying to the said', and 'as soon as it is conveyed
before us it is betrayed in the said that dominates the saying which
states it',[92] nevertheless, Levinas presents the saying as antecedent and
'pre-original' to the said. In fact, Levinas considers this to be one of
the central theses of his book, that 'saying signifies otherwise than as
an apparitor presenting essence and entities'.[93] The Levinasian saying
bears striking conceptual affinity with Schneersohn's *otiyot ha-dibbur*
(letters of speech), which are similarly portrayed as originating prior to
being and its thematization in consciousness. Schneersohn similarly
emphasizes that verbal communication should not be perceived as
an unfurling and unveiling of an original consciousness, for 'in truth,
the letters entirely conceal and hide the concept'.[94] The letters serve
as a sort of code, which enables the listener to understand. However,
the letters and the saying of the sentence, while subordinated to the
concept being conveyed, remain distinct and separate. Because of
their 'primordial source above consciousness',[95] the letters are not
merely a presentation and articulation of the concepts and ideas of
consciousness, but the instantiation of *atsmut* and the idea of the
infinite. Although Levinas locates that origin in a 'beyond-essence'

---

[92] Levinas (2008b), 7.
[93] Levinas (2008b), 46.
[94] Schneersohn (2011), 47.
[95] Schneersohn (2011), 10.

or as a 'transcendence', while Schneersohn uses the term essence (*atsmut*), as mentioned earlier, they both appear to be referring to that which is 'outside any qualification . . . and outside any attribute'.[96] This indescribable quality or this quality of indescription is precisely what is inferred by the term *atsmut*.

Let us now consider how Schneersohn's ideas can relate to Jacques Derrida's deconstruction of the oppositional binary logic that he identifies in the relationship of speech and writing. Ostensibly it would seem that Derrida and Schneersohn situate speech in entirely different positions in the binary opposites they are trying to overturn. For Derrida, speech is emblematic of a metaphysics of presence, which dominates Western philosophy, and which devalues writing as secondary and subsidiary to speech, whereas for Schneersohn, speech is traditionally devalued as merely a phonic signifier of an intellectual or emotional consciousness. I will argue that while their points of departure are noticeably different, their strategies of deconstruction are remarkably similar.[97] Both Derrida and Schneersohn operate a biphasic movement that, on the one hand, exposes and overturns the privileging of one binary element, and simultaneously overcomes the logocentric structures that gave rise to the binary dissonance in the first place.

To consider these possibilities, I will highlight the ways in which Schneersohn's discourses can engage meaningfully with Derrida's project. To be clear, the objective is not to undertake an exhaustive comparison of Schneersohn and Derrida, nor to overlook or ignore the possible differences between them. As stated previously, the goal is to firstly recognize the way in which Schneersohn is already engaged in what was to become known as deconstruction, and furthermore,

---

[96] Levinas (2008b), 16.
[97] Additionally, Schneersohn's idea of speech as 'letters of the trace', while retaining the focus on speech, suggests a type of writing in speech that places him more closely within Derrida's framework than may be initially apparent.

the possibly mutually beneficial outcomes of reading Schneersohn and Derrida in juxtaposition. In harmony with both thinkers, the very act of conveying and translating their thought in a seemingly foreign form should elicit an enhanced version of their ideas. For example, Derrida's outlining of his stages and phases of deconstruction can be helpful when attempting to apply a methodological structure to Schneersohn's discourses. The type of self-conscious reflection that Derrida displays here is largely absent in the discourses; however, the systematic approach of Derrida is strikingly echoed in the flow of ideas in the discourses.

Central to the critical method of deconstruction is a critique of binary oppositional thinking. As Alan D. Schrift has observed, 'for Derrida, the history of philosophy unfolds as a history of certain classical philosophical oppositions: intelligible/sensible, truth/error, speech/writing, literal/figurative, presence/absence, etc. These oppositional concepts do not coexist on equal grounds, however; rather, one side of each binary opposition has been privileged while the other side has been devalued.'[98] Derrida thus describes the process of deconstructing philosophy as initially a tracing and exposing of 'the structured genealogy of philosophy's concepts', which have 'been able to dissimulate or forbid, making itself into a history by means of this somewhere motivated repression'.[99] That is to say, the practice of deconstruction involves, first of all, the revealing of the system in operation that originally constructed the hierarchical system. This deconstruction is described by Derrida as both 'faithful and violent' to Western philosophy, faithful in the sense that it tries to 'respect as rigorously as possible the internal, regulated play of philosophemes',

---

[98] Schrift (1995), 15.
[99] Derrida (1982), 6.

and, simultaneously, violently 'making them slide. . . to the point of their nonpertinence, their exhaustion, their closure'.[100]

This initial stage of deconstruction, where the oppositional binaries of Western philosophy are exposed and undermined, can sometimes overshadow the subsequent strategy to overcome the historic repression of what Derrida labels as a 'logocentric philosophy'. It would, in my view, be overly simplistic to read Derrida as simply inverting the traditional hierarchies, and, instead, privileging the previously subordinated elements of writing or absence, since such a reading would result in a re-inscribing of the hierarchical structure he claims to be overturning. As Derrida himself makes clear, 'we must also mark the interval between inversion, which brings low what was high, and the irruptive emergence of a new "concept", a concept that can no longer be, and never could be, included in the previous regime'.[101] That is to say, the project of deconstruction includes an attempt to reconsider the entire 'regime' that effected the subordination in the first instance.

Based on concerns similar to Levinas, who sought to avoid the assimilation of the idea of infinity into the totalizing demands of the Same, Derrida insists on the use of a 'double gesture', which he calls a 'double writing', that seeks to avoid 'simply neutralizing the binary oppositions of metaphysics', for otherwise, 'the hierarchy of dual oppositions always reestablishes itself'.[102] Derrida is alert to a concern, where rushing to positively affirm the significance of a repressed feature of a hierarchy does not secure the desired overturning of binary opposites. Unless and until the dominating feature of any given hierarchy endures a certain degree of subordination, it will be unable to itself move outside the regime it has perpetuated. Therefore, the

[100] Derrida (1982), 6.
[101] Derrida (1982), 42.
[102] Derrida (1982), 42.

appreciation of writing which Derrida will propose involves a double phasing, which beings by exposing the primacy and dominance of the written sign over meaning and sense. It is, on the one hand, necessary to initially 'traverse a phase of overturning', for otherwise, 'one might proceed too quickly to a neutralization that in practice would leave the previous field untouched, leaving one no hold on the previous opposition, thereby preventing any means of intervening in the field effectively'. However, to stay in this phase 'is still to operate on the terrain of and from within the deconstructed system'. It is specifically through a second phase of writing, involving new concepts evoked in '*différance*' and 'trace', that 'simultaneously provokes the overturning of the hierarchy of speech/writing, and the entire system attached to it, and releases the dissonance of a writing within speech, thereby disorganizing the entire inherited order and invading the entire field'.[103] In this double gesture of writing, Derrida is clearly intent on not just overturning the hierarchical system, but also on using that disruption and the new concepts it spurs to reconfigure the system anew.

Schneersohn begins his analysis of each binary structure by exposing its oppositional structure and the traditional perception, which devalues the role of the recipient. In a manner that is simultaneously 'faithful' and 'violent', Schneersohn likewise works from within the 'regulated play' of the binary while 'making it slide' towards its own 'nonpertinence'. For example, speech is initially described by Schneersohn as a seemingly reduced and devalued form of sense, 'for speech has no content of its own, only that which it receives from consciousness which is higher than it'.[104] Subsequently, Schneersohn positively affirms the primordial element of speech, which works to similarly 'disorganise the entire inherited order' as a type of proto-speech that is akin to Derrida's proto-writing. As Schneersohn claims,

---

[103] Derrida (1982), 41–2.
[104] Schneersohn (2011), 4.

'the entire emergence of consciousness . . . is because of the letters, because of their primordial root higher than consciousness.'[105] In each variation of the provider/recipient relationships that Schneersohn addresses, he initially disrupts the primacy and privileging of the provider and asserts the supremacy of the recipient. Only then does Schneersohn move into the second phase, and holds up speech, for example, as a transformative component within the process of conveying sense. It is with regard to this phase of the project that I would suggest that Schneersohn develops a more considered reorganizing of a new order than Derrida does, and offers an analysis of what Derrida described as having reached an 'absolute limit at this point'.[106] Schneersohn's movement beyond a humbling of sense, towards an appreciation of it as the means to disclose the elusive essential trace that is contained within speech, provides a possible direction for the second phase of Derrida's 'double-writing'.

In his essay 'The Voice that Keeps Silence' in *Speech and Phenomena: And Other Essays on Husserl's Theory of Signs*,[107] Derrida argues how there is an unfailing complicity between idealization and speech, and that the 'history of the *phōnē*' is inseparable from the 'history of idealization'.[108] He explains that in order to understand the way in which speech epitomizes the mastery of objective being, which is the principle of philosophy's determination of being as presence, we need to 'think through the objectivity of the object'.[109] That is to say, the ideal object is independent of any subjectivity that might intend it, and so in order for being to become constituted and realized and to achieve objectivity, it requires a medium that does not impair the presence of the object. 'The ideality of the object, which is only its being-for

---

[105] Schneersohn (2011), 10.
[106] Derrida (1973), 87.
[107] Derrida (1973), 70–87.
[108] Derrida (1973), 75.
[109] Derrida (1973), 75.

a nonempirical consciousness, can only be expressed in an element whose phenomenality does not have worldly form. The name of this element is the voice.'[110] In other words, the substantiation of the ideal self, in a manner which still protects its objectivity, is through the medium of speech. Speech offers a near- transparent projection of, as well as a window into, the supposedly objective self. For since 'phonic sounds . . . are heard . . . by the subject who proffers them in the absolute proximity of their present. The subject does not have to pass forth beyond himself to be immediately affected by his expressive activity.'[111] It is the immediacy and proximity of speech that distinguishes it as a different type of signifier, where there is no spatial reference and no sense of being outside of the signified. The characteristic of speech to 'fade away at the very moment it is produced . . . transforming the worldly opacity of its body into pure diaphaneity'[112] makes it most suited to reinforce the primacy of a transcendent ideality. The sheer transparency of speech, which faithfully conveys the ideal object, demonstrates the way in which speech only confirms the already determined ideal 'without passing through an external detour, the world, the sphere of what is not "his own"'.[113] Speech, for Derrida, is privileged in Western thought, precisely because it reaffirms and maintains the supremacy and dominance of idealization.

Schneersohn makes a similar observation, however, not with regards to the spoken word, but to the language of thought. In the first discourse, Schneersohn differentiates the language of thought from speech in three ways: constancy, interiority and materiality. In contrast to speech where 'there is a time to be silent and there is a time to speak,'[114] a person is constantly thinking, since 'thought is

[110] Derrida (1973), 76.
[111] Derrida (1973), 76.
[112] Derrida (1973), 77.
[113] Derrida (1973), 78.
[114] Ecclesiastes 3:7.

united with the soul, such that it is constantly active'.[115] Just as the soul is constantly enlivening the person, all that which is attached to the soul, including thought, operates constantly. Moreover, unlike spoken words which extend outside of the self, the words of thought remain interior to the self. And furthermore, the language of thought does not materialize and become substantiated in the physicality of breath and sound as it does in the pronunciations of speech.[116] To a certain extent, Schneersohn's distinctions may highlight an incompleteness in Derrida's representation of material-physical speech, which fails to consider in the latter the very qualities he later ascribes to writing. Conversely, Derrida's description of the transparency of speech and its closeness to the sense that it conveys could bring into question whether spoken language is really as distinct from the language of thought as Schneersohn suggests. However, and more importantly in my view, it is significant to appreciate how they are both operating within a similar conceptual framework, albeit with a different target of analysis. The specific locations they each identify as either dominating or being subordinated is less significant than the similarities of the broader structure of their thought, since, and this is especially clear for Schneersohn, the system of binary opposition can be shown to operate on multiple levels and in multiple ways. These manifold examples of hierarchical systems can each inform the broader critique and can thus be seen as complementary rather than divergent. Additionally, as we will ultimately see at the conclusion of the essay, Derrida also arrives at a recognition of the disruptive, and subsequently transformative, nature of speech.

Derrida then goes further, to suggest that speech is not just a coherent expositor of the ideal self; rather, it is the function that makes consciousness possible, for 'no consciousness is possible without

---

[115] Schneersohn (2011), 4; 47. See also, Shneur Zalman of Liady (2002a), Num. 41a.
[116] See Schneersohn (2011), 4–5; 46–7.

the voice. The voice is present to itself in the form of universality, as consciousness; the voice *is* consciousness.'[117] The synonymy of speech and consciousness ensures an absolute proximity between signifier and signified and maintains the signified's control of meaning. For Derrida, this proximity is broken when 'instead of hearing myself speak, I see myself write or gesture'.[118] Derrida's deconstruction of a traditional Western philosophical notion of speech leads him to identify something more primordial in the nonpresence of writing. Writing disrupts the universality of speech and forces the self outside of itself, into a temporal, ungovernable exteriority, which brings into question the absolute objectivity of the self.

In remarkably similar terms, Schneersohn emphasizes the externality of speech in contrast to thought, where speech 'is not for the sake of the self, but for the sake of the other'.[119] Speech thus functions in a manner that suppresses and obscures the presence of the conscious self, enabling an interaction with an other. For Schneersohn, it is specifically the discernible substance and materiality of the spoken word – 'for in truth, the main difference [between the letters of thought and the letters of speech] is in the actual letters, the letters of thought lack substance . . . whereas the letters of speech have tangible substance (*yesh murgash*)'[120] – that allows it to effectively conceal and obscure the immateriality of consciousness, unlike the similarly immaterial language of thought, which faithfully expresses the consciousness it thinks about. Schneersohn would most likely agree with Derrida that this concealing is even more evident in the materiality of the written word; however, the materiality of the written word is already something outside and other than the self, unlike the substance of the spoken word, which is self-generated. Thus,

---

[117] Derrida (1973), 79–80.
[118] Derrida (1973), 80.
[119] Schneersohn (2011), 47.
[120] Schneersohn (2011), 47.

while making comparable and compatible arguments, Schneersohn's preference to identify an otherness within the same could be considered to more effectively disrupt the dominance of the same.[121] Alternatively, perhaps Derrida's preference for writing as the site of disruption more effectively contests the supremacy of the system and regime of idealization, because it is situated at a greater distance from the self.

Derrida, however, goes further than merely establishing writing as a dominant polarity in a maintained binarism of speech and writing; he also recognizes the disruption caused to sense and consciousness by the signification of speech. The very presence of signifiers, even in their most idealized form of speech, disrupts the originality and independence of consciousness. Since consciousness 'needs no signifier to be present to itself', the necessity to justify speech suggests how 'an underlying motif was disturbing and contesting the security of these traditional distinctions from within and because the possibility of writing dwelt within speech'.[122] It is specifically a primordial nonpresence, which is the condition for consciousness and sense, and what is emerging in the exteriority of the signifiers. Once we overcome and pass through the transcendental claim to objectivity, we come to realize that what Derrida calls the movement of difference is not something that happens to a transcendental subject, but, rather, 'it produces a subject'.[123] Here we begin to see the second phase in Derrida's biphasic movement, what he called his 'double gesture', and the reconsideration of the subject as a product, and thus a projection, of a primordial impulse of nonpresence.

Similarly, Schneersohn explains how the primordial spoken letters initiate the expression of consciousness. 'The entire expression of

---

[121] As I will point out shortly, I believe that Derrida comes to a comparable conclusion, notwithstanding his need to use writing as the initial site of disruption.

[122] Derrida (1973), 81–2.

[123] Derrida (1973), 82.

consciousness in the spoken letters is because of the letters, because of their primordial root that transcends consciousness.'[124] Schneersohn, though, makes a distinction between the effect of speech on consciousness that develops prior to actual speech, and its effect after the idea has been spoken. While recognizing the 'movement of difference' that produces the subjective consciousness, Schneersohn notes how this movement transpires 'prior to any actual impact of the letters, meaning prior to speaking'.[125] It is only when 'the letters are actually spoken, meaning when one articulates an idea',[126] that the subject can fully transcend its limited scope of expression and convey what Derrida would call a 'primordial nonpresence', and what Schneersohn would call 'the revelation of the inner and essential light which is beyond revelation'.[127]

As mentioned earlier, this primordial movement is understood by both Schneersohn and Derrida in terms of a trace (*reshimu*). It is worth quoting this section of Derrida's essay more fully:

> The living present springs forth out of its nonidentity with itself and from the possibility of a retentional trace. It is always already a trace. This trace cannot be though out on the basis of a simple present whose life would be within itself; the self of the living present is primordially a trace. The trace is not an attribute; we cannot say that the self of the living present 'primordially is' it. Being-primordial must be thought on the basis of the trace, and not the reverse.[128]

Derrida is careful to not just reproduce the hierarchical impulse by replicating the primordial self in a manner that mimics the universality of consciousness. Instead, a new concept called the trace is introduced,

---

[124] Schneersohn (2011), 10.
[125] Schneersohn (2011), 11.
[126] Schneersohn (2011), 11.
[127] Schneersohn (2011), 11.
[128] Derrida (1973), 85.

which redefines the idea and stability of being. Instead of thinking of being as structured on the notion of an origin, which places the original and primordial as the beginning of a hierarchy, Derrida's trace, which he describes as a 'proto-writing', is always already there from outside itself. The inscription of expression as the condition for being redefines the 'relation of the living present with its outside, the openness upon exteriority in general, upon the sphere of what is not "one's own"',[129] meaning that from the very outset the emanation of the self is predicated on the presence of the other and not of the self. Consequently, 'hearing oneself speak is not the inwardness of an inside that is closed in upon itself; it is the irreducible openness in the inside'. Derrida thus arrives at an altogether different perspective of speech than he originally posited, and recognizes how speech, like writing, is the embodiment of the primordial exteriority of the self.

A similar notion of the trace, or *reshimu*, is utilized by Schneersohn, not in the context of the individual like Derrida, but in his discussion on creation. 'The vessels of The World of Emanation (*atsilut*) originate in the trace (*reshimah*) and the trace is the capacity for finitude in the *ohr eyn sof* before the *tsimtsum*, which are the letters of *atsmut*.'[130] Although Schneersohn's use of the trace is steeped in *kabbalistic* terminology and will be explained more fully in the later chapter on mysticism, for our purposes here it is enough to note how it closely mimics the experience of the speaking subject we have just described. The vessels of *atsilut*, in contrast to the lights that animate them, are the means by which divinity is contained and thus externalized. As in the earlier discussion on speech, these vessels are predicated on the idea of exteriority, which is a manifestation of the trace of *atsmut*. The imprint of otherness and exteriority as the context of being is amplified in Schneersohn's discourses to permeate the entirety of existence, such

---

[129] Derrida (1973), 86.
[130] Schneersohn (2011), 59.

that the finite and separate exteriority of being originates in the most primordial trace of God. These 'letters of the trace,' which manifest in the vessels of *atsilut,* which culminates in divine speech, and which originate in divine essence provide a point of convergence between what we might call Schneersohn's proto-speech and Derrida's proto-writing.

Significantly, Derrida concludes the chapter with the culmination of the second phase of his deconstruction. His disruption of the oppositional binary of sense and speech expression against the indication of writing leads him to construct an entirely different order of relation, which presupposes a primordial trace that makes them all possible:

> Just as expression is not added like a 'stratum' to the presence of a pre-expressive sense, so, in the same way, the inside of expression does not accidentally happen to be affected by the outside of indication. Their intertwining (*Verflechtung*) is primordial; it is not a contingent association that could be undone by methodic attention and patient reduction.[131]

Although only briefly mentioned at the end of the chapter, and not fully developed or explored, Derrida explicates the compatibility of sense, expression (speech) and indication (writing) in the living present on the basis of their primordial association. Before Derrida's deconstruction, the expression of the supposedly ideal object in speech, and furthermore in the indication of everyday writing, undermined the pure objectivity and presence of the self. Now, however, with the awareness of the primordial trace, even the pre-expressive sense is predicated on the exteriority that conditions it. Consequently, there is a harmony of purpose in the entirety of being, where even the supposedly objective nature of consciousness reveals

---

[131] Derrida (1973), 87.

its own subjectivity and vulnerability to the trace. The experience of the self with the outside serves as a

> primordial supplement . . . that comes to *make up* for a deficiency, it comes to compensate for a primordial nonself-presence. And if indication – for example, writing in the everyday sense – must necessarily be 'added' to speech to complete the constitution of the ideal object, if speech must be 'added' to the thought identity of the object, it is because the 'presence' of sense and speech had already from the start fallen short of itself.[132]

In the act of expression, and even more so of indication, the primordial trace is re-established as the constituent component of being, and rectifies the operation of an oppositional binary, which suppresses and betrays the exteriority that inheres in all phases of being. The very compulsion of sense, and subsequently speech, to resort to further external expression in writing betrays the supposed presence of the ideal object in sense. This drive for exteriority is a reflection and an acknowledgement of the deficiency of presence, and the necessity for the enhancement to be found in the otherness of writing. This final twist, where sense is recast as contributing to the disclosure of a primordial trace rather than obscuring it, resembles the proposition of the concluding discourse of Schneersohn's discourses. Schneersohn briefly indicates at the end of the second discourse how once the ontological primacy of the recipient (*mekabel*) is acknowledged, the previously benevolent provider (*mashpia*) is elevated and becomes a recipient itself. Drawing from the imagery of the *midrashic* metaphor of the cups cited at the beginning of the discourses, Schneersohn points out that although a cup is a receptacle of the liquid it receives, and as such functions as a symbol for the receiver, someone may also drink from the cup and then the role of the cup is reversed

---

[132] Derrida (1973), 87.

from being a recipient to becoming a provider. The cup assumes the role of giver and the drinker is the recipient. Quoting a euphemistic Talmudic dictum that 'a man should not drink from one cup and place his eyes on another cup',[133] which warns against extra-marital relations, Schneersohn points out how the husband here is described as a drinker of the cup, in which case 'he is also a recipient'.[134] Thus, the capacity of receiving, which denotes a primordial origin, can be exposed within all aspects of being, and can explain how elements that were formerly polarities can become mutually enhancing.

Derrida's approach is also mirrored in the first discourse of the discourses, where Schneersohn wonders if the provider (*mashpia*) in the form of light, soul or sense is supposedly superior, and its superiority rests on its transcendence and abstraction from the containment and limitation of the vessel, body or speech, 'then it is seemingly surprising the whole idea of the expression of the light and its diminution is seemingly surprising, how it descends and becomes expressed in vessels and letters'.[135] Schneersohn explains how in this movement of the supposedly superior forms of the soul and of consciousness, where they become embodied and expressed in the body and in speech, they acknowledge the primordial origin of the body and speech. In a manner similar to Derrida, Schneersohn describes how the *mashpia* seeks out in the *mekabel* a 'primordial supplement' of sorts: 'because of its primordial origin, it [the body] compels the soul, against its nature, to descend to enliven the body'.[136] While for Derrida this drive and compulsion indicates a primordial and original intertwining of sense and expression, for Schneersohn, this intertwining is not original and occurs only as a result of the act of receiving by the *mekabel*. Here is the key passage in full:

[133] BT *Nedarim* 20b.
[134] See Schneersohn (2011), 23–4.
[135] Schneersohn (2011), 8.
[136] Schneersohn (2011), 9.

On account of their primordial root, the letters cause the light of
the intellect to clothe itself in the letters of speech. However, in the
initial emanation of the intellect's light to become clothed in the
letters of speech – before the letters are actualized (i.e., before one
speaks) – only an external radiance of the origin of intellect (*koah
ha-maskil*) is drawn down to be clothed in the letters of speech.
(This is true despite the fact that this revelation is caused by the
letters, which are the ones that draw the light). But when the letters
are actualized, meaning when the intellectual concept is articulated,
the essence of the letters acts to elicit even the depth and essence
of the *koah ha-maskil*. In other words, the letters compel even the
depth and essence of the light which transcends revelation to be
drawn forth and revealed.[137]

Schneersohn's approach, which insists on the importance of
performing exteriority in order to reconstruct consciousness, affords
greater agency to the speaker or writer than is suggested in the
conclusion of Derrida's essay. Even while demanding the primordial
origin of the trace and the vulnerability to the ideal object which
that inflicts, Derrida, in the final analysis, writes of a primordial
intertwining, which suggests an original and ontic transcending of
presence and idealization in sense and consciousness. Schneersohn,
in contrast, introduces a temporal component, whereby the otherwise
totalizing and idealizing consciousness can become transformed in
the act of speaking, and more broadly, the obscured divine essence
can become unveiled in the messianic future. This temporal
component to Schneersohn's approach can help instil a greater
degree of performative urgency to Derrida's ideas, just as it did in
our discussion about Levinas earlier. For while Derrida affords
significance to writing and its disruption of consciousness, he does
not necessarily advocate an increase in the activity of writing as the

---

[137] Schneersohn (2011), 11.

means to disrupt a system of oppositional binaries. Rather, through understanding the impact of writing, the primordial intertwining of the trace and sense can be appreciated. To a certain extent, Derrida idealizes the notion of writing and abstracts it from its material manifestation. By way of contrast, Schneersohn insists on the actual performance of the *mekabel*, whether as speech, or the body or, as we will shortly see, as the mother, in order to achieve the transformation of any given hierarchical order.

Through this close reading of Derrida's essay, we have come to appreciate how Schneersohn's discourses can be seen as antedating many of the key aspects of deconstruction. The way in which the exteriority of speech and its impact on consciousness is described by Schneersohn closely resembles Derrida's valuing and privileging of the indication of writing. Furthermore, Derrida's imagery of a trace functions in a similar way to Schneersohn's *reshimu*. Moreover, juxtaposing these distinct thought traditions and bringing them into discussion has helped highlight and emphasize what may sometimes be overlooked in Derrida's philosophy. The important 'double gesture', which reconstructs the deconstructed objectivity of sense, is foreshadowed and more heavily emphasized in Schneersohn's discourses. Additionally, the more self-conscious approach of Derrida and the classification of his methodology can offer a more structured framework with which to engage with Schneersohn's system.[138]

Derrida is not generally regarded as a 'Jewish' thinker in the way that Levinas might be, and therefore bringing him into discussion with Schneersohn reflects to a greater extent than it may have done with Levinas the philosophical relevance of Schneersohn beyond

---

[138] Among the major obstacles to engagement with traditional rabbinic thought for scholars trained in philosophy is an unfamiliarity with the technical terminology and the organization of ideas in these texts. This section of the chapter has demonstrated how Schneersohn's ideas can be more easily understood when juxtaposed with concepts and themes that are familiar to the philosophical scholar.

the limited confines of Jewish thought. Nevertheless, Derrida's Jewish heritage as well as his complicated engagement with Jewish thought might suggest that Schneersohn's thought is of relevance and significance only to other Jewish thinkers.[139] To counter this argument, let us now bring Schneersohn's discourses into a dialogue with Julia Kristeva and her idea of the semiotic, and in this way, Schneersohn's thought can more obviously be seen to reach beyond the boundaries of what commonly constitutes Jewish thought.

For our purposes here I will present a close reading of 'From One Identity to an Other' in Julia Kristeva's *Desire in Language: A Semiotic Approach to Literature and Art*.[140] First, I will identify ways in which Schneersohn can be seen as a forerunner to a number of Kristeva's ideas, and then I will consider the ways in which her ideas can inform and be informed by Schneersohn's discourses of 1898. Unlike Levinas and Derrida, who place less emphasis on positing a valuable function for an emasculated 'sense', Kristeva is consistently clear that any disruption of the oppositional binary, in her case between the symbolic and the semiotic functions of signification, can be considered only within the framework of symbolic signification. In that way, her work can be considered as more naturally aligned, and in tune, with Schneersohn. Additionally, Kristeva's invocation of the Platonic *chōra*, which as a receptacle and as the maternal, exemplifies for her the site of the pre-thetic, situates her work clearly within Schneersohn's concerns, and his own linking of the primordial origin of speech and of the maternal.

To better understand Kristeva's approach, it is important to familiarize ourselves with the specific terms she uses to orientate her ideas. The two

[139] On Derrida's engagement with Judaism and Jewish thought, see Srajek (1998); Ofrat (2001); Wolfson (2002). I will have more to say on Derrida's relation to Jewish mystical thought at the outset of Chapter 4.
[140] Kristeva (1980), 124–47. The original French version, '*D'une identité l'autre*', was first published in Kristeva (1975) and then reprinted in Kristeva (1977), 149–72.

polarities of the oppositional binary she intends to disrupt are usually described as the symbolic and the semiotic. The symbolic function in language is the way in which consciousness confers meaning, while simultaneously constituting the identity of the speaking subject. Kristeva explains that whether linguistics is studied comparatively, and seeks to find laws across families of languages, or comes in the form of philology, which attempts to decipher the meaning of one language, 'a common conception of language as an *organic identity* unites them'.[141] According to both the comparativists and the philologists, language is assumed to be the appropriation of a specific meaning or structure by a speaking subject. Hence, this organic identity 'implies that language is the possession of a *homo loquens* within history',[142] and that language is a symbolic structure to convey meaning.

Alternatively, Kristeva points out how structural linguistics, through Saussure, developed a system of signs that was distinct from the speaking subject, and differentiated between the signifier and the signified. In this way, 'structural linguistics could not become a linguistics of speech or discourse' since in order to 'move from sign to sentence the place of the subject had to be acknowledged'.[143] However, Kristeva argues that, far from diminishing the symbolic function in language by separating the subject from the sign, structural linguistics problematized the absence of the subject. In this way, the role of generative grammar in reinstating the subject is not an alternative to structural linguistics, but, rather, a correction, which nevertheless maintains the same presuppositions as structuralism, that there is a subject which generates meaning.

Kristeva situates her reading of modern linguistics in the context of the philosophy of Edmund Husserl. She quotes Husserl's *Logical*

---

[141] Kristeva (1980), 126.
[142] Kristeva (1980), 126.
[143] Kristeva (1980), 128.

Investigations where he posits the sign as an expression of meaning: 'The articulate sound-complex, the written sign, etc., first becomes a spoken word or communicative bit of speech, when a speaker produces with the intention of "expressing himself about something" through its means.'[144] Consequently, the act of signification is achieved through the intention of endowing meaning by the subject, which he calls the transcendental ego. Kristeva concludes how, for Husserl, 'the subject is henceforth the operating thetic consciousness' and 'any linguistic act . . . is sustained by the transcendental ego.'[145] Through introducing the philosophy of Husserl, Kristeva has situated the structuralism of modern linguistics within a phenomenological framework. As a result, the operating consciousness of the subject under discussion entails a notion of transcendence, which in turn creates a deeper divide and a distancing of the individual subject or meaning structure from the act of signification.[146]

To summarize, Kristeva examines the recent history of linguistic theory and associates it with Husserl's philosophy of phenomenology. She claims that every language theory is predicated on a conception of a subject who posits meaning. This positing of meaning by a definite subject is referred to as the symbolic.[147] In contrast, Kristeva will highlight an anterior and premonitory aspect to language, which is heterogeneous to meaning, and manifests in the rhythms and intonations of speech. She calls this disposition the semiotic.

Drawing from her research on child language acquisition in pre-phonological children as well as her research into psychotic discourse, Kristeva detects a '*heterogeneousness* to meaning and signification . . . detected genetically in the first echolalias of infants as rhythms and intonations . . . which is later activated as rhythms, intonations,

---

[144] Husserl (1970), 276–7; Kristeva (1980), 129.
[145] Kristeva (1980), 130.
[146] See Kristeva (1980), 124.
[147] See Kristeva (1980), 134.

glossalalias in psychotic discourse'.[148] These semiotic operations also exist in adult non-psychotic language, albeit in a less pronounced manner, and most evidently, according to Kristeva, in poetic language. Unlike prosaic language, where the coherence and meaning of the conscious idea is most prominent and pronounced, poetic language emphasizes the elements of language that appear to be devoid of signification. As such, the semiotic function within language, while inseparable from the symbolic function within a signifying practice, can at times operate 'through, despite, and in excess of it'.[149] The musical and syntactically disruptive aspects of poetic language at times disturb and challenge the thetic and predicative aspects of language, thereby undermining the transcendental ego of Husserl's phenomenology.

Schneersohn similarly expresses an onomatopoeic theory of language and distinguishes between intellectual consciousness and the pre-thetic 'letters of speech'. At first glance, it appears that Schneersohn's letters of speech are necessarily vocalized phonetic letters, and sounds and noises alone, which do not constitute coherent speech, would not reflect and instantiate a pre-thetic semiotic function. While Kristeva's semiotic is even more anterior in the 'body's drives observable through muscular contractions and the libidinal or sublimated cathexis that accompany vocalizations',[150] Schneersohn insists on the substantiation of discernible letters.[151] However, Kristeva herself later observes how, while a phoneme belongs to the symbolic function of language, it also 'tends towards autonomy from meaning so as to maintain itself in a semiotic disposition near the instinctual drives' body'.[152] Additionally, Schneersohn, while

[148] Kristeva (1980), 133.
[149] Kristeva (1980), 133.
[150] Kristeva (1980), 134.
[151] See Schneersohn (2011), 51–2.
[152] Kristeva (1980), 135.

emphasizing the importance of discernible letters, still recognizes the impact and relevance of sound in the transformative impact of speech on consciousness. In the first discourse, Schneersohn notes how when the words of prayer are pronounced loudly and with more intensity, it triggers a greater intentionality and devotion in the person praying. He explains how sound provides the material component of the letters, and it is specifically the material aspect of speech that is rooted deepest within the self. Therefore, through intensifying the materiality of the letters, their impact increases on a person's intellectual and emotional consciousness.[153] Although not addressed explicitly by Schneersohn, I expect he would be very accepting of the rhythmic and musical value of language highlighted by Kristeva, albeit in the context of and in consort with coherent speech.[154]

Kristeva warns that any challenge to the dominance of consciousness and the symbolic function must still consider the subject who expresses meaning in a communicable sentence between speakers. Invoking Derrida, Kristeva criticizes the attempts to deconstruct phenomenology, and argues that 'such "deconstructions" refuse (through discrediting the signified and with it the transcendental ego) what constitutes one function of language though not the only one'. Kristeva goes further and insists that 'any reflection of significance, by refusing its thetic character, will continually ignore its constraining, legislative, and socializing elements . . . such a reflection will become lodged in a negative theology that denies their limitations'.[155] As I have outlined earlier, I think this is an unfair criticism of Derrida; however, it gives further credence to my claim that deconstruction's second movement is often missed by its readers. Importantly, Kristeva is acknowledging how our appreciation of the semiotic must be

[153] Schneersohn (2011), 7–8.
[154] For Schneersohn on music, see Schneersohn (1989), 95.
[155] Kristeva (1980), 131.

understood within its operating context, where it is inseparable from the symbolic function. As I emphasized earlier, Schneersohn similarly goes to great lengths to understand the function of the provider, once the importance of the recipient is established. In this way, the schema of Schneersohn's thought, while found in Levinas and Derrida, is more explicitly expressed in Kristeva.

To fully appreciate how Kristeva explains the function of the symbolic when the semiotic is pronounced in poetic language, I will quote a key passage at length:

> the signifying economy of poetic language is specific in that the semiotic is not only a constraint as is the symbolic, but it tends to gain the upper hand at the expense of the thetic and predicative constraints of the ego's judging consciousness. . . . However elided, attacked, or corrupted the symbolic function might be in poetic language, due to the impact of semiotic processes, the symbolic function nonetheless maintains its presence. It is for this reason that it is a language. First, it persists as an internal limit of this bipolar economy, since a multiple and sometimes even incomprehensible signified is nevertheless communicated; secondly, it persists also because the semiotic processes themselves, far from being set adrift (as they would be in insane discourse), set up a new formal construct; a so-called new formal or ideological 'writer's universe', the never-finished, undefined production of a new space of significance. Husserl's 'thetic function' of the signifying act is thus re-assumed, but in different form: though poetic language unsettled the position of the signified and the transcendental ego, it nonetheless posits a thesis, not of a particular being or meaning, but of a signifying apparatus: it posits its own process as an undecidable process between sense and nonsense, between *language* and *rhythm* . . . between the symbolic and the semiotic.[156]

---

[156] Kristeva (1980), 134–5.

Kristeva provides us with two ways in which the heterogeneity of semiotic processes relies on, and benefits from, the symbolic function of language. Firstly, it facilitates the communication of an otherwise uncontainable multiplicity of semiotic aspects of poetic language. Secondly, the function of consciousness is 're-assumed' as a proponent, not of a determined meaning, but of an indeterminacy that opens up within the subject this other scene of pre-symbolic functions.[157] Subsequently, this newly configured subject, which no longer imposes the intentions of its consciousness, and acknowledges its own heterogeneity, is referred to by Kristeva as a questionable *subject-in-process*. This 'questionable subject-in-process exists in an economy of discourse other than that of thetic consciousness',[158] and seeks to convey the instinctual rhythmic and intonational drives of the body within a signifying structure.

These two functions of symbolic language, communication of the pre-symbolic and at the same time preserving its indeterminacy, were already conceived of by Schneersohn in the discourses: the primordial roots of speech, women and the body are not 'in an active state',[159] for in their source they are essential qualities that lack expression. Although these recipients typify the notion of otherness, they lack the impulse and thus the capacity to convey and articulate the separateness they exemplify. Therefore, the expressive qualities of the providers enable the otherwise hidden essential qualities of the recipients to be revealed.[160] Moreover, just as in Kristeva, where the symbolic functions of language, while facilitating the communication of the semiotic, remain faithful to the indeterminacy and uncontainable multiplicity of the semiotic, Schneersohn similarly re-assumes the signifying apparatus. Here is the key passage in full:

[157] See Kristeva (1984), 27.
[158] Kristeva (1980), 146.
[159] Schneersohn (2011), 17; 99.
[160] Schneersohn (2011), 99–100.

The essence of consciousness becomes internally grasped in specific details; however, the essence of consciousness shines in each detail, even in its most tangential detail. Therefore, all the details are in a state of wondrousness, and are not so distinguishable and restricted, since they are all connected with the essence.[161]

Schneersohn's symbolic function, which he calls the details of consciousness, expresses the pre-thetic 'essence of consciousness', while simultaneously transcending the usually limiting and restrictive categories of consciousness itself. This is a particularly difficult section in the discourses to comprehend; however, with the help of the poetic in Kristeva, we can propose here a significant enhancement to Schneersohn's explanation. Poetic language more naturally models how the semiotic can at once exceed and be expressed in the signified than in prosaic speech and language, and further demonstrates the benefits of juxtaposing Schneersohn and Kristeva's thought.

Let us summarize some of the key points we have addressed in this chapter. Schneersohn's examination of language, both in content and in form, foreshadows some of the defining features of postmodern thinking. His concern about a misplaced privileging of consciousness over spoken language leads him to reject the implications of a hierarchical order. To receive is not seen as an inferiority; rather, it indicates a primordial origin. Consequently, the relevance of consciousness is reimagined as the medium to convey the essential quality of speech. Moreover, through engaging Schneersohn's ideas in conversation with Levinas, Derrida and Kristeva we have been able to appreciate to a greater extent the possibilities these modes of thinking entail. These conversations have attempted a 'fusion of horizons' and endeavoured to produce a novel dialogical encounter between distinctive thought traditions. Whether considering 'the saying',

---

[161] Schneersohn (2011), 105.

'proto-writing' or 'the semiotic', we have been able to observe parallel trends of thought, as well as notable differences. In the next chapter we will expand these conversations and explore Schneersohn's ideas concerning gender and how they anticipate the reimagining of the female and the maternal body in postmodern thought.

3

Gender

In the previous chapter we examined Schneersohn's innovative and extensive exploration of the function of speech and its relationship with and impact on consciousness. His ideas were then brought into conversation with more contemporary figures who have developed strikingly similar understandings of language. These conversations sought to overcome a presumed interiority of Schneersohn's thought that has hitherto left him outside existing discussions in the philosophy of language. In this chapter I will attempt a similar examination of Schneersohn's philosophy of gender in his discourses of 1898 and consider the ways in which they can inform and be informed by an engaged dialogue with Levinas, Derrida and Kristeva. I will suggest how Schneersohn's understanding of the female, especially in her erotic encounter with the male, resists even more potently than in the previous chapter an exclusionary impulse towards him.

He enlivened us from the days . . .[1]

Schneersohn describes how the function of the *sephirah* of *malkhut* (itself referred to invariably as the female) as the creator of souls is

---

[1] Hosea 6:2.

comparable to a woman in the maternal role.[2] He first contrasts the communication of knowledge from a teacher to a student to an act of reproductive sexual intercourse: that whereas knowledge, even knowledge of physical things, is transferred in the form of conceptual abstractions that are non-physical, the sexual reproductive act involves the transference of physical semen.[3] Furthermore, the communication of knowledge does not involve a transference of the intellectual ability of the teacher, but merely an intellectual concept that can be appreciated only by a student who already possesses a sufficient level of their own intellectual ability. For 'no amount of intellectual communication can affect someone who is incapable of intellectual thought and who is inherently not an intellectual person. Hence the popular saying, "A head cannot be placed (on a person's shoulders)".[4] Thus, the communication of intellect is possible only when the recipient already possesses some level of intelligence, yet in the physical semen of the father, 'the very essence of the [father's] intellect[5] is actually communicated'. Through the semen of the father a new person with intellect is reproduced. Schneersohn is highlighting what may at first seem like a conceptual anomaly, namely, that a person's intellectual abilities can be conveyed to a greater extent through the non-intellectual physical semen than through intellectual ideas themselves.

Schneersohn elaborates further on this distinction between verbal intercourse and sexual intercourse, the former being a communication of an intangible intellectual concept whereas the latter involves the transference of a physical and tangible 'drop' of semen. The reason for

---

[2] See also Shneur Zalman of Liady (2002a) Deut. 94a; Ibid., *Shir ha-Shirim* 1a. An early source for this similitude is found in *Deut. Rab.* 2:37.

[3] As is common in rabbinic texts, Schneersohn opts for euphemistic terminology and refers to the semen simply as 'a drop'.

[4] Schneersohn (2011), 4. This phrase is quoted frequently in *Habad* texts, for example, Schneersohn, S. (1988), 314; Schneersohn (1984b), 64.

[5] As well as the whole essence of his being.

this distinction, he explains, 'is because in communicating intellect, only its radiance is conveyed – not the essence and substance of the intellect'.[6] That is to say, the act of intellectual communication is not an attempt to reproduce intellect itself but, rather, to convey intellectual concepts to an already equipped intellectual mind. While it might appear more logical to assume that an intangible communication would be more capable of conveying essential qualities such as intelligence, in fact, because intangible communication is in closer conceptual proximity to the intellect, 'we are forced to say that only a radiance [of the intellect] is conveyed – not its essence'. The essence of something is by definition not on display or ordinarily conveyed; only a 'radiance' and reflection of the thing is communicated through tools that are substantively similar to the conveyed matter. By contrast, with regards to sexual intercourse, Schneersohn continues, 'the very essence of the (father's) intellect is actually communicated, to the extent that it creates a complete soul with intellect and all the faculties of the soul. . . . This is because the essence is conveyed in this outflow (of semen), and so a new creation comes into being that is literally a reproduction of (the father)'.[7]

The notion that an essence can be transmitted only through physical, not spiritual, channels is explained in light of the *kabbalistic* idea expressed in *Sefer Yetsirah*: 'their beginning is lodged in their end'.[8] A person's essence, including their intellectual abilities, can be transferred specifically by means of the physical; Schneersohn explains that the highest and most primal – the essence – manifests itself specifically in the lowest and most peripheral – the semen. That is to say, in an ordered system of cause and effect, it would be unexpected for the effect to be able to influence let alone supersede the

---

6   Schneersohn (2011), 4.
7   Schneersohn (2011), 4.
8   *Sefer Yetzirah* (1965), 28a. This idea is further elaborated in Schneersohn, M. M. (1975), 450.

cause, since the entirety of the effect is an outcome of the cause. Yet, the emerging pattern of certain effects being capable of disrupting the ordered system and being able to express the seemingly inexpressible suggests a quality in the effect that is not dependant on the cause. The *kabbalistic* formula for this phenomenon is to say that whatever is most original and essential is 'lodged' and embedded in the most final and trivial. The idea that there is an inherent supremacy in the most final and trivial, by virtue of the fact that they are final and trivial, further enhances the novelty of the idea. For the task of disrupting the binary between intellect/speech and male/female is not achieved by reversing or equalizing the roles, but by maintaining the superficial representation of the parts while 'gifting' a quality to the apparently inferior component. It is central to the argument that this quality which is found in the recipient is not organic, but, rather, imposed from the outside, further accentuating the finality and triviality of its state.[9]

Schneersohn notes that notwithstanding the primal origin of the semen, the reproduction of the father by means of the semen alone does not produce a child, for 'the drop must be drawn into and clothed in the womb of the woman, who absorbs the drop'.[10] Moreover, it is specifically the quality of receptivity in the mother that allows for the reproduction of a child. Schneersohn invokes the Talmudic statement that 'additional understanding (*binah*) was given to a woman than to a man'[11] as referring to this creative capacity of women to bear children. For while the semen contains the potential of the new-born, 'it cannot produce a new creation; this can only be accomplished through the female. For it is with her power that the new-born is

---

[9] One hasidic thinker defined this principle as follows: in the situation where a refined quality is not suited to express something, then a crass quality is no longer inferior in its ability to express the very same thing. See Ushpal (1975), 17.
[10] Schneersohn (2011), 4.
[11] BT *Niddah*, 45b.

created as a literally new creation.'[12] In *Habad* literature, *hokhmah* (wisdom) is described as the initial expression of a concept prior to detailed analysis or appreciation. This insightful flash is then received in *binah* and is thoroughly examined and given detail and definition. This role of *binah* as recipient and then catalyst for a more profound appreciation of the concept than was originally possible in *hokhmah* is treated as archetypal for all things that function as a recipient, and hence the woman's ability to enhance upon the original transmission from the man is described by the Talmud as her possessing an added measure of this *binah* quality.[13] In contrast to earlier and subsequent *Habad* texts that primarily represent reproduction through the lens of the father,[14] Schneersohn gestures here towards a gynocentric understanding of reproduction, which he develops more fully in the second discourse, where the woman is the most significant contributor to the generation and birth of a child. The extension of the theme of receptivity to the female enhances our conception of the receptivity of *malkhut*; we learn how it is not merely a container like a cup, or a conduit as implied by the analogy of speech, but, rather, the main contributor to the 'birth' of the souls by virtue of the beginning being fixed in the end.

To expand his explanation of the provider/recipient paradigm in human reproduction, Schneersohn invokes the metaphor, which is prevalent throughout rabbinic literature, of the relationship between God and the Jewish people as being comparable to the relationship between a groom and a bride, respectively.[15] Furthermore, the midrash

---

[12] Schneersohn (2011), 4.
[13] See Schneersohn (2011), 11.
[14] For an example in earlier *Habad* thought, see Shneur Zalman of Liady (1978), 6b where the process of reproduction is principally linked to the father, and the mother's participation is portrayed as an incubator where the child 'waits for nine months' until it becomes formed. For an example in later *Habad* thought, see Schneerson, M. M. (1998), 458; (2000), 98. Schneersohn himself also presents this perspective in his annotations to Shneur Zalman's *Tanya*, see Schneersohn, M. M. (1989), 112.
[15] *Deut. Rab.* 2:37.

broadens the comparison and describes the giving of the Torah as being the wedding day and the consummation of the marriage.[16] From the background of this imagery, Schneersohn explores the nature of sexual intercourse and the resulting conception, gestation and production of a child. As we saw with regards to speech, the attempt to understand the metaphor is not merely as a means to better understand the subject, but, rather, it serves to extend the original concept further than was previously possible.

Schneersohn iterates two defining features of the female in a reproductive sexual encounter: she is both the cause of the transmission of the male's essence in the physical semen, and the one who produces the child. Schneersohn suggests that the example of the human female more strongly demonstrates her innate quality of essence than even the example of the supernal female (*malkhut*), which will be discussed more fully in the next chapter. For whereas the supernal female (*malkhut*) is a part of The World of Emanation and all its inherent attachment to God, the female as a created entity that perceives itself as an independent entity is not merely an indicator of a source beyond herself, but, in her perceived separateness, the very presence of that source itself. The extent to which the subjective human experience can be thoroughly unaware of any connection with God is a manifestation of divine essence that can only be hinted at by the *sephirah* of *malkhut*. This essential quality is present in all of humanity in a general sense but is more specifically evident in the maternal role of women.

Initially, Schneersohn establishes the basic physiology of reproduction, albeit couched in the *kabbalistic* terms of 'a drop of male waters' (semen) and 'a drop of female waters' (ovum):[17]

[16] *BT Ta'anit* 26b; *Num. Rab.* 12:8.
[17] Wolfson translates *tipat ma"n* more literally as female orgiastic fluid, which is more consistent with classical rabbinic and medieval Jewish understandings of female physiology. I have chosen to translate it as ovum in line with developments in medical

Just as the male bestows the drop of male waters, the female contributes the drop of female waters. The drop of female waters, however, serves as a receptacle to receive the drop of male waters from the male. Now even though the power of procreation comes from the drop of male waters, the drop of male waters by itself cannot conceive, except when it is received in the drop of female waters.[18]

After establishing the need for both male and female roles to produce a child, Schneersohn then goes further and argues that the female plays the primary role in the production of the child: 'Indeed, the primary formation of the foetus in its 248-limbed structure is due specifically to the drop of female waters.'[19] Although the male semen is instrumental in what Schneersohn describes as 'filtering' of the ovum, 'selecting the good and the choice components and removing the rest', and then 'from the best elements, the foetus is formed; from the remainder, the placenta is formed, and (later) is expelled',[20] it is the female who causes the development and birth of a new entity.

Schneersohn goes on to explain and 'justify' the role of the male in the production of the child:

The male initiation is necessary, however, because that which is 'essence', does not lend itself to revelation. Consequently, (this essence, or state of being) does not act at all. Similarly, the Essential power invested in the female lies dormant. The male emission, however, is akin to a revelation of essence, and therefore its power of procreation is more apparent. (To be sure, the male alone [also] cannot procreate or conceive at all, since he provides merely the aspect of revelation and not the actual essence). He awakens in the female the power to procreate and to conceive so that she can bring

understanding in the late nineteenth century that would possibly have been familiar to Schneersohn.
[18] Schneersohn (2011), 16.
[19] Schneersohn (2011), 16.
[20] Schneersohn (2011), 17.

into actual being – but she, the recipient, by herself actually creates. This is because of her original superiority.[21]

Similar to speech, the female is able to accomplish more than her apparent superiors, due to her actual superior origin and source in essence. Thus, not only is it specifically through her receptivity that the reproductive semen flows from the male provider, but she alone also has the ability to create and develop the child. This portrayal of the centrality of the mother's role in reproduction is markedly different from earlier Jewish sources and offers an important link between a theory of gender and the earlier discussion on speech and language.

The erotic reproductive encounter, which has historically been seen by many as the site that reinforces and is emblematic of the patriarchal system, is identified by Schneersohn as the precise location of its disruption. The divine-like creative female stimulates and arouses in the male an otherwise inaccessible reproductive force that she alone transforms through her maternity into offspring. This repetition of her own independence, separateness and otherness situates the female as both the most precise incarnation of these unique divine qualities and the means for their reiteration. However, the extreme implication of this absolute independence and otherness is a stasis that remains inert and impotent without the male propensity for expression. The sexual encounter remains the critical site of our understanding of gender relations, but for Schneersohn it exemplifies a perversion of an inherited patriarchal structure. His reconstructed gynocentric order embraces the profundity of a passive and receptive female that orchestrates her own emergence as the 'mother of all living things'.[22]

Before engaging Schneersohn's philosophy of gender with Levinas, Derrida and Kristeva, let us review the historic representation of the

---

[21] Schneersohn (2011), 17.
[22] Genesis 3:20.

role of the mother in the conception and gestation of a child, where
Schneersohn diverges considerably from a largely patriarchal tradition
and heritage. In early Greek thought, for instance, there is a tendency
to dichotomize existence in general into hierarchized dualisms.[23] The
table of Pythagorean opposites presents a view of the world divided
between determinate forms such as light, good and straight in contrast
to irregular and disorderly ones such as dark, bad and curved. The
identification of male with the determinate forms and the female
with the irregular ones contributed to the idea of male superiority in
line with the Pythagorean contrast between form and formlessness.[24]
In the *Eumenides*, for example, Apollo expresses in stark terms the
differing paternal and maternal roles in the production of a child:

> The mother to the child that men call hers
> Is no true life-begetter, but a nurse
> Of live seed. 'Tis the sower of the seed
> Alone begetteth. Woman comes at need,
> A stranger, to hold safe in trust and love
> That bud of her life – save when God above
> Will that it die.[25]

Clearly, the role of 'life-begetter' is exclusively paternal, and the
maternal role is here reduced to merely containing the seed that
generates itself into a child.

In both Plato and Aristotle, these gender differences were
incorporated into their broader distinction of form and matter.
For Plato, it was necessary for humans to exemplify in themselves
the broader reality of a distinction between knowable form and
unknowable matter. The ultimate goal was to liberate the rational soul

[23] See Lloyd, G. E. R. (1966); Lloyd, G. (1984).
[24] See Lloyd, G. (1984), 3.
[25] Aeschylus (1952), 235.

from the 'follies of the body'.[26] Plato's equating of male with form and female with matter encourages the notion of male superiority just as form is superior to matter. As Genevieve Lloyd has noted, 'The rightful dominance of mind over body, or of superior over inferior aspects of the soul, brings the knower into the required correspondence relations with the forms, which are in turn seen as superior to matter.'[27] As we can see, the role of the female becomes inextricably linked with the role of the body, and the superiority of the soul over the body is replicated in the superiority of the male over the female.

These notions of gender difference were further developed with regards to sexual reproduction, most notably by Aristotle, who saw the male semen as the principal reproductive agent, establishing the father-right and reducing the maternal role to a subordinate status.[28] From the very start of his *Metaphysics*, Aristotle presents the binary thought of Pythagoras's 'Table of Opposites', wherein male/female correlates with good/bad.[29] This correlation of the feminine with bad entails a further subordination of the maternal matter to the paternal form. For despite her portrayal by Aristotle as a life-giver and nurturer, she is secondary to the true creator and nurturer, which is the masculine principle of reason.[30] Specifically, Aristotle was of the view that men contribute form while women contribute matter in the process of reproduction, which he compares to the process of carpentry:

> Thus grasping the widest view of each, [the male principle] as maker and mover, and [the female principle] as that which is acted on and moved, the thing that comes to be is not made one from

---

[26] Plato (1997), 58 (*Phaedo* 67a).

[27] Lloyd, G. (1984), 7.

[28] Although Galen, who recognized the importance of women in reproduction, is often portrayed in contrast to Aristotle, he nevertheless maintained that the male seed is superior to the female. See Connell (2000).

[29] Aristotle (1984), 1559 (*Metaphysics*, 986a 22–26).

[30] See Pessin (2004), 29.

these, except as a bed is from the carpenter and the timber, or as the sphere is from the bronze and the form.[31]

The female, for Aristotle, provides the raw materials that the male shapes into progeny. This representation of gender attitudes in Aristotelian thought and its subsequent influence on the direction of Western philosophy has undergone a thorough critique by Sophia M. Connell in her *Aristotle on Female Animals*. Connell argues that there are a range of interpretative methods that attempt to deal with issues of consistency and coherence in Aristotle's thought and many feminist scholars 'imbibe second-hand scholarship coming from this interpretative tradition'.[32] She contends that a close analysis of Aristotle's works does not support the contention that he is particularly responsible for the subjugation of women to a dominant patriarchy. Notwithstanding Connell's intervention, which I consider having merit, for our purpose it is sufficient to assert that the Platonic and Aristotelian traditions as they were received and interpreted, especially during the Middles Ages, did indeed contribute to the dichotomization of existence into hierarchized dualisms. As such, the patterns of Western thinking in the modern period were fashioned to consider femaleness in general, and maternity in particular, as subordinate and inferior to maleness and paternity.

The maternal role and the perception of the body in classical rabbinic Judaism was notably different from its Hellenistic surroundings. Daniel Boyarin has explained that rabbinic Judaism in late antiquity, in contrast to prevalent Hellenistic thought, defined the human being as 'a body – animated, to be sure, by a soul – while for Hellenistic Jews (such as Philo) and (at least many Greek-speaking) Christians (such as Paul), the essence of a human being is a soul housed in a body'.[33]

---

[31] Aristotle (1984), 1132 (*Generation of Animals*, 729b14–19).
[32] Connell (2016), 15.
[33] Boyarin (1993), 5.

He goes on to clarify, however, that this definition does not imply a complete undoing of the implications of Greek hierarchical thought; in fact, 'the insistence on embodiment and sexuality as the foundational primitives of human essence almost ineluctably produces gender and sex-role differentiation as dominant characteristics of the social formation'.[34] While role differentiation does not inevitably manifest as a hierarchical system, and there is evidence in classical rabbinic thought of a non-hierarchical orientation, this differentiation lends itself to being appropriated in hierarchical thought systems.

In later medieval Bible and Talmud commentary there is, indeed, such a predominance to diminish the female contribution to reproduction, advancing a predominately androcentric portrayal of human genesis. For example, on the verse in Leviticus (12:2), which refers to a woman producing seed and giving birth to a son, the medieval exegete Bahye ibn Asher (1255–1340) interprets it to mean that the woman passes on the seed: 'For it is entrusted to her from the man, just like the seed of the earth is implanted in the earth and emerges in its time . . . for the children are his'.[35] This interpretation is emblematic of the emphasis on the centrality of paternity in reproduction, as well as the secondary role of the mother as a mere facilitator of the father's reproduction.

The explicitness and extensiveness in which *kabbalistic* thought uses gender imagery to characterize the divine could suggest the adoption of a gender polarity that places equal value on each autonomous gender. Subsequently, Schneersohn's restoration of both the biological and the sephirotic female as ontically distinctive and superior to the male could potentially be traced back to earlier *kabbalistic* formations of the same theme.[36] However, Elliot Wolfson

---

[34] Boyarin (1993), 10.
[35] Bahye ibn Asher (2007), 64.
[36] For an extensive treatment of this subject, see the recently published Idel (2019).

has argued that the *kabbalistic* recognition of feminine aspects of the divine is, in fact, portrayed as an undesirable gender bifurcation of an original male androgyne. Moreover, the female is commonly perceived as originally part of the male, and the goal becomes the restoration of the female to the male. According to Wolfson, 'although kabbalists clearly describe the divine in terms of male and female, in the final analysis the dualistic posture gives way to a metaphysical monism that can be expressed mythically as the male androgyne'.[37] Consequently, while the explicit gender imagery of *kabbalistic* texts may appear to naturally augment the developments in Schneersohn's discourses, upon closer examination the former further entrench a phallocentric mentality, further pointing to the innovative direction of Schneersohn's thought.[38]

Perhaps most significantly, even in *Habad* texts, which serve as the primary conceptual influence on Schneersohn's thought, the reproductive role of the father is privileged over that of the mother. In Rabbi Shneur Zalman of Liady's foundational work, the *Tanya*, he says as follows:

> Just as a child is derived from his father's brain . . . in that (even) the nails of his feet come into existence from the very same drop of semen, by being in the mother's womb for nine months, descending degree by degree, changing continually, until even the nails are formed from it. Yet (after all this process) is it still bound and united with a wonderful and essential unity with its original essence and being, which was the drop (as it came) from the father's brain.[39]

Here, the mother's role is presented as a mere transitory stage of the foetus's development, in order to ultimately establish its eternal

---

[37] Wolfson (1995), xiii.
[38] See Wolfson (1995), 79–121.
[39] Shneur Zalman of Liady (1978), 6a–b.

connection with the father. As has been shown earlier, Schneersohn develops a radically alternative understanding of the mother's role in reproduction: not merely as a transitory incubator but, rather, as the principal creative force that produces the child.

As we have seen with Schneersohn, for Levinas, the disruption of hierarchical binaries similarly leads to a consideration of the feminine and the maternal. He endeavours to disrupt a patriarchal dominance in the erotic and reproductive encounter, which involves a reappraisal of femininity and maternity. As we will shortly discover, while Schneersohn focuses on the passivity and creativity of the mother *vis-à-vis* the father, Levinas ultimately emphasizes the subjectivity of the mother in relation to her child.

At the conclusion of *Totality and Infinity*, Levinas brings the ideas of his book to their culmination with the claim that the ethical relation begins with an encounter with feminine alterity. However, it is specifically in the erotic encounter, and moreover, an erotic encounter that gives rise to paternity, where Levinas locates the truest form of the ethical encounter. He observes how 'a notion of being founding transcendence . . . seemed to us to be inscribed in the erotic relation'. Furthermore, the erotic is to be 'analysed as a fecundity', where 'the subject enters into relation with what is absolutely other . . . the feminine . . . the relation with it is a relation with its absence'.[40] Some feminist thinkers have taken issue with Levinas's apparently androcentric approach, which emphasizes the passivity of the woman (an absence) and her seemingly highest value as a means for reproduction.[41] Some scholars have argued that Levinas is not attempting to delineate actual male and female roles in the ethical relation, but is, rather,

---

[40] Levinas (2008a), 276–7.
[41] For scholarly criticism of Levinas's use of the feminine as the site of the absolute other, see de Beauvoir (1997, 6) and references cited by Sandford (2000), especially in chapter five (82–109). See also, Chalier (1982); (2002); Brody (2001); Chanter (2001); Sikka (2001).

developing an ontological category that is not exclusive to women.[42] However, what these critiques reveal is a reluctance to appreciate the impact of Levinas's disruption of traditional binaries where the same, consciousness and the male, are privileged. For Levinas, extending perceived male qualities of activity and dominance to women, misses the point of challenging the traditionally derogatory portrayal of the female as passive. To successfully overcome patriarchal dominance requires a radical reappraisal of feminine passivity and alterity, which for Levinas are the very qualities that condition ethical living.[43]

Levinas was aware of the feminist backlash against him and his conception of the female as the absolute other. In a 1982 interview he acknowledges that he 'used to think that otherness began in the feminine' and that he thought 'that the feminine was otherness itself'. Importantly, he refuses to retract from this position, but he explains that it is 'a very strange otherness: woman is neither the contradictory nor the opposite of man, nor like other differences'. As we experience throughout Levinas's work, otherness is not a polarity of sameness, but, rather, the ground on which sameness is possible. 'It is not like the opposition between light and darkness. It is a distinction that is not contingent, and whose place must be sought in relation to love.'[44] While Levinas's language in his earlier works might understandably trigger fierce feminist opposition, it simultaneously exposes the prevalence of an entrenched binary thinking that asserts female difference in opposition to what is male. For Levinas, the 'beyond object and face and thus beyond the existent' of the feminine is not perceived as 'a freedom struggling with its conqueror, refusing its reification and its objectification, but a fragility at the limit of non-being'.[45] The feminine is thus not seen as an alternative to the masculine, but, rather, as that

---

[42] See Perpich (2001), 47.
[43] See Rosato (2012), 349; Handelman (1991), 206.
[44] Levinas (2006), 97.
[45] Levinas (2008a), 258.

which brings the masculine into question. Especially in fecundity, the maternal feminine 'evinces a unity that is not opposed to multiplicity, but in the precise sense of the term, engenders it'.[46] Through the female capacity for reproduction and hence multiplication, the unity and dominance of the masculine I is disrupted. 'In a situation such as paternity the return of the I to the self . . . is completely modified . . . neither the categories of power nor those of knowledge describe my relation with the child.' For whereas in other spheres the impulse for domination either through power or knowledge allows the self and the same to have a sense of ownership and control, the reproduction of the self in paternity 'is neither a cause nor a domination'. The child is thus a multiplication of the self that exists separately from it and underscores the ontological importance of fecundity. 'Sexuality is in us neither knowledge nor power, but the very plurality of our existing . . . in existing itself there is a multiplicity and transcendence.'[47] It is specifically through what Levinas calls a 'phenomenology of eros' that rests upon the biologically empirical erotic relation with the feminine that the otherwise dominating and all-knowing self of the masculine comes into relation with transcendence.[48]

Significantly, in *Otherwise than Being*, Levinas moves beyond a focus on the feminine as the other to the masculine and emphasizes, instead, the idea of maternity itself. He explains how the presence of the child (the other) in the mother (the same) is a situation of supreme vulnerability that makes one hostage to another person, which for Levinas is the highest possible situation for any person. In this way, Levinas can be seen as seeking to overcome the criticism that in *Totality and Infinity*, he excluded women from his project of ethical

[46] Levinas (2008a), 273.
[47] Levinas (2008a), 277.
[48] See Derrida (2001), 97–192, for his critique of *Totality and Infinity*, and especially footnote 92 where Derrida remarks on the male-centred approach, and that uniquely among metaphysical writings it is impossible that it could have been written by a woman.

living. Through maternity, a woman can similarly encounter the other to the point of substitution where the mother can become a 'complete being "for the other".[49]

There are a number of comparisons and divergences in the way Levinas and Schneersohn go about disrupting the traditional patriarchal supremacy in the erotic encounter. It is notable how they both see the reproductive sexual encounter as exemplary of where the traditional dominance of the male can be disturbed. Instead of focusing on sexual difference as an abstracted binary, they pay attention to the performative sexual relationship of men and women. I consider this to be significant as it foresees the disruption of patriarchal supremacy not so much through a theoretical reconsideration, but as an informed physical intervention. Just like with speech mentioned in the previous chapter, where only the actual spoken words can elicit the effusion of the essential self through consciousness, so too is it only in the actual erotic encounter where paternal virility is realized. Additionally, they both emphasize the quality of passivity in the female, which places her prior to the self-identity of the male. As Schneersohn notes, while 'the root of the female is higher than the root of the male',[50] her primacy is manifest specifically in her identity as a recipient (*mekabel*). Her essential source is naturally inactive as it replicates a divine self-sufficiency that is indifferent to any impulse for exteriority. This quality manifests itself in her passive recipient state.

Where they diverge is in their treatment of maternity: Levinas focuses on the alterity of the child within the mother, thus repeating and intensifying the ethical relation between the male and the female in the erotic encounter, whereas Schneersohn emphasizes the creativity of maternity in the production of the child, which fails to address the subjectivity of the mother in relation to the child. These

---

[49] Levinas (2008b), 108. See Rosato (2012).
[50] Schneersohn (2011), 92.

divergences could be instructive and helpful. Through recognizing and appreciating the creative capacity of the female, which is a result, and not in spite of, her passivity, it may be possible to assuage some of the criticisms that are levelled against Levinas, and that accuse of him of being disparaging in his stereotyping of women. Comparably, through welcoming the more developed notion of women as subjects in the maternal relation, there is scope to explore more substantially the idea of the woman as provider (*mashpia*), which is only hinted at by Schneersohn in the discourses. While recognising the various ways we can observe how Schneersohn and Levinas disrupt binary systems, it is also important to note that the stated aims of their projects were different. Schneersohn was trying to give purpose and meaning to the religious observance of his followers, whereas Levinas was attempting to place ethics as prior and original to philosophy. Nevertheless, the marked similarity of their approach in unsettling the range of polarities in binary thinking can allow us to view them as mutually complementary. Schneersohn can provide insight as to how ethics and, more importantly, the ethical relation can condition social interaction,[51] and the more extensive treatment of the subject in Levinas can provide additional inspiration to the religious adherents in their commitment to Torah study and the fulfilment of *mitsvot*.

To a greater extent than Levinas, Derrida throughout his work is preoccupied with the theme of sexual difference. Derrida's starting point is a perception of Western metaphysics that purports a distinct 'male firstness', which he labels as a 'phallogocentrism'.[52] To

---

[51] It is noteworthy that during the delivery of the *discourses* in 1898, Schneersohn made two interruptions to deliver the same stand-alone discourse, which dealt with the importance of brotherly love. See Schneersohn (2011, 225–55). See also, Wolfson (2009b, 210), where he suggests that the project of Schneersohn's successor, Rabbi Menahem Mendel Schneerson (1902–94), where there is an emphasis on the primacy of the other as well as a more developed role for women, is premised on the intellectual framework established by Schneersohn in the discourses of 1898.

[52] Derrida (1988), 171.

better understand the meaning and intent of this neologism, let us first explain what Derrida means by logocentrism. Logocentrism is defined as 'the metaphysics of phonetic writing', which presumes that meaning can be made present through words and signifiers. In this construction, rational meanings are the dominant category in their binary relation with the systems of language. Drawing from Lacan's concept of phallocentrism, which views the phallus as the transcendental signifier, Derrida combines the two concepts and sees in binary and hierarchical systems the imprint of masculine dominating presence and feminine absence. Derrida's deconstruction seeks to expose how in each of these binary structures the dominating logo-phallic presence is, in fact, dependent and reliant on the absence of the signifier which 'condition and subtend its appearance'.[53] Moreover, he critiques what he calls a 'reactionary feminism' which conceives of sexual difference as an opposition. This 'dialectical opposition neutralizes or supersedes the difference' and 'insures phallocentric mastery under the cover of neutralization every time'.[54] In a manner akin to Schneersohn, which was discussed earlier, Derrida is alert to the potential of a mere inversion and thus repetition of a gender hierarchy. More specifically, he foresees how an attempt at neutralizing sexual difference will just further embed male dominance and lead to the erasure of the feminine. A central contention of deconstruction is that the conceptual edifice of a dominating logos/phallus presupposes the absence of the other and is conditioned by it. Therefore, in our context, female alterity and its perceived lack is what undergirds male dominance. As we described previously, Schneersohn similarly questions the supposed superiority and dominance of phallic elements. Notably, this questioning imitates and complements his probing of a dominating consciousness and its

---

[53] Feder and Zakin (1997), 47.
[54] Derrida (1988), 175.

relation to language, which we discussed in the previous chapter, and notwithstanding the possible differences between Schneersohn and Derrida, the discourses should be seen as an early iteration of deconstructing phallogocentrism *avant le lettre*.

Derrida portrays sexual difference in terms of presence/absence, which parallels Schneersohn's *mashpia/mekabel* (provider/recipient) paradigm. The decisive move that disrupts the phallogocentric perspective for both of them is a shift in our notion of these terms. For Derrida, presence presents as a stability with an ontological confidence that resolves the inadequacy of an absence. Presence is then exposed as being reliant on this absence, thereby laying bare its instability and ontological uncertainty. Similarly, the *mashpia* is initially portrayed as the supposedly superior and dominating force in its relationship with the *mekabel*. Ultimately, Schneersohn demonstrates that the very impulse to provide belies an instability, which seeks out the unchanging and secure indifference of the *mekabel*. Absence and receptivity are thus reconceived not as a polarity of presence and provision, but as the elements that undermine the very axioms of the phallogocentric discourse they sustain.

Derrida's wide-ranging thoughts on women, gender and sexual difference can at times appear apart from or in conflict with Schneersohn in his discourses. For example, a Derridean critique of gender identities in the discourses might accuse them of making essentializing ontological claims. Moreover, the insistence on the limited category of the biological woman in the discourses might be seen as inhibiting the emergence of a genuine *différance* that can deconstruct the axioms of Western metaphysics. In truth, these are questions that have been levelled against Derrida himself by several feminist scholars.[55] Nevertheless, it is important to restate that there is

---

[55] For example, see Feder and Zakin (1997), 24.

no intention of claiming that these texts align with certain perceived tenets of contemporary feminist thought. They do, however, reconceive models of sexual difference that have proven fundamental to Western thought and society, and provide possibilities for a post-phallogocentric culture.

From the broader context of sexual difference, Derrida arrives at a consideration of the maternal body. In certain ways, Derrida repeats and replicates a Levinasian reading of maternity, which at first accentuates the mother's absence. 'The mother is the faceless figure of a *figurant*, an extra. She gives rise to all the figures by losing herself in the background of the scene like an anonymous persona.' However, it is specifically this capacity that places her outside and beyond the symbolic system. 'Everything comes back to her, beginning with life; everything addresses and destines itself to her. She survives on the condition of remaining at bottom.'[56] As we saw in Schneersohn's discourses and in Levinas, the centrality of the mother is not despite her position in a hierarchical system but because of it.

More generally however, it is difficult to get a clear grasp of Derrida's approach to the maternal body. At times he seems to be deeply engaged with the notion of motherhood in its most biological and empirical sense, and yet, at other times he appears to be using maternity as a loose metaphor for language or the state. Kelly Oliver suggests that the reason the maternal body is a 'blind spot' for Derrida is that 'he associates the maternal body with nature or God'.[57] Unlike his more coherent and developed theory of writing and gender, it is perhaps specifically in the maternal where Derrida comes up short. For while language and gender reflect similar dynamics, the impact of the empirically situated biological encounter of sexual relations, which leads to pregnancy and birth, is the most potent demonstration

---

[56] Derrida (1988), 38.
[57] Oliver (1988), 66.

of the phenomena we are trying to describe. For whereas language and gender difference exist within their own internal loops and merely demand a reappraisal of an existing system, the creative mother forces us to think beyond any system or structure. As such, Derrida perceives the maternal as a key disruptor of the metaphysical structures he seeks to overcome.

As we mentioned earlier, Schneersohn similarly considers the maternal as the more significant example and demonstration of a *mekabel* that disrupts the perceived dominance of the *mashpia*. He describes his linguistic paradigm in conditional terms, where speech, for all its transformative effects on consciousness, cannot reproduce it. Consequently, the absence of speech merely enables us to reappraise and reassign value to an existing system that remains limited in what it can communicate. However, in maternity, a far more profound change occurs. He goes so far as to identify in the maternal body an immensity that exceeds even the workings of the metaphysical and sephirotic female (*malkhut*), which for all its creative force which we will discuss at length in the next chapter, is not capable of reproducing itself. For Schneersohn, the creative mother upends all our assumptions about male dominance, forcing us to reconsider how being is constructed and anticipating the similar deconstructive moves in Derrida's thought.

In our discussion so far, we have observed how both Levinas and Derrida centre their ideas concerning women on their maternal role. For Levinas, the female is an alterity that erotically disrupts the totalizing sameness of the male. Moreover, in her pregnancy she herself becomes disrupted and held hostage by the absolutely dependent otherness of the child. For Derrida, the absence of the mother enables the emergence of being and existence in a way that exceeds sexual difference alone. Kristeva deals at greater length with an understanding of motherhood and femininity than Levinas and Derrida, and her theory of language is often more directly linked to her theory of maternity. She notes the dominant representation of femininity as motherhood and how some *avant-garde* feminist groups have subsequently rejected motherhood, thus accepting the limitations of this traditional representation. However, she proposes that the 'resorption of femininity within the Maternal' may not just be a reduction which 'represents no more than a masculine appropriation of the Maternal', but maybe 'one might detect in it . . . the workings of enigmatic sublimation'.[58]

Drawing from Plato's *Timaeus*, she introduces the idea of a *chōra*, which she identifies as 'receptacle, unnameable, improbable, hybrid, anterior to naming, to the One, to the father, and consequently, maternally connoted to such an extent that it merits "not even the rank of syllable"'.[59] In Plato, the recipient is compared to the mother and is regarded as necessary for the production of offspring, but since it is unstable, uncertain, ever changing and becoming, Plato does not consider it divine.[60] For Kristeva, however, the mother's body becomes the site that precedes the intentionality of the child's thetic consciousness, and prepares the child for 'entrance into meaning and signification (the symbolic)'.[61] This semiotic *chōra* is described elsewhere by Kristeva as 'preceding the positing of the subject. Previous to the ego thinking within a proposition, no Meaning exists, but there *do* exist articulations heterogeneous to signification and to the sign.'[62] This grounding of the semiotic qualities of language in the maternal body, concomitantly associates the symbolic function of language with the father. Hence, the paternal symbolic function in structural linguistics and in Husserlian phenomenology 'constitutes itself at the

[58] Kristeva (1986), 163. See also, Kristeva (1980), 238.
[59] Kristeva (1980), 133. Derrida also makes extensive use of Plato's *chōra*. See Derrida (1995), 89–127. See also, Rickert (2007) for similarities and differences between Kristeva and Derrida on their use of the idea.
[60] See Plato (1997), 1253 (*Timaeus*, 50d); see Kristeva (1984), 239.
[61] Kristeva (1980), 136.
[62] Kristeva (1984), 36.

cost of repressing instinctual drive and continuous relation with the mother', and conversely, 'the unsettled and questionable subject of poetic language . . . maintains itself at the cost of reactivating this repressed instinctual, maternal element'.[63]

In our earlier discussion in the previous chapter on the reassuming of the symbolic function to express the semiotic, I argued that Kristeva's locating of her argument within poetic language can be helpful when understanding Schneersohn's approach to the subject. In this instance, in contrast, I would suggest that Schneersohn's explanation in the discourses of the paternal role, once the significance of the maternal function has been acknowledged, is more elaborate and detailed than what we find in Kristeva's work. Kristeva merely intimates how she intends to renew the paternal function as follows:

> It is probably necessary to be a woman (ultimate guarantee of sociality beyond the wreckage of the paternal symbolic function, as well as the inexhaustible generator of its renewal, of its expansion) not to renounce theoretical reason but to compel it to increase its power by giving it an object beyond its limits.[64]

Kristeva is here sketching out the possible outcome of a reassumed paternal role. She emphasizes how the destruction of the dominance of the paternal in the presence of the maternal must lead to the renewal and regeneration of the former. This renewal can only come about through the 'inexhaustible generator' that is the maternal, which provides the paternal with insight into something beyond its prior limits.

Schneersohn similarly parallels his insights on language with his understanding of gender, where the maternal is synonymous with speech and the paternal is likened to consciousness.[65] Unlike Kristeva,

---

[63] Kristeva (1980), 136.
[64] Kristeva (1980), 146.
[65] Schneersohn (2011), 16–17.

however, who seamlessly intertwines her exposition on language and gender, Schneersohn's approaches them individually. He explains how the ontological primacy of the mother and her creative maternal function is reflected in her receptivity: 'The actual reproduction is exclusively the power of the recipient (the mother), because of her superior source.'[66] However, as in the other instances of recipients, the mother is unable to actualize her reproductive qualities, and is thus dependent on a reassumed paternal function, which activates the mother's creativity:

> Therefore, the essential quality of reproduction is found specifically in her, but it requires the effusion of the semen (*hamshakhat ha-mayin dekhurin*), because something essential (*ha-atsmi*) is not capable of self-activation . . . he arouses the reproductive function in the recipient which enables the procreation.[67]

The father, in a manner similar to the other providers considered in the discourses, is aware of the supremacy of the mother and her supernal source. Consequently, her presence exposes and challenges the inability of the father to procreate as she can, which in turn arouses him to become intimately engaged with the mother. The sexual reproductive act in the discourses entails an elevation of the father because of his proximity with the mother – that is to say, the man becomes a father only because of the maternal creative function. This exposition closely mirrors Kristeva's hints at the end of her essay and helps situate how her paternal symbolic function can be compelled by the maternal to reach beyond its limits.

Through this dialogue between Kristeva and Schneersohn's discourses it has become clearer how Schneersohn was already concerned with the relationship of the symbolic and the semiotic over

66 Schneersohn (2011), 17.
67 Schneersohn (2011), 17.

half a century before they became prominent themes in Kristeva's thought. Moreover, juxtaposing their ideas and bringing them into dialogue has enhanced and elucidated otherwise difficult and terse sections in their respective texts. For example, Kristeva's choice to situate her thought within poetic language[68] offers an expanded and more accessible conception of language in Schneersohn, and Schneersohn's portrayal of the reproductive sexual encounter suggests a way to understand the renewal of the paternal function, which Kristeva only hints at.

This chapter has further demonstrated the relevance of Schneersohn's thought to modern philosophical concerns. The purposeful dialogue developed here between the traditional rabbinic thought of Schneersohn and the modern philosophy of Levinas, Derrida and Kristeva indicates again how overlooking traditional rabbinic thinkers in the study of philosophy, as well as reading traditional rabbinic thought in isolation from other thought traditions, reduces the scope of our understanding and knowledge of these traditions. In the next chapter the focus will turn to Schneersohn's mystical and metaphysical concerns in the discourses. The binary implications of divine mercy and justice are expanded to notions of transcendence and immanence, and to a new perception of an original cosmogony and an ultimate eschatology.

---

[68] See Levinas (2008a), 263, for a suggestion of a link between poetry and the feminine.

4

Mysticism

In the previous chapters we examined Schneersohn's portrayal of a range of supposedly oppositional binary relationships, and how there, in fact, inheres a primary significance to the supposedly secondary and inferior component in these relationships. Schneersohn argues that speech, women and the body while functioning as recipients of intellect, men and the soul, respectively, are actually the condition for, and initiators of, all the beneficence that they receive. Moreover, through the act and function of receiving they make possible the manifestation and disclosure of what is ordinarily concealed and inexpressible. Schneersohn explained how this transformative quality of the recipients is due to their innate originality and primacy in God. The passive and non-expressive qualities of the recipients and their apparent independence and separateness mirror the very same qualities in the essence of God and thus indicate their primordial origin in the divine essence.

While Schneersohn's concern with language and gender in the discourses of 1898 lend themselves to an engaged discussion with contemporary philosophical thought, the primary focus of the discourses is on the mystical and the metaphysical. Schneersohn teases out the implications of metaphysical binary structures such as divine 'mercy and justice' as presented in the *midrash*, as well as the themes of *sovev* and *memale*. As with language and gender, Schneersohn seeks to reconstruct a new vision whereby these contrasting forces reinforce each other and function harmoniously. Ultimately, the discourses will present how, through commitment to the divine commandments in the Torah, these metaphysical models will manifest in the world in the messianic era.

Unlike in the previous chapters on language and gender, this chapter will not attempt a sustained dialogue between Schneersohn and Levinas, Derrida and Kristeva. Apart from some analysis of the concept in *tsimtsum* and how it can inform some enigmatic *kabbalistic* motifs in the writings of Levinas, some comments on the idea of messianicity and *khora* in Derrida, and the use of Kristeva's explanation of the heterogeneity of the semiotic becoming constituted in and expressed through the symbolic, I have purposefully chosen to not engage extensively with what some consider to be mystical overtones in the writings of these thinkers. As I laid out in the introduction, the purpose of this study is to create the circumstances where it is possible for these thinkers to constructively engage with each other and observe where there might be a convergence of concerns. In the previous two chapters I have demonstrated the potential for such a dialogue; however, in this chapter my aim is to analyse the primary context of Schneersohn's philosophy within *Habad* mystical thought. The presentation of the broad schema of Schneersohn's thought in the previous sections and its parallels with postmodern thought will hopefully allow the philosophically trained reader to engage with the topics in this section more easily. And while I recognize that for others there is a desire to discover latent Jewish mystical dimensions specifically in the works of Levinas and Derrida, my objective here is to propose how a new discourse, which does not seek to dissolve the different thought traditions of the interlocutors, may become possible. Thus, notwithstanding the attempt later in this chapter to directly engage Levinas and Derrida with Schneersohn's *kabbalistic* and mystical themes, it remains important to acknowledge the limited and narrow scope of their familiarity with original *kabbalistic* sources. Such an acknowledgement is not intended to cast doubt on the validity or worthiness of this exposition, but, rather, to avoid a situation where correlation is mistaken for causation. Just as it would be both anachronistic and confusing to incorporate Schneersohn in the canon of postmodern thought, it would, in my view, be a similar oversimplification to strongly identify Levinas with the Jewish mystical tradition. In fact, what makes the previously mentioned insights of the alignment of Levinas's thought with Schneersohn all the more interesting is how they were able to emerge reasonably independently of each other. This approach allows for a broadening of ideas where each thinker's positions can become expanded into categories that were previously unexplored and avoids a methodological approach that reduces the apparent diversity of thought into a supposed unity.

These fundamental limitations of relating Levinas to mystical Jewish thought are even more pronounced when considering Derrida.[1] Susan Handelman observes how the common concern of transcending and transgressing boundaries makes it wholly natural to link *kabbalistic* and poststructuralist themes.[2] Indeed, and as I have shown in this book, there is considerable value in engaging thinkers such as Derrida with rabbinic thinkers who engage with Jewish mystical thought. The problem as I see it, however, is that Derrida himself, as well as the scholarly literature on this topic, engages with *kabbalah* through a Scholemian lens and mainly overlooks the vast tradition of mysticism that abounds in contemporary rabbinic works. As I have written at greater length elsewhere, the ignoring of the extensive post-Luria rabbinic *kabbalistic* writings of the modern period within contemporary academic Jewish mysticism

---

[1] On Derrida and Kabbalah, see Wolfson (2014), 154–200, and the references he cites there. Wolfson goes to considerable lengths to advise caution when approaching the topic of Derrida and *Kabbalah*. See also, Bielik-Robson (2021), 389–418, for a more strident approach towards the *kabbalistic* dimension of Derrida's thought.

[2] Handelman (1982), 217.

leaves the field at best deficient and at worst, distorted.[3] Derrida was adamant that his work has no relation to mysticism in general and Jewish mysticism in particular. 'I'm not mystical and there's nothing mystical in my work . . . . When I say I am no mystic, above all no Jewish mystic, as Habermas maintains somewhere . . . I'm not only personally not mystical, but I question whether anything I write has the least trace of mysticism.'[4] While there is no need to take Derrida's self-appraisal as the definitive word on the possible mystical nature of his work, and notwithstanding the irony of Derrida of all people insisting on absolute categorical boundaries, it is nonetheless sensible to recognize Derrida's limited exposure to, and lack of familiarity with, Jewish mystical thought. This chapter will hopefully contribute to a widening of scholarly resources needed for a meaningful discourse between Jewish mysticism and contemporary thought, and further demonstrate the necessity for a greater engagement with mystical post-Luria rabbinic literature.[5]

The particular idiomatic format of *Habad* texts will inevitably prove difficult for the uninitiated scholar, and they may require some initial help and direction in order to appreciate the material. The scholar seeking to gain familiarity with the nearly 500 volumes of primary texts of *Habad* thought will encounter a number of obstacles. The subjects they discuss are not neatly arranged in a manner where ideas progress in a linear format. Furthermore, many topics have multiple interpretations and there is little attempt to dogmatically assert a conclusive reading, often leaving the reader to determine which interpretation any given text may be following.[6] Add to all

---

[3] Leigh (2021), 86–92.
[4] Rötzer (1995), 47.
[5] For examples of scholarly engagement with mystical post-Luria rabbinic literature, see Wolfson (2009b); (2013); (2016).
[6] A common Yiddish refrain among initiates of *Habad* thought when trying to decipher a difficult text is 'it all depends in which context the discussion is being held' (*es vent zich vu m'redt*).

this a whole range of idiomatic and idiosyncratic phraseology, and it becomes understandable why so few scholars have attempted to engage with *Habad* thought in a comprehensive way. In our analysis of the discourses of 1898, we encounter all the above obstacles. To help orientate the reader I will present here a brief schema of some key themes in *Habad* thought that will be extremely pertinent to the discussions in our text.[7]

Atsmut ve-Eyn Sof – God's Essence and Infinitude:[8] One of the foundations of *Habad* thought is that God's being is beyond any categorization or definition. For were God to be defined or categorized as, say, wise or kind, that would problematically suggest that God has a definable form. The term used to connote this idea is *atsmut* (essence), and it is used specifically to indicate something that is non-differentiated and non-composite.[9] A possible consequence of the idea of *atsmut* is that human beings would never be able to achieve an understanding of God, since the human intellect is limited in its ability to comprehend a non-differentiated entity. Any human experience of, say, divine wisdom or kindness, would thus have to be described as relative and not truly indicative of God, who always remains beyond the differentiated categories of wisdom and kindness. Moreover, the idea of *atsmut* would render the innumerable descriptions of God in Scripture as being wise, kind and benevolent, as descriptions of human perceptions of God.

Together with the idea of *atsmut*, God's being is defined as *eyn sof* (infinitude). Infinitude is not understood in the binary terms of

---

[7] There is a noticeable gap of any comprehensive discussion of the main themes and concepts in the scholarship on *Habad*. In the main, I have relied on the extensive material in the wide-ranging but incomplete *Sefer ha-Erkhin Habad* (Kahn and Lipskier (1975)).

[8] See Schneersohn (1989), 214; (1991), 940.

[9] The *Habad* texts when attempting to indicate essence typically invoke the phraseology of Rabbi Judah Loewe of Prague (1526–1609) in his *Gevurat Hashem*: 'God's essence is simple and not differentiated in any way ... and we cannot know God's being ... for God is simple in an absolute simplicity' (*pashut be-takhlit ha-peshitut*).'

finiteness and infiniteness that would indicate that God is not restricted or limited, but, rather, as a perfection and completeness that does not exclude any quality from God, even finiteness.[10] This perfection of God ensures, unlike the idea of *atsmut*, that God can be truly grasped in the finite and relative confines of human understanding and experience. God is no longer understood as being *necessarily* non-differentiated, but, rather, God has all the advantages of not being differentiated, and none of the deficiencies of a categorized entity. At the same time, together with this advantage, God's perfection also includes all the advantages of differentiated entities, namely, that they can be humanly grasped.

Ohr Eyn Sof – The Light of Infinitude:[11] *ohr eyn sof* refers to the revelation of God that precedes creation and it is called 'light' to indicate its similarity to the light of the sun. Just like sunlight is a mere reflection of the sun and is incomparable to it, so too the *ohr eyn sof* is incomparable to God. Conversely, just like the sunlight is attached to the sun and reflects the sun's qualities, so too the *ohr eyn sof* reveals the perfection of God. Thus, contained within the *ohr eyn sof* is both the quality of finiteness and that of infiniteness; nevertheless, the dominant feature of God's perfection in the *ohr eyn sof* prior to creation is God's quality of infiniteness. God's quality of finiteness will subsequently emerge only through the act of *tsimtsum*.

Tsimtsum – Creation: Prior to creation there was God (*atsmut eyn sof*) and God's self-reflection (*ohr eyn sof*) that expressed the infiniteness of God. In order to facilitate the creation and the emergence of differentiated finite entities, God brought to the fore

---

[10] This idea of *eyn sof* is commonly attributed to Rabbi Meir ibn Gabbai (1480–1540), who states in his *Avodat ha-Kodesh*: 'The *eyn sof* is absolute perfection, just as It has the quality of infiniteness so too It has the quality of finiteness, for if you were to say that It has the quality of infiniteness but does not have the quality of finiteness, you cause Its perfection to be lacking.'
[11] See Kahn and Lipskier (1975), 40–278.

the divine quality of finiteness. This quality of finiteness is depicted as *otiyot* (letters), which provide the components for the creative divine speech in the *sephirah* of *malkhut*.

Eser Sephirot – Ten Attributes:[12] God's presentation in the form of differentiated entities so that humans can actually engage with God is called *sephirot*. Therefore, when God is described as wise or kind, it is truly indicative of the instantiation of God in the *sephirah* of *hokhmah* (wisdom) or *hesed* (kindness) and is not just a relative description of human experience. The division of ten distinct attributes depicts the emergence of the quality of finiteness of God in the *sephirot*. These ten categories are portrayed as each consisting of an *ohr* (light) and a *keli* (container) that mediates the transition from formlessness to a distinct definition. There is disagreement among the early *kabbalists* as to the exact constitution of these lights and containers and as to the question of whether the differentiation of, say, wisdom and kindness already exists within the *ohr*, or whether these forms are superimposed on the *ohr* by the *keli*. The ten *sephirot* are anthropomorphically arranged to broadly reflect a cognitive process that transitions from an abstract self-contained mind, through an emotional connection to something external to itself, and ultimately leading to an actual engagement with the other. The *sephirot* thereby signify a diminution of the infiniteness of God and the development of a differentiated interface that can engage with human beings. The process begins with the awareness of a concept in *hokhmah* (wisdom), which is then analysed in *binah* (understanding), resulting in an appreciation of the concept's relevance in *da'at* (knowledge). Once the concept is appreciated in *da'at* it can trigger the three primary emotional responses of *hesed* (lit. kindness, associated with love and a drawing close) or *gevurah* (lit. severity, associated with fear and a pulling away) or *tipheret* (lit.

12 See Kahn and Lipskier (1976), 57.

beauty, associated with a blending and harmonizing of *hesed* and *gevurah*). Each of these three emotional traits is closely linked with the intellectual *da'at* that spurns them and remains at a distance from an actual interaction with anything external to itself. In order to move further towards such an external encounter, a less self-conscious version of these emotions emerges in the form of *netsah* (lit. victory), *hod* (lit. splendour) and *yesod* (lit. foundation), respectively. The process reaches its culmination in the final *sephirah* of *malkhut* (lit. sovereignty, associated with speech) where the previously aloof and self-contained God communicates the creation. In the discourses of 1898, the *sephirah* of *malkhut* is regarded as the instantiation of God's quality of finiteness, which in turn originates in *atsmut eyn sof*. In contrast, the previous six *sephirot* (often referred to with their *kabbalistic* moniker *ze'ir anpin* (*z"a*)) are regarded as expressions of God's quality of infiniteness found within the *ohr eyn sof*.

This brief primer provides a starting point to engage with some of the primary terms, themes and issues within *Habad* thought. However, it remains vital to remember how all the aforementioned descriptions do not constitute a rigid and fixed system of thinking, and all the themes mentioned undergo regular revisions across the *Habad* corpus of literature. Even within Schneersohn's oeuvre itself there are significant shifts in his interpretation of key themes. Consequently, readers should remain mindful of how the philosophy of Schneersohn in the present chapter reflects his approach in the discourses of 1898 and does not necessarily reflect his thinking in the round. While keeping that in mind, it is noteworthy how several of the later developments in Schneersohn's thought can be found in embryonic form in our discourses.[13]

---

[13] For example, while it would not be until 1912 that Schneersohn would embrace a theory of *sephirot* where their definitions as distinct from each other would encompass both the *ohr* and the *keli*, there is already a tentative adoption of this approach in 1898 as we will discuss shortly.

'He will revive us from the two days'[14]

On 18 September 1898,[15] Schneersohn delivered the second instalment out of eight of his series of discourses. Unlike the first discourse, which he delivered the day before, that is predominately occupied with an exploration of human speech and is presented in relatively accessible terminology, the early part of this discourse is more enmeshed in the technicalities of metaphysical *kabbalistic* thought.[16] Some commentators on the text suggest that this noticeable change to a more laconic tone may reflect the tangential nature of the point being made at the outset of the discourse.[17] I would add that among Schneersohn's audience would consist of a range of intellectual abilities, and it is possible that he would vary his style in order to cater for a variety of expertise. However, I disagree with the contention that this subject is of secondary importance to the main theme of the discourses, and the present discussion will be integral to the conclusion of the discourses, where the necessity of the provider in the provider/recipient relationship will be outlined.[18] With that in mind and to make the next section more accessible, I will make a few preparatory remarks on the kabbalistic concepts that are germane to both this discourse and the continuation of the discourses.

The process of creating the physical and finite world is described as at first requiring a series of emanations whereby the non-composite and non-differentiated essence of the divine could create composite and differentiated metaphysical existence. This process

---

[14] Hosea 6:2.
[15] Corresponding to the second day of *Rosh Hashanah* (Jewish New Year).
[16] Rabbi Ya'akov Landa (1893–1986) notes that in 1918 when a group of students questioned Schneersohn on a difficult *kabbalistic* passage in one of his discourses, he replied, 'what has kabbalah got to do with you,' suggesting that he did not intend for his students to labour over the terse *kabbalistic* passages. See Altein (2006), 107.
[17] See Paltiel (2010).
[18] In fact, throughout the discourses we find a switching between a more dense and technical style of writing to a more expansive and explanatory style.

of emanation consists of myriads of levels and degrees, and at each stage in this process the emanation is concealed and reduced until it is possible to create entities that are not overwhelmed by, and hence subsumed in, the divine presence. A key stage in the crossover from an overwhelming divine presence to a stable created existence is called The World of Emanation (*olam ha-atsilut*). The World of Emanation consists of ten general stages of emanation (*sephirot*) that are called wisdom (*hokhmah*), understanding (*binah*), knowledge (*da'at*), kindness (*hesed*), strictness (*gevurah*), beauty (*tiferet*), victory (*netsah*), glory (*hod*), foundation (*yesod*) and sovereignty (*malkhut*). This discourse is particularly interested in the interplay between sovereignty (*malkhut*) and the six emanations that precede it. Being the tenth and the last of the emanations, *malkhut* embodies the idea of receptivity, as it receives its energy from the other emanations. *Malkhut* is described as the female (*nukvah*), while the preceding six *sephirot* are called the male (*dekhar*). Since the transition that enables the creation of the physical world is identified as taking place in The World of Emanation, the analysis of created reality is heavily focused on the intricate interaction between the particulars of this stage.

Furthermore, a foundational idea in *Habad* thought is that the physical world, in contrast to the *sephirot*, falsely perceives itself as an independent and self-sustaining entity. These physical entities are not overwhelmed by the divine presence and are entirely unaware of their dependence on the Creator, thereby feeling stable and self-sufficient. *Habad* thought concludes that since only God can be truly stable and self-sufficient, and not preceded by anything else, then only God is capable of creating entities with a similar self-awareness. Therefore, in a paradoxical way, the very quality that obscures the creations' awareness of the Creator, namely their apparent self-sufficiency, is the quality that denotes their intimate association with the essence of God. This raises the question of how the creation, which is mediated by *sephirot* in The World of Emanation that are aware of their dependence on God, can create entities with a sense of independence from God. The emanations are just a radiation from the essence of God and are deeply aware of their connectedness to their source; this lack of independence makes them incapable of creating a world with a perceived independence from God.[19] Therefore, for all the structure and apparatus of The World of Emanation that facilitates the creation of the physical world, it does not sufficiently explain how the process of creation is possible. Regardless of how reduced and diminished an emanation becomes, it will still remain an emanation of God that is defined by its connectedness to God.

It thus becomes necessary to identify and locate an essential power of God (*koah ha-atsmut*) within The World of Emanation, which can explain how entities with a perception of independence could be created. This discourse explains that the location of this creative power of God is in the *sephirah* of *malkhut*. The passivity and lack of expression of *malkhut* connotes a lack of active connection to a higher source, unlike the emanations whose active expression of God reflects a connectedness and attachment to God. In this sense, *malkhut's* separateness and detachment is akin to the essence of God that is entirely independent and self-sufficient. Consequently, *malkhut* is able to convey this essential quality and create entities that believe in their own autonomy.

However, *malkhut* alone is incapable of creating the physical world, and she requires the activity of the six *sephirot* that precede it to activate her creative power. Although she has the exclusive ability to replicate and reproduce the quality of divine separateness and independence, this ability will always remain inactive, since by her nature she is unaware of, and thus indifferent to, the motivation for creation. By contrast, the six preceding *sephirot* are fully aware of the

---

[19] The primary text for this idea is Shneur Zalman of Liady (1978), 129a.

divine motivation for creation due to their attachment to God, yet on their own, lack the ability to actually create a separated physical world. These differences result in a co-dependency of the six preceding *sephirot* and *malkhut* in the process of creation. This dependency has a significant impact on the six preceding *sephirot* which, in order to activate this creative power in *malkhut*, gain access to this essential quality of God (*koah ha-atsmut*). In this way, the six preceding *sephirot* also become a vehicle for the essential creative power of God by virtue of their engagement with *malkhut*. This concept of the elevation of the six preceding *sephirot*, albeit by dint of *malkhut*, will play a crucial role in the latter part of the series of discourses as mentioned before.

In summary, a provider/recipient relationship that aims to reproduce the self-sufficiency of the recipient (such as in creation) achieves an essential communication in a manner that is not seen in some of the previously discussed provider/recipient relationships. For example, speech can have a transformative effect on the communication of ideas, but it relies on a suitable listener who is already familiar with similar ideas. In the absence of an erudite interlocutor the communication will fail to convey the ideas that would have been greatly enhanced by speech. The present discussion, however, involves a recipient comparable to the maternal body who does not just convey an enhanced version of the provider, but also produces and creates a version of itself. *Malkhut* conveys the essence of God that she contains in the creation of the world, similar to the way a woman conveys her essence in the creation of a child, as discussed in the previous chapter. The objective of the first section of this discourse is to further entrench the principle that the recipient does not merely receive from the provider, but also, in fact, gives far more in return. The first discourse discussed this principle with regards to speech as recipient of ideas and emotions, and the body as recipient of the soul. Schneersohn extends this principle to the relationship of *malkhut*, as recipient of the six preceding *sephirot* in The World of Emanation.

Malkhut is described in the *Zohar* as 'not having anything of her own',[20] and as being dependent on the six preceding *sephirot*. Yet, for Schneersohn, the very condition and the catalyst for the giving of the six preceding *sephirot* is the presence of *malkhut*. The outcome of this interplay is the creation of the world, which in turn determines the very fabric of existence: that the provider/recipient relationship is reciprocal and that the recipient is the key transformative element in all relationships. Quoting from Song of Songs (3:11) and the *Zohar*,[21] the six preceding *sephirot* are compared to a king who achieves his greatness and receives his crown only on the day of his coronation when the people, the subjects of his rule, anoint him as their king. The concept of a coronation in *Habad* thought is the arousal of the will to rule in the monarch. Since the will to rule is a very deeply concealed faculty of the soul, it requires the people, through their submission to the king, for its arousal and revelation. Once this will to rule is uncovered, the whole being of the king is elevated to a state of greatness.[22] *Malkhut* is synonymous with the people and is the condition, the cause and the reason for the emanation of the crown (*keter*) in the six preceding *sephirot*. Whereas according to the proscribed order of emanation, there is no effusion of the crown in the six preceding *sephirot*, when these *sephirot* enter into relations with *malkhut*, it benefits from 'an effusion of a greater supernal radiation, which is the radiation of The Crown'.[23] The reason why *malkhut* is capable of this distinction is that her origin is higher than that of the six preceding *sephirot*.[24] The extension of this principle of the profound

---

[20] *Zohar* I:249b; II:215a.
[21] *Zohar* 3:5a; 2:235a; *Zohar Hadash Tisa* 44a; *Hukat* 51d.
[22] See Schneersohn (1988), 324, for an extensive treatment of this theme.
[23] Schneersohn (2011), 15.
[24] See *Zohar* III:292a. See also, Shneur Zalman of Liady (2002a), Lev. 19b. Whereas both six preceding *sephirot* and *malkhut* are effusions from the crown, Schneersohn distinguishes between the innermost level of the crown (*atik*) and its exterior (*arikh*). See *Ets Hayyim, Sha'ar Arikh Anpin*, 7.

relevance of the recipient to *malkhut* unlocks a new dimension in the principle that will have a significant impact on the direction of the series of discourses. In contrast to the example of speech that can only communicate an emanation of the self (*hashpaʾah hitsonit*) but is unable to convey the self itself, *malkhut* (the supernal female), similar to the biological female, is capable of reproducing her innate essential selfhood.

Schneersohn then extends the provider/recipient paradigm to the relationship between the Torah and the people of Israel. Drawing on imagery from Song of Songs, the discourse imagines the revelation at Sinai as a wedding day with God as the groom, the people of Israel as the bride and the Torah as that which consummates the union.[25] The Torah is thus an essential transmission of God comparable to the seminal emission of the male, discussed earlier, who is able to produce an essential copy of himself. This essence of the male is specifically conveyed in physical semen; similarly, the Torah and *mitsvot* are expressed in the physical components of the world. Some traditions in Jewish thought fail to see any inherent meaning in the physicality of material *mitzvot*, and for them this physicality serves merely as a necessary medium due to a human inability to engage with God in a transcendent way. Schneersohn, by contrast, appreciates how 'the beginning is lodged in the end,' and divine essence is specifically expressed in the most final and peripheral material elements. Consequently, the performance of a *mitzvah* using the physical components of the world is not treated as a sign of human frailty, but, rather, as the necessary site for connecting with the essence of God.

In accord with earlier examples of provider/recipient models, the receiving of the Torah by the people of Israel demonstrates, says Schneersohn, that the people of Israel are the very cause of

25 Song of Songs 3:11; see *Mishnah Taʿanit* 4:7.

the essential divine transmission of the Torah. Just as the letters of speech and women are the very condition for consciousness and male presence, so too the people of Israel are the very condition that elicits the revelation of the Torah. This insight has potentially far-reaching theological and social consequences. *Hareidi* communities have developed a theology that places Torah and its study as the highest ideal, often to the detriment of other religious concerns and ideals. Conversely, Schneersohn appreciates a profundity in the people of Israel that undergirds the Torah system. This idea plays a critical role in contemporary *Habad* activism and informs its philosophy of outreach. Whereas in the *Hareidi* community the highest ideal is a lifetime of Torah study, in *Habad* circles the ultimate achievement is to go on *shlihut* (become emissaries) and connect with disengaged Jewish people, often in far-flung locations.

Furthermore, this deconstruction of the hierarchical binary between Torah and Israel does not lead to an inversion that disadvantages the Torah. Rather, because the source of Israel is higher than the source of the Torah, it is able to enhance and elevate the Torah itself. The transmission of the Torah prior to its reception by the people of Israel is only an effusion of the essence but not the essence itself, yet when it is received and performed by the people of Israel, it becomes a conduit for the essence itself, just like the supernal and biological male as described earlier. However, just as in the case of the mother, the people of Israel's quality of essence is naturally dormant and non-expressive and requires stimulation and arousal from the provider. Therefore, every activity of the people of Israel must be according to the Torah in order to arouse the essential quality of the people of Israel, but the reason why that activity is impactful is that it is performed by the people of Israel.

This 'deconstruction' of a 'logocentric' religious system of thought distinguishes Schneersohn's Jewish theology not only from other religious traditions, but also from other major strands of

Jewish thought. Whether it be the logocentric assumptions of early Christian critiques of Judaism as a religion of law as opposed to faith, medieval Jewish apologetics of *mitzvot*, Reform Judaism's rejection of supposedly outdated religious practices or *Hareidi* hyper-emphasis on Torah study, Schneersohn presents an alternative premise for Jewish theology, identity and observance. The Jew in particular, and the physical world more generally, are understood to be the instantiation of God's independence who through the Torah and *mitzvot* realise their purpose.

Return! O Israel . . .[26]

Schneersohn now returns to the *midrash* on which the discourses are structured and focuses on the contrasting forces of justice and mercy. It is important to stress again that the term 'justice' (*din*) is used here to connote the strict basis and application of the law rather than an emphasis on fairness,[27] and 'mercy' (*rahamim*) suggests a contrasting force that can override the limitations and constrictions of such strict justice. These two forces will provide the setting for a broader and more encompassing application of the earlier discussion on oppositional binaries. According to the *midrashic* material under discussion, the original intention was to create the world with the attribute of justice, but creation was ultimately enacted through the joint forces of God's attributes of justice and mercy. These attributes are depicted in Genesis as the divine names *Elokim* and YHVH. The opening question posed at the beginning of the series of discourses was why God, who is good and seeks to do good,[28] would consider

---

[26] Hosea 14:2.
[27] In Hebrew, terms such as *mishpat* or *tsedek* more closely denote fairness.
[28] See Schneuri (1991), 5.

creating the world with the attribute of justice rather than mercy.[29] The third, fourth and fifth discourses present a range of explanations for why God would have initially desired to create the world with justice as described in the *midrash*. The presentation of a plurality of explanations is common in *Habad* writings and is reminiscent of a rabbinic approach found consistently in *midrashic* and Talmudic texts. This juxtaposing of contrasting and sometimes contradicting interpretations of the same material suggests a belief in the polysemic nature of text, as well as an epistemological pluralism that does not seek a dogmatic and singular resolution to the given concerns. The way in which the discourses first acknowledge and then expand upon justice's desirable quality reflects the broader objective of constructing a positive and mutually beneficial system whereby both justice and mercy together enable the fulfilment of creation. Schneersohn will offer over the next three discourses two contrasting explanations that will seek to define the attribute of justice as not merely the function of enacting punishment but also the condition for meaningful divine service.

The origin of the coupling of the divine names with the attributes of justice and mercy as described in these *midrashim* has been the subject of considerable scholarly attention, especially within the field of Philo studies.[30] The subject of the relationship between divine names and attributes was already examined by Zacharias Frankel (1801–85) in his *Ueber den Einflus der palestinensichen Exegese auf die alexandrinische Hermeneutik*,[31] where he claimed that Philo's knowledge of rabbinic thought was entirely superficial and is reflected in his inverted schema of the relationship between the divine names and attributes, matching justice with the YHVH and mercy with

---

[29] See Schneersohn (2011), 2.
[30] See Philo; Coulson and Whitaker (1930), 77.
[31] See Frankel (1851), 26.

Elokim.[32] The theme of the two divine attributes is explored more generally and distinctly from the writings of Philo by professor of Jewish Law Suzanne Last-Stone.[33] Stone explains that 'the rabbis posit a complex schema in which mercy and justice are combined in one divine figure possessed of two distinct attributes or measures – strict justice (*din*, which also connotes law, argument, logic and punishment) and mercy (*rahamim*) . . . the rabbis conceived of justice and mercy as two polarities of a paradoxically unified divine whole'. She goes on to describe how according to the rabbinic tradition 'the various names of God appearing in scripture refer to these two attributes of God',[34] and provide the framework for interpreting divine action in the Bible.

According to Israeli scholar Yehudah Liebes, the parable of the cups can be traced back to Homer in the *Iliad* (24: 527–34) and in Plato's *Republic* (379d)[35] and claims that the most direct source for both Philo and the rabbis is Plutarch's *Moralia* (369c):

> Nature brings nothing which is not combined with something else, we may assert that it is not one keeper of two great vases who, after the manner of a barmaid, deals out to us our failure and successes

---

[32] In contrast, Arthur Marmorstein (1882–1946) links the relationship between the rabbinic concept of divine justice and mercy as represented in the divine names with the similar idea expressed by Philo. See Marmorstein (1927). See also, Marmorstein (1932) where he responds to critics of his 1927 monograph, defending his claim by arguing how the seemingly inverted format of Philo's schema, in fact, reflects an earlier and more authentic representation of the rabbinic idea. Marmorstein's argument was not widely accepted since it relied on a single proof text, which was later found to be deficient; nevertheless, his general thesis was examined further by Nils A. Dahl (1911–2001) and Alan F. Segal (1945–2011) in their 1978 article 'Philo and the Rabbis on the Names of God'. They claim that even though Marmorstein's proof was inconclusive, his general intuition may have been correct. They conclude that it is not possible to ascertain which schema is attested to in the earliest sources, and, in fact, is not significant in relation to the primary point of the harmonization of the divine attributes that is attested to by the joining of the divine names. Shlomo Naeh (1997) performs a critical analysis of the Philonic text and the *midrash* under discussion. He suggests that both Philo and the Rabbis based their parable on an earlier interpretation of Psalms 75:9: 'there is a cup in the hand of the Lord of unmixed wine, full of mixture . . .'

[33] See Last-Stone (1996).
[34] Last-Stone (1996), 8.
[35] See Liebes (2000).

in mixture, but it has come about, as the result of two opposed
principles and two antagonistic forces, one of which guides us
along a straight course to the right, while the other turns us aside
and backward, that our life is complex, and so also is the universe.

Considering the *midrash* in light of this source in Plutarch can help
us appreciate Schneersohn's initial question. Even though justice is
a divine attribute, why would God desire to only 'deal out to us our
failure . . .' and 'turn us aside and backward'? However, in order to
answer this question of why God intended to create the world with
justice, Schneersohn will proceed to describe the attribute of justice
in a manner that is not readily apparent in either the earlier rabbinic
or Greek sources.

The third discourse was delivered on the Sabbath between the New
Year and the Day of Atonement[36] and draws its title from the reading
of the prophets from that Sabbath.[37] The *Habad* discourses delivered
on this Sabbath are traditionally focused on the concept of *teshuvah*
(return/repentance) and tend to focus on the more applied nature of
hasidut, referred to as *avodah* (service), rather than its conceptual
nature, known as *haskalah*.[38] Accordingly, this discourse provides an
extensive exploration of a contemplative process geared to eliciting
three levels of love of God and which reaches its culmination in the
act of *teshuvah*. However, while accentuating the applied aspects of
his thought, Schneersohn continues to develop the central conceptual
theme of his series of discourses, and weaves the two objectives,
avodah and *haskalah*, into a continuous theme.[39]

[36] Friday, 23 September 1898.
[37] *Hosea* 14:2.
[38] This term should not be confused with its common usage as a name for the Jewish
Enlightenment.
[39] During the course of my research, I was approached by a *Habad* follower and was
challenged whether I would include the *avodah* sections of this discourse in the book or
would focus only on the *haskalah*. This comment reflects how the continuity between
conceptual and applied aspects of *Habad* thought are not always appreciated even by its
seasoned readers.

The discourse makes an important claim at its outset that the entire purpose of the *midrash* under discussion, which describes the divine method of creation, is in order to give guidance and instruction as to how the people of Israel should conduct themselves in their divine service.[40] This claim is instructive in how it allows us to appreciate the orientation of the series of discourses. For Schneersohn, his extensive analysis of this *midrash* and the construction of an abstract cosmo-ontological theory is in order to apply his findings to a newly informed mode of religious practice. Consequently, although we have been drawing comparisons between Schneersohn's thought and broader currents in twentieth-century philosophy, it is important to remember that Schneersohn's thought is situated in the very specific context of encouraging his followers to lead meaningful religious lifestyles. I would argue that the specific demands of Jewish religious life could be viewed as prompting the very questions that Schneersohn is seeking to address. Whereas the dominant narrative in both *Habad*[41] and many other Jewish schools of thought[42] speaks of the need for form to dominate matter (*hitgabrut ha-tsurah al ha-homer*), the material and embodied nature of Jewish ritual observance can be viewed as leading Schneersohn towards an alternative, and in his view more satisfactory, answer to the perceived dualistic conflict between the embodied nature of Jewish ritual observance and a transcendent religious experience.

Schneersohn's initial solution for God's consideration to create the world with the attribute of justice is in order to instil fear of punishment (*yirat ha-onesh*). If divine justice conditioned the fabric of reality, then all creatures would be aware of the consequences of their actions and would guard themselves from sin. This explanation

---

[40] Schneersohn (2011), 25.
[41] For example, see Schneerson, M. M. (1995), 30.
[42] For example, see Seidler (2013), 118–19.

might appear normative to some religious traditions; however, Schneersohn feels compelled to offer a justification for invoking it here. Throughout *Habad* literature there is an especial aversion to divine service that is premised on personal gain or survival, suggesting that such behaviour is itself sinful.[43] Schneersohn explains that whereas divine service that is self-serving is, indeed, problematic, it is less problematic than actual forbidden acts, and can therefore be considered worthwhile, albeit begrudgingly. This explanation suggests that God considered creating the world in this manner to guarantee higher levels of obedience.[44] The value of obedience that the attribute of justice would invoke is primarily in the guaranteed fulfilment of the divine will. Schneersohn, however, goes further, and suggests that beyond achieving a basic level of religious commitment, this initial consideration to create the world with the attribute of justice would also inspire the practitioner to achieve the highest form of divine service (*avodah ha-amitit*). The discourse explains how a world created by the attribute of justice would not only ensure greater obedience and fewer transgressions but would also enable a more complete performance of the divine precepts. The exacting and demanding attribute of justice would prompt a responding degree of self-censure in the creations. This notion already finds expression in a number of Talmudic[45] and *kabbalistic*[46] sources that the discourse cites, where justice is identified with an act of self-censure and critique.[47] When individuals critique themselves, to the point of 'their heart becoming crushed within them',[48] they are able to remove the concealing forces of the body and access the deepest love of the soul.

---

[43] See Shneur Zalman of Liady (1958), 31; Schneersohn M. M. (1977), 2029.
[44] See Schneersohn (2011), 25–7.
[45] See for example, *BT Berakhot* 30b.
[46] See for example, *Zohar* III:178b; III:168a.
[47] See *BT Sotah* 47a.
[48] Schneersohn (2011), 27.

Were the world to be created with the attribute of justice, it would inspire people to be self-censorious, thereby achieving the highest levels of divine service. To explain this idea more fully, Schneersohn describes levels of divine service that reach their highest perfection through an intense critique of the human condition.

The love the soul has for God is divided into three categories commensurate with the verse in Deuteronomy (6:5): 'And you should love the Lord your God with all your heart, with all your soul, and with all your might.' The discourse proceeds to explain the way to achieve these three forms of love, drawing closely from earlier *Habad* texts.[49] The love of God with all your heart and soul are described as products of an intense contemplation on the nature of reality, and on how matter is dependent on and thus subservient to the form that animates it. Consequently, lusting after and indulging in the matter component of anything alone severs the natural unity that inheres in it. Contemplating the way in which everything is animated by a divine form and how all creations are 'truly subservient to the divine light within them' should arouse a person to a 'great wanting, yearning and love to Godliness,'[50] and to no longer desire the materialism of the world.

It may seem that Schneersohn is presenting here an entirely different perception of the relationship between the soul and the body than in the previous discourses, and some *Habad* scholars have suggested that this section of the discourses could be treated as on a tangent from the broader theme.[51] I would posit that perhaps

---

[49] See Shneur Zalman of Liady (2001), 85c; Shneuri (1989), 573; Schneersohn M. M. (1968), 1855.

[50] Schneersohn (2011), 30.

[51] From a private discussion with Rabbi Michoel Golomb, a lecturer in *Habad* thought at the central *Habad yeshivah*. He argued that discourses at this time of the year traditionally focused on *teshuvah* and even though Schneersohn was in the middle of a set of discourses, he quite understandably devoted a section of this discourse to concepts not directly relevant to the overall theme of the discourses.

in light of the strong affirmation of the role of the body and the physical in the previous two discourses, Schneersohn wanted to clarify to his listeners a potential misunderstanding. It is imperative to recognize that whereas the body and the material are rooted deeper in the essence of God, in the context of their detachedness and unawareness of their source, they can lead a person away from a connection to God. Therefore, it is still valuable, and sometimes necessary, to maintain a perspective of the superiority of the soul over the body, in order to achieve a love for God. Nevertheless, as will be developed shortly, even in this state, the body remains the cause and catalyst for the highest expressions of the soul. Schneersohn will describe how the soul, even prior to its descent into the body, already has a love of God. However, it is specifically through the sense of estrangement that the soul experiences while in the body that the soul is able to reach a deeper and more profound love of God.

The discourse observes how the two forms of love, 'all your heart' and 'all your soul', remain limited within the context of the divine engagement with this world, not to mention the limited capacity of the contemplator's intellectual and emotional abilities. These two forms of love are expressed as the desire to escape the confines of the material world and cleave to the divine light that animates the world, and as the desire to increase the awareness of the divine presence in this world through the observance of the Torah and its commandments. The divine engagement with this world, which is the subject matter of this contemplation, is described as merely a 'ray' and 'effusion' (*ziv ve-ha'arah*) of God and is considered insignificant in the context of the essence of God. Consequently, the impact of these forms of love is an intensification of the divine engagement with the world, in a manner of *ziv* and *ha'arah*, but does not reach beyond that. Conversely, the third form of love – with all your might – is associated with the very essence of the soul (*mehut ve-atsmut ha-nefesh*), and expresses itself as a complete nullification of the self (*bitul kol metsiuto le-gamri*), and in an expiration of the soul (*kelot ha-nefesh*) in its yearning for the divine essence.[52] Unlike the love forms described earlier that operate within the limits of expression of the faculties of the soul, 'love with all your might' expresses the unlimited essence of the soul that is rooted in the essence of God.

However, the stimulus for this love is a reaction to the distress and anguish felt by the soul from its embodied experience. The soul, notwithstanding the restrictions imposed upon it by an embodied experience, is in a constant state of love and desire for Godliness. Through contemplating the limits and restrictions the soul experiences in the body and how this situation distances it from Godliness – an act of self-censure and critique – the soul can be intensely aroused to escape the confines of the body.[53] Thus, the very cause of estrangement of the person from God serves as the catalyst for the most intense love and reconnection of the person with God. This process is identified as being synonymous with *teshuvah* (repentance),[54] since the act of penitence is a request for forgiveness from a power that transcends and exceeds the normative legal bounds of divine service. When the penitent goes above and beyond the limited requirements of divine service, they can elicit the necessary forgiveness to overcome past deficiencies. Through past deficiencies the penitent is propelled towards a more exceptional divine service, similar to a 'love with all your might'. The normative bounds of divine service involve a legal framework where disobedience is punished, whereas through the act of *teshuvah*, a person is able to be pardoned for their transgression. Schneersohn invokes the *midrash* that describes *teshuvah* as one of

---

[52] For references to kelot ha-nefesh in earlier *Habad* works and other non-*Habad* works, see Wolfson (2009b), 318fn50.
[53] Schneersohn (2011), 33.
[54] Schneersohn (2011), 34.

the things that preceded the creation of the world,[55] placing *teshuvah* beyond the limitations of divine engagement with the world.[56]

By explaining that only when creations behave judgementally with themselves can they connect with the essence of God and subsequently reveal that essence in the world, the discourse has attempted to explain why an otherwise merciful God would intend to create the world with justice. The intense presence of the attribute of justice would highlight the incongruity of mundane existence and inspire in people the desire to cleave to God. However, the sheer intensity of such a divine service would have been unbearable – 'He saw that the world could not survive' – and required a more balanced approach – 'So he mixed with it the attribute of mercy'. The intensity of being in a constant state of complete nullification of the self to the point of expiration of the soul, however desirable from the perspective of achieving the most sublime divine service, is beyond most people's capabilities. Therefore, the world was created together with mercy, yet it remains coherent and understandable why a God, who is good, would want to create the world with justice.

As will be discussed in more detail shortly, if we interpret justice in the *midrash* as an overwhelming and extremely present expression of God as we do here in the third discourse, then the addition of mercy connotes a curtailing and reducing of divine expressiveness. It could be argued that this approach is more in tune with a straightforward reading of the sentiment of the *midrash*, which appears to indicate that the addition of mercy was a sort of compromise and cooling down of justice. However, the next two discourses will attempt to understand the motivation for creating the world with the attribute of justice from an entirely different perspective than the one presented here. Instead of the attribute of justice signifying an exacting and involved presence

---

[55] See BT Pesahim 54a.
[56] See Schneersohn (2011), 37.

of God that will arouse people to be exacting and judgemental with themselves, the fourth and fifth discourses will explain how creation with the attribute of justice is an act of self-censorship by God that conceals and hides God's presence.[57]

The date-palm and the willow . . .[58]
on the eighth day . . .[59]

The title of discourse 4 is drawn from the mishnah in the tractate of *Sukkah* that details the rules regarding the taking of the four kinds (*arba minim*) on the festival of Tabernacles (*Sukkot*) when it occurs on the Sabbath. Following an initial query on the differences between the rules concerning the blowing of the horn (*shofar*) on the Jewish New Year (*rosh ha-shanah*) and the taking of the four kinds when they occur on the Sabbath, as they did in 1898, the discourse provides a short summary of the conclusions of the previous discourse. The discourse then proceeds to offer an alternative explanation for the motivation to create the world with the attribute of justice than was proffered in the previous discourse. The present explanation, which will be treated to a prolonged examination that will reach its conclusion only at the end of the fifth discourse, rests on an entirely opposite premise than the first explanation. Whereas in the previous discourse Schneersohn argued that the attribute of justice would facilitate a higher level of intensity in divine service due to the practitioner's exposure to divine intensity, in this discourse Schneersohn will assert that the attribute of justice serves to conceal and hide the divine presence.

---

[57] Ultimately, the discourses will show preference for the second explanation in its final account of the *midrash*; however, this first version is maintained throughout as a valid alternative construction of reality.
[58] Mishnah *Sukkah* 4:1–2.
[59] Numbers 29:35.

This concealment allows for the emergence of apparently distinct and autonomous created beings that are unaware of their origin, which is a necessary prerequisite for an advanced level of divine service.

In order to reach this conclusion, the discourse will present a detailed description of a cosmic order that is drawn from earlier *kabbalistic* and *Habad* texts.[60] This cosmic order is extrapolated from Isaiah 43:7: 'Everyone that is called by My name (*shemi*), and whom I created (*berativ*) for My glory, I formed him (*yetsartiv*), yea I made him (*aseetiv*).' The discourse explains how 'created, formed and made' refer to the three supernal worlds called *briah* (creation), *yetsirah* (formation) and *asiyah* (action), whereas *shemi* indicates the highest world of *atsilut* (emanation). Throughout kabbalistic thought there is an attempt to explain how it is possible for finite and limited existence to have emerged from an infinite creator. In the Zoharic tradition there is much emphasis on a process of emanation referred to as the ten *sephirot*, which serve as a bridge between the creator and the created. These ten *sephirot* constitute the world of *atsilut* (emanation)[61] and the transition from divinity to creation. The creation *ex nihilo* takes place through these ten *sephirot* of the world of *atsilut*.[62] In later Lurianic *kabbalah* the concept of *tsimtsum* is expanded upon to suggest that, prior to the emanation of the ten *sephirot*, God withdrew in order to allow for an 'empty space' wherein the world could be created. *Tsimtsum* is fundamental to the *Habad* conception of reality and in

[60] Schneersohn (2011), 40. See also, Schneersohn S. (2000), 470; Schneersohn (1984a), 68.
[61] See Scholem (1954), 205–43; Jacobs (2006), 27–43; Shneur Zalman of Liady (1998), 896–921.
[62] Schneersohn identifies the lowest rung of the world of *atsilut* (emanation) – *malkhut* – as the key location for the transition from unlimited Godliness to finite existence. *Malkhut* (lit. sovereignty,) as discussed in the earlier discourses, is the process whereby the infinite Godliness of *atsilut* is concealed and hidden in order to create finite worlds. During the months prior to the delivery of these discourses, Schneersohn was engaged in a thorough study of a foundational discourse of Rabbi Shneur Zalman of Liady on this subject, see Schneersohn (1980).

these two discourses will play a crucial role in understanding creation as described in the *midrash*.

The concept of *tsimtsum* underwent a thorough and forensic examination in the works of each of the *Habad rebbes,* and it is beyond the scope of this chapter to present a complete appraisal of their readings and innovations. Still, for the purpose of better appreciating the novelties in Schneersohn's 1898 writings, I will first present a general schema of the treatment of *tsimtsum* in *Habad* thought.[63] Rabbi Shneur Zalman, the founder of the *Habad* system of thought, professed a strong allegiance to the writings of Isaac Luria,[64] but, as we will see, he carefully developed an original version of the Lurianic *tsimtsum* that sought to overcome a version of theism that placed the created world entirely outside of God, while at the same time attempting to maintain God's immutability. A reading of Luria's *tsimtsum* that involved God's withdrawal (*tsimtsum kipshuto*) and God's absence from creation was unacceptable according to Rabbi Shneur Zalman's notion of divine unity. At the same time, if God participates in the act of creation (*tsimtsum she-lo kipshuto*), the newly emerged creation suggests a change in God that would be equally unacceptable.

To overcome these problems, the *Habad tsimtsum* is dependent on a clear distinction between God (*atsmut*) and the expression of God (*ohr eyn sof*).[65] Characteristics that identify something as essential (*atsmi*) in *Habad* thought are self-containment and a lack of dependency on anything else. An *atsmi* is not interactive and is not perceptible by anything other than itself. In contrast, what is classified as expressive (*giluy*) is reliant on an original luminary and is interactive in its aim to express its source. God (*atsmut*) is therefore

---

[63] See also my earlier presentation of this theme in Leigh (2021).
[64] Shneur Zalman of Liady (1987), 89.
[65] On the emergence prior to *tsimtsum* of divisions and distinctions in God, see Schneersohn (1984a), 101.

conceived as that which has no origin and cause, and moreover has no compulsion to be expressive. In contrast, the expression of God (*ohr eyn sof*) does have an origin – in God – and serves to convey divine qualities such as omniscience and omnipotence.

Habad thought explains the motivation of God to create a world as the desire to create an entity that is sufficiently independent to willingly subject itself to divine sovereignty. However, the infinite and luminescent nature of the *ohr eyn sof*, which expresses divine omniscience, precluded the emergence of sufficiently independent beings that could satisfy this desire for divine sovereignty (*ta'anug bi-melukhah*), which is the desire for a seemingly independent and separate entity to submit their will to God. Consequently, when the objective of creation to create separate entities that would submit their will to God was conceived by God (*atsmut*), it stood in conflict with the objective to convey the exclusivity of God by the expression of God (the *ohr eyn sof*). Subsequently, the act of *tsimtsum* was interpreted by Rabbi Shneur Zalman in a manner that rejected the notion of God (*atsmut*) actually withdrawing from any void; rather, the impact of *tsimtsum* was, instead, on the *ohr eyn sof*. Obscuring the *ohr eyn sof* made the creation of an apparently independent entity possible.[66]

The distinction between God and the expression of God aimed to resolve the concerns that *tsimtsum* brought about a change in God, by stating that the *tsimtsum* affected only the expression of God. This would seemingly allow for a more literal reading of *tsimtsum*, where the expression of God is actually removed; however, the *tsimtsum* is still not interpreted literally (*kipshuto*) by Rabbi Shneur Zalman; rather, the *ohr eyn sof* is described as being concealed and suppressed but not removed. Similarly, just as the withdrawal (*siluk*) is not

---

[66] On the division of *ohr eyn sof* before the *tsimtsum* into three levels: 'the essence of the light' (*etsem ha-ohr*), 'the light that is revealed only to Itself' (*ha-ohr she-be-giluy le-atsmo*) and 'the light that is relevant to the worlds' (*ha-ohr ha-shayakh le-olamot*), see Schneersohn (1991), 247–9.

interpreted as an actual removal of the *ohr eyn sof* but its concealment and the suppression of its opposition to creation, so too the resulting so-called empty space (*makom panui*) is understood as being empty of only the expressiveness of the *ohr eyn sof* that would oppose creation. Through this suppression of the *ohr eyn sof* there is sufficient 'space' for the emergence of a trace (*reshimu*) of God (*atsmut*). This idea of *reshimu*, which originates in the school of Israel Sarug (d. 1610), is identified with God's ability of limited expression (*koah ha-gvul*) that prior to the *tsimtsum* was overwhelmed and concealed by God's ability of unlimited expression (*koah ha-bli gvul*), namely, the *ohr eyn sof*. Through the act of *tsimtsum* this divine ability for limitation emerges in the place now no longer saturated with God's infinite expression.[67] The act of *tsimtsum* is then understood as a diminishing of the ability of the *ohr eyn sof* to overshadow and overwhelm the essential divine quality of finiteness. This interpretation of the *tsimtsum* overcomes the problem of any type of actual removal of both God and the *ohr eyn sof*.

Drawing on the imagery of engraving in the *Zohar's* account of creation,[68] Rabbi Shneur Zalman and subsequent *Habad* thinkers emphasize the identification of letters (*otiyot*) with the trace (*reshimu*). As will be expounded shortly, letters exemplify the essential qualities of separateness and independence that inhere in God, and thus serve as a fitting contrast to the expressive *ohr eyn sof*. The letters of the *reshimu* are thus considered to be at the very epicentre of created reality and provide the link between God and creation. This linguistic metaphor found its fullest exposition in the 1898 discourses of Rabbi Shneur Zalman's great-great-grandson, Rabbi Shalom Ber Schneersohn.[69]

---

[67] For one of the clearest descriptions of this idea, see Schneersohn (1998), 30–44.
[68] See *Zohar* I:15a: 'He engraved engravings in the Supernal Purity.'
[69] For the most comprehensive example of this interpretation of *tsimtsum* in Rabbi Shneur Zalman's writings, see Shneur Zalman of Liady (2002a), Lev. 54a.

As we described in the earlier chapters, Schneersohn's conception of speech and language involves a sharp distinction between the phonetic pronunciations of spoken letters (*otiyot ha-dibbur*) and the intellectual or emotional content of an oral communication. Schneersohn contends that there is no obvious link between the articulated phonemes and the concepts they convey, and that the vocalization of somatic letters is not to be thought of as the product and expression of a conceptual idea or emotional state, but to a certain extent constitutes their concealment and suppression.[70] However, ultimately, through speech the ideas are able to achieve far greater depth and clarity. As discussed at length in the first discourse, the ontological primacy of spoken language in general and, more specifically, the physically vocalized component, letters of speech (*otiyot ha-dibbur*), enable speech to 'force' the faculty of intellect to express itself to a greater extent than it would out of its own initiative. Prior to speaking a person can develop an idea using their intellect together with their faculty of thought, a process that will initially be limited to the intellectual development of that person. However, beyond this, through expressing the idea in speech, an essential dimension of the self is triggered and filters through to the intellect, thereby expanding the horizons of the original idea.

In the present discourse, Schneersohn returns to the theme of speech and expands upon his earlier exposition. For whereas he had previously stated how the component, letters of speech, are not considered to be generated by the intellect or emotions and ontologically precede any state of intellectual or emotional consciousness, he now emphasizes that the emergence of these letters in a tangible and discernible form, and not just as mere sounds, occurs by way of that consciousness. Schneersohn observes that while the letters of speech (*otiyot ha-dibbur*)

---

[70] See Schneersohn (2011), 47.

may originate from a primordial source within the self, they lack, on their own, the capacity to articulate and convey that sublime source. As explained earlier, the characteristics that identify something as essential (*atsmi*) in *Habad* thought are self-containment and a lack of dependency on anything else, in contrast to what is classified as expressive (*giluy*) that displays its reliance on an original luminary. Consequently, were these letters (as essential and primordial) to become isolated from the coherence of intellectual or emotional consciousness, they would fail to communicate the profundity of their source since they lack the quality of expression.

This line of reasoning is similar to his earlier explanation of the necessity of the male in the process of reproduction, since the female's creative ability would remain dormant without the stimulation of the male. Schneersohn's appreciation for the superior origin of the letters does not lead him towards a reification of a nonsense. Such a position would merely invert the traditional Platonic and Aristotelian hierarchical relationship between consciousness and speech and would result in the degradation of consciousness. Instead, he recasts intellectual and emotional consciousness from being the true inner meaning of speech as conceived in much of Western and rabbinic thought, to becoming the necessary tools to convey the sublime qualities that are here assigned to speech. As was explained at length in the second discourse with regards to the purpose of the expressive male in conveying the essential quality of the female, similarly here, the expressive character of the intellect serves to provide the framework in which the essential quality of speech can be voiced.

This conceptualization of the relationship between consciousness and speech provides Schneersohn with a distinctive framework in which to describe the *tsimtsum*.[71] The *ohr eyn sof*, which is analogous

---

[71] See Schneersohn (2011, 58–66) for the full exposition of this understanding of the *tsimtsum*.

to consciousness, is suppressed in order to allow for the emergence of the *reshimu* (the trace), which is compared to the letters of speech.[72] The key terms used to express this notion of *tsimtsum* are *ohr* (light) and *otiyot* (letters/signifiers). Light denotes the quality of attachment to and dependence on a luminary thereby being a true reflection of it; furthermore, the deference of light to its source is highlighted to indicate how light lacks an identity beyond the reflection of its source. By contrast, letters, and signifiers more generally, denote something separate and detached from their source. Consequently, the term used to describe divine manifestation in a manner of attachment is 'light', and the term used to describe divine manifestation in a manner of separation is 'letters'.

Prior to the *tsimtsum*, the *ohr eyn sof* was fully expressed, and totally overshadowed the *otiyot ha-reshimu*, to the extent that 'the letters were not in existence at all (*bi-behinat metsiut klal*).'[73] However, through the process of *tsimtsum* – portrayed as divine speech – the *ohr eyn sof* becomes concealed and the letters are able to emerge. Schneersohn asserts, as he did regarding the phonetically articulated letters of human speech, that the letters of the trace (*otiyot ha-reshimu*) precede and are rooted deeper in God's essence (*atsmut*) than the *ohr eyn sof*. Since an essential quality of God is self-containment and independence from anything else, the inanimateness of letters and their division from each other is identified with God's essence. Schneersohn's cosmogony sees *tsimtsum* not as the removal or concealment of God, but as the process that facilitates the emergence of the more essential divine qualities of autonomy and self-sufficiency, which were previously obscured by the quality of attachment exhibited by the *ohr eyn sof*.[74] The act of *tsimtsum* could be described as a removal (*siluk*) of divine

---

[72] Schneersohn (2011), 46–7.
[73] Schneersohn (2011), 59.
[74] See Schneersohn (2011), 88.

qualities (*giluyim*) to allow for the emergence of God ('*she-elokut atsmo yihye be-behinat metsiut yesh*').[75]

However, even this qualified 'removal of the light' (*siluk ha-ohr*) is not understood 'simply' (*kipshuto*), that is, that the *ohr eyn sof* was removed; rather, the overwhelming presence of the *ohr eyn sof* is itself overawed by the supreme essential quality of the *reshimu*. Subsequently, the newly enlightened *ohr eyn sof*, similar to intellectual and emotional consciousness mentioned earlier, becomes the expressive device to confer divine essence to the finite world. Just as in the case of the aforementioned letters of speech, the divine essence is not naturally in a state of expression ('*eyno be-geder pe'ulah li-f'ol*')[76] and as such it relies on the expressive tool of the *ohr eyn sof* to actualize the creation of the world. Even though the problem that *tsimtsum* is said to resolve was the impossibility of creation (*lo hayah makom le-amidat ha-olamot*) due to the intensity of the *ohr eyn sof*, according to Schneersohn, the post-*tsimtsum ohr eyn sof* is not so much a diminution of its intensity, but an enhancement of its awareness of the essential quality that inheres in the separateness of creation. Whereas previously the *ohr eyn sof* was singularly focused on expressing the virtue of attachment to God, and thus found the separateness of the *otiyot ha-reshimu* and creation in general as anathema, after the *tsimtsum*, the *ohr eyn sof* is able to appreciate the profundity of separateness as a divine quality. The *tsimtsum* is thus not presented as a cataclysmic event that altered the components of reality by removing something or other, but as a continuous moment of clarity, when the essential origin and purpose of both the *otiyot ha-reshimu*, as a trace of God, and the *ohr eyn sof*, as its tool of expression, becomes pronounced.

This extended exposition of *tsimtsum* and creation offers an entirely different perspective on the intention of creating the world with the attribute of justice. Unlike the third discourse that suggested that such a

---

[75] Schneersohn (2011), 59.
[76] Schneersohn (2011), 99.

creation would result in an intensive presence of God, these discourses argue that creation with the attribute of justice would result in an intense concealment of divine expression. The 'judgemental' and self-censuring act of *tsimtsum* that facilitates the emergence of apparently independent and autonomous creations provides the setting for a meaningful divine service where people freely choose to subject themselves to the divine will. The fourth and fifth discourses have offered an understanding of justice as the limitation and restriction of the expressiveness of God, in contrast to the third discourse's explanation that focused on the self-judgement of the human individual. As a consequence, however, this initial intention to create the world with only justice would have utterly concealed the expression of God, and the demands on the creations to constantly self-motivate and remain dedicated and committed to a completely obscured God would prove too difficult. A creation made purely with the attribute of justice would have generated a complete sense of separateness and unawareness of God among the creations, which would have ultimately undermined the objective of creation. Therefore, there was a need to combine mercy with justice. Divine revelation in the form of the Torah, occasional miracles and righteous individuals would temper the extreme divine obscurity of the justice-induced *tsimtsum*. As a result, the created reality would have enough divine exposure to be aware of God's presence and still remain sufficiently free from divine intrusion to independently choose obedience to the divine will.

This portrayal of the *tsimtsum* in the fourth and fifth discourses can provide a useful framework to better appreciate certain themes in Levinas's thought. Levinas engages and utilizes the concept of *tsimtsum*, and his association with *kabbalistic* themes has been the subject of considerable scholarly research.[77] Levinas himself remarked in a 1982

---

[77] A dominant line of enquiry in Levinas scholarship has been whether or not there is a discernible presence of *kabbalistic* influence on the thought of Levinas; for example, see Mopsik (1991); Cohen (1994), 241–73; Ajzenstat (2001), 139–99; Chalier (2002),

interview how 'there is even in *Totality and Infinity*, the evocation of the *tzimtzum*'.[78] However, Levinas's own rejection of *kabbalah* in 'its Hasidic excesses',[79] and his positive regard for the non-hasidic thought of Hayyim of Volozhyn, have resulted in a limited focus by Levinas scholars on an affinity between Levinas and aspects of hasidic thought. The evocation of the *tsimtsum* in *Totality and Infinity* appears most clearly at the end of section 1, where Levinas affirms the importance of separateness: 'Infinity is produced by withstanding the invasion of a totality, in a contraction that leaves a place for the separated being.'[80] For the Infinite to be truly infinite and not restricted and limited to a totality, which precludes multiplicity and separateness, there must be a contraction (*tsimtsum*), which allows for the emergence of independent beings. Furthermore, the 'multiplicity and limitation on the creative Infinite is compatible with the perfection of the Infinite; they articulate the meaning of this perfection'.[81] Instead of assuming the perfection of the Infinite as a unity, Levinas states how specifically through the separation, which is enacted through creation, the Infinite can become pronounced and expressed. Creation is thus understood as the possibility for separate and independent beings, 'for an existent is an existent only in the measure that it is free, that is, outside of any system . . . creation *ex nihilo* breaks with system, posits a being outside of every system'.[82] Levinas is seeking to overcome the totality of a system where separateness is seen as an ontological 'fallenness', where beings limit each other in their finitude. The contraction of the Infinite in creation *ex nihilo* rejects a system of totality that seeks

---

77–106; Wolfson (2006), 193–224; Meskin (2007), 49–77; Fagenblat (2010), 60–1. Here, by contrast, I will focus on the way in which rabbinic texts that have been explicitly influenced by *kabbalah* can inform our understanding of Levinas, regardless of any biographically identifiable encounter between Levinas and kabbalistic texts.

[78] Wyschogrod (1989), 107.
[79] Levinas (2007), 150.
[80] Levinas (2008a), 104.
[81] Levinas (2008a), 104.
[82] Levinas (2008a), 104.

unity and, instead, projects the infinite quality of limitation and separateness. Levinas recognizes how the resultant created beings are, nonetheless, dependent on the Infinite for their existence; however, he describes it as 'an unparalleled dependence: the dependent being draws from this exceptional dependence, from this relationship, its very independence, its exteriority to the system'.[83] In what he calls 'the paradox of creation', Levinas is describing how the separated being is the articulation of the Infinite, and the preservation of its separateness and independence 'opens upon the idea of Infinity'.[84]

This Levinasian exposition of the *tsimtsum* contains striking parallels to the *Habad* version of the *tsimtsum* outlined earlier. The totalizing impulse of an infinity that resists a multiplicity and separateness is akin to the notion of *ohr eyn sof*, in which there needs to be a contraction-*tsimtsum* to 'withstand the invasion of a totality'. The outcome of overcoming this totality-*ohr eyn sof* is not a diminution of the infinite-*atsmut*: 'this separation is not simply a negation',[85] but the 'articulation'[86] of its very infinitude. The use of the term 'articulate', could be interpreted as pointing towards his ideas on the *Saying* and the *Said*, where he develops the *kabbalistically* evocative idea of the *trace*. In the reading that follows, I suggest that Schneersohn's overt connecting of his linguistic theory to *tsimtsum* can inform our reading of Levinas and more clearly link the evocation of the *tsimtsum* in *Totality and Infinity* and the trace (*reshimu*) in *Otherwise than Being*.

As outlined earlier, Schneersohn likens the process of *tsimtsum* to the articulation of speech. In the abstract terminology of *tsimtsum*, the infinite light (*ohr eyn sof*) is removed, leaving behind a trace (*reshimu*) in an empty space (*makom panui*), to allow for the emergence of a

[83] Levinas (2008a), 104–5.
[84] Levinas (2008a), 105.
[85] Levinas (2008a), 105.
[86] Levinas (2008a), 104.

finite world. Schneersohn compares this process to a suppression of the sensible thematized content of spoken language, and an emphasis on the somatically produced symbols of speech. Through concealing and suppressing the primacy of the cognitive self, which takes the form of the sensible and rational content of language, a transcendence beyond cognition can emerge in the act of speaking. Schneersohn regards the *tsimtsum* not in terms of divine absence, but as an act that allows for the emergence of the divine essence (*atsmut*). Similarly, for Schneersohn, language at its most semiotic and somatic articulates an ontological primacy that is prior to any meaning and sense. This overt coupling of language and *tsimtsum* by Schneersohn could helpfully associate and connect what may be perceived of as two distinct threads in Levinas's thought.

Furthermore, having already established in *Totality and Infinity* how the separation brought about by the *tsimtsum* 'is the very constitution of thought and interiority',[87] Levinas in *Otherwise than Being* introduces the idea of the trace and its representation in speech to convey the meaning of created existence: 'A trace is sketched out and effaced in a face in the equivocation of a saying. In this way it modulates the modality of the transcendent.'[88] The transcendent, by definition, is not presentable and is not in a mode of expression, hence, it is specifically through the trace of a saying that the transcendent can be articulated. Schneersohn explains how the trace (*reshimu*) is the 'capacity for limitation (*koah ha-gvul*)' in God, which he calls 'the letters of *atsmut*'.[89] Prior to creation, meaning before the *tsimtsum*, this divine quality of limitation, separateness and independence was not discernible. However, after the *tsimtsum*, when 'the light (*ohr*) was removed from the letters, the letters became revealed'.[90] That is

---

[87] Levinas (2008a), 104.
[88] Levinas (2008b), 12.
[89] Schneersohn (2011), 59.
[90] Schneersohn (2011), 59.

to say, this ability of limitation and separateness, which manifests in the seeming independence of creation and creations and is invariably referred to as the letters or the trace, is rooted and originates in 'the letters of *atsmut*'. The trace/*reshimu* is thus, for both Schneersohn and Levinas, the presentation of the infinite/*atsmut* in the Saying/*otiyot* of a Said. With the aid of Schneersohn's explicit association of speech with the dynamics of *tsimtsum*, we can now understand how Levinas's own theory of speech can be situated in his evocation of the *tsimtsum*. Levinas's use of 'trace' as a term to depict the infinite is seemingly not coincidental and is coherently linked with the contraction (*tsimtsum*) that is evoked in *Totality and Infinity*.[91] This 'linguistic turn' in Schneersohn's *tsimtsum* enables us to appreciate the thematic link between Levinas's deployment of *tsimtsum* in *Totality and Infinity* and his focus on the trace in the saying in *Otherwise than Being*, and it can be appreciated for the way in which it constructively extends the ideas of Levinas in new directions. Moreover, an appreciation of the philosophical potential of Schneersohn's *tsimtsum* can point to ways in which the thought of other modern philosophers who have engaged with the concept of *tsimtsum*, such as Franz Rosenzweig, as well as other modern linguistic thinkers who do not explicitly engage with the concept of *tsimtsum*, might similarly be illuminated in new ways. The objective here is not to claim a possible influence or even confluence of ideas, which might imply a historical claim, but an attempt to show how Schneersohn and Levinas might mutually illumine each other.[92]

Let us now consider how Schneersohn's understanding of the letters of *malkhut*, which guarantee the perceived separateness of creation, can inform a metaphysical reading of Derrida. While many

---

[91] Beyond these technical references, Schneersohn also offers a useful structure with which to decipher the notoriously difficult writing of Levinas in *Otherwise than Being*.

[92] See Wolfson (2014, 179) for a similar observation on the relationship between Derrida and *kabbalah*.

have read Derrida solely as a rejection of a metaphysics of presence and of any centred transcendental signification, from our reading of Schneersohn we should now be able to discern in Derrida a number of key metaphysical insights.[93] As mentioned at the beginning of this chapter, I am more cautious than other scholars in my reading of *kabbalistic* motifs in Derrida due to his own limited knowledge of the topic; however, conversely, I may be more ambitious in attempting to use more contemporary mystical Jewish thought to expand the horizon of Derrida's texts.[94]

In *Dissemination*, Derrida makes overt reference to mystical Jewish thought and how he considers it relevant to his own project.[95]

> The Kabbalah is not only summoned up here . . . it also cooperates with an Orphic explanation of the earth . . . . Interestingly, through the importance it gives to the dot, the air, etc., this Orphic explanation also describes an analogue of the *pleroma*, which is a sort of original space, a pneumatic layer (*tehiru*) in which the *zimzum*, the crisis within God, the 'drama of God' through which God goes out of himself and determines himself, takes place.[96]

For Derrida, *tsimtsum* plays the role of removing divine presence and innovating the notion of nonpresence to allow for created presence. Significantly, in that removal there emerges 'the dot, the air, etc', which is the original space that will become an important dimension of Derrida's later use of the Platonic idea of the *khora*[97] – an undefinable original space, which he describes as 'the

---

[93] For a summary of existing scholarly attempts to envisage a metaphysical dimension in Derrida that is informed by *kabbalah*, see Bielik-Robson (2021), 390fn6.

[94] See Wolfson (2021), 141–89, where he similarly attempts to make use of Rabbi Solomon Eliashiv (1841–1926) to inform a reading of Heidegger.

[95] My understanding of Derrida in this section has greatly benefited from Wolfson (2014), 154–200, and Bielik-Robson (2021), 389–418.

[96] Derrida (1981), 344.

[97] See Bielik-Robson (2018), 26–9, and how she links *tsimtsum* and *khora* in Derrida's writings.

undifferentiated atmosphere in which the first present seems to congeal or take shape, a sort of origin of the world and of sensible certainty, mimed with "the false appearance of a present".[98] Not to be understood as a generative source for presence but as what makes it possible, 'The air *is* the *apeiron* of Presocratic physiology, the *tehiru* of the Kabbalah, the possibility of presence, of visibility, of appearance, of voice, etc.'[99] In this reading of the Lurianic *tsimtsum*, Derrida attempts to posit a decentred origin that no longer acts as a foundational generator of presence. Consequently, the emergence of presence in the vacated space betrays its own supposed stability and, in fact, disseminates the differentiated, separate and detached reality of the decentred space that made it possible.[100] Like Schneersohn, this differentiated original reality is understood linguistically. 'My own presence to myself has been preceded by a language. Older than consciousness, older than the spectator, prior to any attendance, a sentence awaits 'you' . . . . There is always a sentence that has already been sealed somewhere waiting for you where you think you are opening up some virgin territory.'[101] While Derrida initially employs dramatic language of a 'crisis within God' to describe the Lurianic *tsimtsum*, he appears to reject any notion of it being a problem that requires fixing. '*Numbers* are thus a kind of cabal or cabala in which the blanks will never be anything but provisionally filled in . . . going on forever and not in the expectation of any Messianic fulfilment.'[102]

Derrida's subtle deployment of *kabbalistic* themes can benefit from Schneersohn's more detailed and developed examination earlier. In Schneersohn's schema, differentiated passive existence (*yesh*

[98] Derrida (1981), 345.
[99] Derrida (1981), 347.
[100] Derrida (1981), 342.
[101] Derrida (1981), 340.
[102] Derrida (1981), 345.

ha-nivra) becomes a manifestation (mirror-play)[103] of an ultimate differentiation in God (*yesh ha-amiti*), which is made realizable by way of an active animated presence (*ohr eyn sof*). This mellowing of the divide between the active and the passive transforms the relation between God and his creation and challenges Derrida's assertion that 'reduced to its textuality, absolutely disseminated, the *Kabbalah*, for example, evinces a kind of atheism'.[104] Schneersohn would readily accept that the *tsimtsum* radically reconsiders the dominance of the *ohr eyn sof*, what Derrida might call *theion*,[105] and thus provisionally evinces a kind of 'atheionism'. However, because of his contention that the *tsimtsum* is not an event, drama or crisis in God (*theos*) at all, not only does the *tsimtsum* not lead to an atheism, but it also actually enables the emergence of the essence of God (*yesh ha-amiti*). As we will see even more explicitly towards the end of the *hemshekh*, this doctrine of *tsimtsum* reverses and thus revolutionizes the traditional picture. The reconfigured *ohr eyn sof* does not overflow the created beings, and, instead, allows them to experience a degree of the exclusively divine quality of autonomy. Thus, the *tsimtsum* fulfils its function of complicating the binary opposition of God and the world, not despite, but specifically because of, the ontological autonomy of created beings that it ensures.

Additionally, Schneersohn's reconfigured *ohr eyn sof* that becomes the means by which this ontological autonomy can be realized is somewhat akin to Derrida's 'hollow phallus' that, having been decapitated, no longer acts as the potent symbol of presence, and, instead, 'guarantees the innumerable passage of dissemination and

---

[103] See Derrida (1981), 354–5: 'The mirror-play (*Spiegel-Spiel*) of world is the round dance of appropriation . . . it lightens the four into the radiance of their simple oneness. Radiantly, the ring joins the four, everywhere open to the riddle of their presence . . .'
[104] Derrida (1981), 344.
[105] See Derrida (2002), 94.

the playful displacement of the margins'.[106] This sentiment is more pointedly addressed in Derrida's essay 'Faith and Knowledge', where he distinguishes between revelation and revealability and poses the following questions: 'is revealability (Offenbarkeit) more originary than revelation (Offenbarung), and hence independent of all religion? ... Or rather, inversely, would the event of revelation have consisted in revealing revealability itself, and the origin of light, the originary light, the very invisibility of visibility?'[107] With these questions, Derrida is positing how it is precisely in the presence of revelation that the absence of the 'nocturnal light' emerges. This idea parallels the double gesture we explored in our section on language and reappears here as a newly understood mode of revelation. No longer at odds with the hidden and concealed, revelation becomes the method by which the autonomous and differentiated essence of God is disseminated.

It is worth pointing out that Derrida's rejection of a messianic dimension in *Dissemination* is revised in his later works to comprise what he calls a messianicity in contrast to messianism. Messianicity does not denote a traditional eschatology that suggests a return to a once pristine origin; rather, it heralds an ultimate coming to terms with the indefiniteness of existence. As we will shortly see in the final two discourses in the series, Schneersohn will present a model of messianic redemption that reflects these tensions. Schneersohn presents two messianic options: the first possibility would restore the primacy of the undifferentiated *ohr eyn sof* as it was prior to the *tsimtsum*. This option, which seems quite similar to the messianism Derrida critiques, is deferred for the preferred second possibility, which glorifies the instantiation of God's differentiated being in existence. Schneersohn's messianic vision is far more deterministic than anything Derrida would consider; however, it definitely

[106] Derrida (1981), 342.
[107] Derrida (2002), 54–5.

leans towards a messianicity that does not dream of restoring and reinforcing ancient binary oppositions.

In this case as in many others, Schneersohn's more clearly outlined treatment of Jewish mystical thought provides important context and maps out helpful contours of thought in which to decipher the often terse and elusive writing of Derrida. Whereas in our discussion on language, it was Derrida's more developed categories that helped us perceive broader possibilities in Schneersohn, the reverse is the case in our present discussion. Let me highlight once again that these conceptual opportunities become more possible when there is a dialogical encounter as advocated for in this book, and the urge to blur distinctions is resisted. The goal here has been to begin this style of conversation and demonstrate its merits, thereby encouraging further fruitful exchanges in the future.

'These are the histories of . . .'[108]

In the third, fourth and fifth discourses, Schneersohn explained why God would want to create the world solely with the attribute of justice in two ways. Firstly, justice refers to the way God will interact with people, being exacting with people so they will not sin, and also to facilitate intense divine service. The problem he identifies with this plan is the way in which punishments would be too severe for anyone who sins, and the divine service would be too intense for people to bear. Alternatively, justice refers to the limitations and restrictions placed on the *ohr eyn sof* to enable the creation of separated beings. Here the problem lies in the complete obscuring of God from creation, which would unfairly require a person to constantly muster

---

[108] Genesis 2:4. The sixth discourse was delivered on 14 October 1898.

immense feelings of devotion to remain obedient. In this discourse Schneersohn adds a further complication: how according to the second interpretation of creation with the attribute of justice where there would be an intense concealment of the divine presence, there would be the added problem of facilitating evil as a result of this divine obscurity.[109] The introduction in the earlier discourses of the attribute of mercy was portrayed as a means of ameliorating the previously mentioned problems. A system of justice combined with mercy would allow for a more tolerant form of justice and an appreciation for *teshuvah* (repentance), according to the first interpretation, and a less extreme obscuration of the *ohr eyn sof*, according to the second interpretation. In the present discourse Schneersohn explains how the attribute of mercy combined with the attribute of justice can also achieve the elimination of the *kelipot* and of evil.[110]

Let us explain in more detail. In the previous discourse Schneersohn explained how a diminution of the *ohr eyn sof* by the attribute of justice leads to the emergence of the discernible letters of *malkhut*, the implications of which is that the delimiting of the

---

[109] The exposition thus far accords with the second interpretation of the purpose of creating with the attribute of justice found in the fourth and fifth discourses, that the attribute of justice conceals the *ohr eyn sof*. Schneersohn explains parenthetically (2011, 76) how it is also compatible with the first interpretation found in the third discourse: that the purpose of creating with the attribute of justice is in order to be exacting and strict with people so that they are a) obedient, and b) they can serve God in the most optimal way. Drawing on the imagery of the *Sefer ha-Zohar*, which refers to the *kelipot* as the whip of God (*retsu'ah le-eloka'ah*), Schneersohn explains how the attribute of justice needs to have tools of enforcement to encourage obedience. Notwithstanding the divinity of the attribute of justice, the meting out of justice through punishment would be a destructive act that requires destructive forces associated with evil.

[110] See Schneersohn (2011), 78. The basis of this explanation is a reading of the *midrash* in *Genesis Rabbah* 12:3: 'These are the histories of the heaven and the earth when God created them, on the day when *Havayah Elokim* made earth and heaven.' Rabbi Avuha said: 'wherever it says *eileh* (these) it invalidates what is stated previously, what did it invalidate? *Tohu va-vohu va-hoshekh*.' In another version of this *midrash* (*Exodus Rabbah* 30:3), Rabbi Avuha is more explicit: '. . . What did it invalidate? God created heaven and earth and examined them, and they were not pleasing to God, and God returned them to *tohu va-vohu*. When God saw this heaven and earth, they were pleasing to God. God said: these will have a history; therefore, it states: "these are the histories of the heaven and the earth. But the earlier ones, they did not have a history."'

ohr eyn sof is not understood as something that happens to it by an external factor, but, rather, as an in-built component of the *ohr eyn sof* itself. Schneersohn thereby depicts a transcendental order that already resists an oppositional system of revelation and concealment or of presence and absence. The revelation of the *ohr eyn sof* is not controlled and restricted by the concealing force of the letters of *malkhut*; instead, the *ohr eyn sof* is already conditioned to self-regulate itself to facilitate the emergence of the letters. The objective of these letters is 'in order that there will be finite creations . . . for then it is possible to have sovereignty (*melukhah*) over them'.[111] Since 'there is no king without a nation' there is a necessity to create separated beings, so they can submit their will to God. Therefore, the creation of the world with the attribute of justice is one in which all expressions of God automatically function to conceal the divine presence. In this discourse, Schneersohn recognizes that as a consequence of the extensive contraction of the *ohr eyn sof*, and its concealment by the letters, there entails the creation of not just finite and servile creations but 'completely separated beings which . . . are the *kelipot* (lit. Shells – evil forces)'.[112] Whereas the goal of reducing the overwhelming presence of the *ohr eyn sof* is to facilitate the circumstances where sovereignty and obedience are possible, the impact of creating the world with the attribute of justice alone is a situation where absolute separation and disobedience are also made possible. Accordingly, creation with the attribute of justice as described in the first verse of Genesis is read by Schneersohn as the cause of the creation of evil: since '*Elokim* (attribute of justice) created the heavens and the earth' (Gen. 1:1), 'the earth was *tohu, vohu, and* darkness' (symbols of *kelipah* and evil) (Gen. 1:2). From this perspective, the existence of evil is a natural consequence of creating with the attribute of justice.

---

[111] Schneersohn (2011), 72.
[112] Schneersohn (2011), 72.

If you want sufficiently independent human beings to freely submit themselves to the divine will, you create the possibility that they will choose the alternative and transgress the Torah and *mitzvot*.

The concern that Schneersohn is raising could be understood as an ethical uneasiness regarding the attribute of justice, and how it facilitates the presence of evil. He is worried how evil will persist in either a creation devoid of any supra-physical awareness, or one in which an intensely present God will need to mete out punishment. However, replacing it with the attribute of mercy is also not a solution. The attribute of mercy, which is capable of forgiving sin and wrongdoing, might augment a culture of permissiveness and indifference to sin, and thereby lead to a further proliferation of evil, albeit for different reasons. To better understand the possible apathy to sin of the attribute of mercy, Schneersohn expounds on the nature of mercy in the *sephirotic* realm. Unlike the attribute of justice which, as mentioned earlier, is denoted by the divine name *Elokim*, the attribute of mercy, as described in the *midrash*, is synonymous with the divine name *Havayah*, which in turn is associated with the *sephirah* of *hokhmah*. *Hokhmah* is portrayed as being aloof from specifics and particulars that characterize the other intellectual faculties of *binah* and *da'at*. The understanding and comprehension of *binah* and *da'at* can often lead to an intolerance of alternative perspectives, whereas *hokhmah* is indifferent to any opposing views. *Hokhmah* is the initial encounter with a concept prior to any detailed exposition; however, far from being a superficial awareness it is described as a consciousness of the fundamental point of the concept that transcends the definitions it acquires in a detailed exposition. At this stage of consciousness, the idea is so real that any suggestion to the contrary does not intrude or disturb the certainty of *hokhmah*. By contrast, comprehension of an idea with the faculty of *binah* involves an engagement with the detailed specifics of a concept, which inevitably leads to a delimiting of the idea. At this point, an opposing idea encroaches on the certainty of *binah* and can arouse anger and frustration, which can ultimately lead to even more negative character traits. Once in the realm of proofs and argumentation, there is an acute awareness of conflicting approaches that can contest the veracity of one's approach. By contrast, when someone holds deep convictions, the existence of alternative perspectives fails to unsettle their certainty and confidence. Hence, the creation of the world with the attribute of justice would be an active cause for the presence of evil, whereas the tolerance of the attribute of mercy might lead to an apathy towards its existence, such that if, instead of combining mercy with justice, mercy would replace justice, the apathy and indifference of mercy would be a passive cause of a state of affairs where evil could go unchecked. Schneersohn thus interprets the *midrash* – where the two attributes are combined – as the necessary condition for overcoming an evil that is at once not an inevitable outcome of justice, and at the same time is also not passively tolerated by mercy.[113]

Schneersohn has thus explained how the combination of the attribute of mercy with the attribute of justice is necessary to avoid the proliferation of evil. This interpretation introduces a new consideration, and possibly an important corrective, to the earlier discourses. As discussed earlier, Schneersohn's innovative and positive approach to the physical world has the potential of unintentionally leading his listeners and readers towards a more materialistic approach to divine service. With such an approach, there would be a fear that Schneersohn's adherents might themselves become estranged from God. A mindset and an approach that emphasize the concealment and absence of divine expression could themselves accidentally lead to a forgetting of the divine purpose of creation. By emphasizing how, notwithstanding the emergence of the essence of God in creation

---

[113] See Schneersohn (2011), 78–9.

through the concealment of the *ohr eyn sof*, there exists the very real danger of being completely unaware of God and God's presence, Schneersohn is ensuring his followers remain vigilant in their interaction with the physical. In the next discourse, Schneersohn will continue with his attempt to present a balanced approach to reconsidering the assumed oppositional forces exemplified by justice and mercy and will offer two ways to understand the manner in which the divine attributes can combine and exist harmoniously.

'You remembered the earth . . .'[114]

In the final section of the discourses, Schneersohn concludes his exposition of the *midrash* that was introduced in the first discourse. Drawing from his earlier descriptions of orality and femininity, he presents a distinctive ontology that attempts to disrupt a simple binary distinction between the supra-physical (*ruhaniyut*) and the physical (*gashmiyut*). This binary distinction, which has often been portrayed as emblematic of Western thought, will not be eradicated, but will, instead, undergo a reconstitution of significant consequence. In a manner similar to the way speech and the female were described as being synonymous with the most primordial and essential, *malkhut* (itself referred to as 'letters' or 'the female') and the apparently self-sufficient world it creates, is described as being commensurate with the essence of God (*atsmut*). Equally, just as the essential characteristic of speech and the female depends on the expressive ability of intellect and the male, respectively, so too *malkhut* must rely on the revelatory capacity of the *ohr eyn sof*. Henceforth, the *ohr eyn sof*, which had previously been characterized as being antagonistic to the separateness

---

[114] Psalms 65:10. The seventh discourse was delivered on 28ᵗ October 1898.

associated with *malkhut*, now becomes the vehicle by which the essence of God, which defies the binary distinction of attachment and separateness, becomes revealed. The *ohr eyn sof* is akin to a supra-physical reality that initially transcends and appears superior to the physical realm created by *malkhut*. However, Schneersohn proposes that through dedicated divine service the essential nature of physical existence can be exposed and unveiled through the *ohr eyn sof*. This harmonization of *malkhut* and the *ohr eyn sof* will be equated with the harmonization of the attributes of justice and mercy described in the *midrash*.

In the final two discourses, Schneersohn will focus on the attribute of mercy, so let us briefly summarize the accumulated sense of the attribute of justice and its role in creation. The third, fourth and fifth of the discourses we examined previously gave two alternate interpretations of the impact of creating the world with the attribute of justice. In the third discourse Schneersohn described a world that would be overwhelmed by God's presence and attentiveness, whereas in the fourth and fifth discourses he interpreted justice as the means by which God becomes obscured from the world. In the previous (sixth) discourse, Schneersohn added how according to both interpretations there would be a proliferation of evil that could be ameliorated only through the combination of the attribute of mercy with the attribute of justice. In this penultimate discourse of the series, he focuses solely on the second interpretation of justice, namely, the obscuring of the *ohr eyn sof* by the letters of *malkhut*.

Schneersohn will present two schemas for mapping the *midrashic* terminology onto *kabbalistic* concepts. The first approach will identify the concealing letters of *malkhut* with the attribute of justice and the revelatory *ohr eyn sof* with the attribute of mercy, where the resulting combination of the two attributes will imply a transformation of *malkhut*. Instead of concealing the *ohr eyn sof*, *malkhut* will become the organizational tool to convey the intense revelation of the *ohr eyn sof.* The second approach will classify the self-limiting *ohr eyn sof* as the attribute of justice and the essential origin of *malkhut* as the attribute of mercy. In this schema the combination of the attributes entails a transformation of the *ohr eyn sof* into a means by which to reveal and convey the essence of God.

A significant shift in the interpretation of the *midrash* takes place at this stage in the discourses. Until now, Schneersohn has taken a more straightforward and natural reading of the *midrash* as an explanation of the creation narratives in Genesis. In the third, fourth and fifth discourses the suggestion is that Genesis 1 depicts the original intention of creation with the attribute of justice (*elokim*) and Genesis 2 (*havaya-elokim*) is how the world was actually created with the combined attributes of justice and mercy. In the sixth discourse there is a slight adjustment and Genesis 1 depicts the actual creation of the world with the attribute of justice that was tempered with the attribute of mercy with the creation of man on the sixth day, and Genesis 2 is understood as a second phase of creation. The concluding discourses, however, move beyond reading the *midrash* as being concerned with cosmogony alone and introduce messianic and eschatological themes. This new interpretation of the *midrash* will explain how Genesis 1 depicts the actual creation of the world with the attribute of justice that will reach its perfection in the future messianic era when it is combined with the attribute of mercy as depicted in Genesis 2. This shift in interpretation of the midrash has a significant effect on the individual and their role in creation. Whereas the earlier interpretation demands a deeper awareness of reality, now a person is expected to be the agent of change to transform reality. I will suggest shortly how this pivot from a slightly passive to a more active role in creation provides an important ideological underpinning of contemporary *Habad* thought and activism. In the meantime, another notable impact of this new approach is to no longer treat the combining of the attribute of mercy as a sort of compromise and watering down of the intensity of the attribute of justice. Notwithstanding how this would be the more natural and obvious reading of the text, Schneersohn's new approach presents an altogether more ambitious and aspirational dimension of the *midrash*.

Schneersohn explains how the attribute of justice (*malkhut*) initially conceals and obscures the attribute of mercy (*ohr eyn sof*); however, when the attribute of mercy is expressed, it transforms the previously constraining force of justice into the very tool of its expression. 'The impact of the letters then is not to conceal, rather the opposite, to reveal, that the *ohr* should be revealed through them . . . and not like it is presently when the letters of *malkhut* conceal the *ohr*.'[115] To explain how the attribute of justice is capable of expressing and not obscuring the attribute of mercy (the *ohr eyn sof*), Schneersohn introduces an analogy of the way a teacher conveys an idea to a student. The nature of the teacher/student interaction is always dependent on the teacher adapting their knowledge according to the abilities of the student. In the instance where a student is disproportionately inferior in comprehension to the teacher, such as a small child in relation to an acclaimed genius, then 'the teacher is required to entirely conceal the entire depth of his wisdom, and only express a miniscule amount',[116] so that the student is not overwhelmed and confused. Conversely, when the student is advanced, it may be possible to convey the entirety of the idea. Nevertheless, even with an advanced student it is still necessary to present the concept in an orderly fashion and not share the full complexity and depth of the concept as it is present in the mind of the teacher. This effort on the part of the teacher, which on the one hand is a *tsimtsum* and concealment, still conveys the entirety of the concept, and allows the advanced student to ultimately reach a level of comprehension comparable to that of the teacher.

---

[115] Schneersohn (2011), 82.
[116] Schneersohn (2011), 82.

Using this analogy, Schneersohn describes the two ways in which *malkhut* conveys *ohr eyn sof* to the creation. The manner in which *ohr eyn sof* becomes obscured in *malkhut* such that it becomes entirely concealed from creation, similar to a profound idea that is conveyed to a small child, describes the process of creation with the attribute of justice. By contrast, when the attribute of mercy is combined with justice, then the full force of the *ohr eyn sof* is conferred on creation by *malkhut*, similar to the teaching of a profound concept to an advanced student. The *ohr eyn sof* still needs the containment of *malkhut* so as not to overwhelm the creation; however, through that containment the creation is able to experience the full expression of the *ohr eyn sof*.[117] As was explained in the fourth discourse, the degree of separateness of the letters of *malkhut* (*yeshut ve-hagshamat ha-otiyot*), which conceals the expression of the *ohr eyn sof*, is a result of a self-imposed *tsimtsum* by the *ohr* itself. Consequently, when the *ohr eyn sof* is manifest and revealed and no longer restricting itself, the resultant letters of *malkhut* no longer conceal the expression of the *ohr*.[118] Unlike the limiting and concealing letters of *malkhut* that emerge from the attribute of justice alone, the combination of the attribute of mercy produces a translucent and diaphanous form of letters that regulates the transmission of the *ohr eyn sof*.

This first explanation, while removing the oppositional dimension of the binary relationship between the *ohr eyn sof* and *malkhut*, does so by privileging the *ohr eyn sof*. This explanation identifies the shortcoming in creating the world with the attribute of justice as the diminution of the *ohr eyn sof* by *malkhut*, and its resolution through combining with the attribute of mercy and allowing the *ohr eyn sof* to become manifest. The removal of the oppositional stance of *malkhut* does not bring about an equalization of the binary correlates, but,

---

[117] See Schneersohn (2011), 85.
[118] See Schneersohn (2011), 87.

rather, leads to a further subordination of *malkhut* to the *ohr eyn sof*. In this explanation, *malkhut* is presented as a type of transparent conduit for the *ohr eyn sof* that is valued primarily for its lack of interference with the *ohr eyn sof*.[119]

Appreciating the limitations of this interpretation and its failure to build on the positive qualities associated with *malkhut* in the earlier discourses, Schneersohn introduces towards the end of the discourse an alternative explanation, an explanation that completely reconfigures the implication of combining the attribute of mercy with the attribute of justice. The first explanation identified the attribute of justice with the *sephirah* of *malkhut* and the attribute of mercy with the *ohr eyn sof*, whereas in the second explanation the attribute of justice is identified with the *ohr eyn sof*, and the attribute of mercy with the primordial root of *malkhut*, namely, the essence of God (*atsmut*). Instead of suggesting how a revelation of *ohr eyn sof* reconstitutes the functioning of *malkhut*, the discourse now suggests how a revelation of *malkhut* can redefine the status and function of the *ohr eyn sof*.[120]

As was explained in the fourth and fifth discourse, the *ohr eyn sof* is only an expression of God and not God (*atsmut*), and to express God it must by definition be, to an extent, other than God. By contrast, the self-contained and static characteristics of *malkhut* are synonymous and akin to the independence and self-sufficiency of *atsmut*. Subsequently, when the origin of *malkhut* in *atsmut* (attribute of mercy) is triggered, the *ohr eyn sof* (attribute of justice) becomes the means by which to convey and express the very essence of God. This second explanation and the question as to how the *ohr eyn sof* is able to convey *atsmut* will be the central focus of the following and final discourse.

[119] See Schneersohn (2011), 86.
[120] See Schneersohn (2011), 88–90.

'For every pleasure . . .'[121]

On his thirty-ninth birthday, Schneersohn delivered the eighth and final discourse of the *hemshekh* of 1898.[122] The discourse will attempt to explain, according to the interpretation introduced towards the end of the previous discourse, how the *ohr eyn sof* is able to express and reveal the very essence of God (*atsmut*). Schneersohn also broadens the discussion from the *midrashic* themes of justice and mercy to the kabbalistic categories of *memale kol almin* (lit. fills all the worlds) and *sovev kol almin* (lit. encompasses all worlds). *Memale* indicates how God is expressed in a manner that is commensurate with, and akin to, the restrictions and limitations of the world. In contrast, *sovev* indicates how God, while being expressed in the world, remains unrestrained by the limitations of the world. An analogy for *memale* would be individualized intellectual expression that corresponds to differing intellectual abilities, as reflected in the intellectual development of a person from childhood to maturity. *Sovev*, by contrast, is comparable to a person's will and desire, which, while expressing itself through the intellectual and emotional faculties, is not restricted or confined by them. The existence of instinctive drives and impulses in a person are not so closely dependent on age and maturity. In the context of these discourses, *memale* refers to the *ohr eyn sof* while *sovev* refers to the essence of God (*atsmut*).

The final discourse will attempt to explain how the previously incompatible *ohr eyn sof* can now function as an able tool to express the essence of God. Schneersohn will argue how his earlier definition of the *ohr eyn sof*, as a ray and impression of God that seeks to reflect the all-powerfulness of God, is transformed when a radical definition of divine omnipotence and omniscience presents itself in the guise of

[121] Psalms 119:96.
[122] 4 November 1898.

the apparently distinct and autonomous existence of creation. At that moment, the perception of reality is fundamentally altered, wherein specifically the physicality of the world is appreciated for its divine character, and the supra-physical *ohr eyn sof* is recognized as merely a ray of the divine that conceals the divine essence. Subsequently, and in a similar manner to consciousness and the father described earlier, the supra-physically orientated *ohr eyn sof* becomes a recipient of the essential quality of the physical. Consequently, instead of the *ohr eyn sof* merely expressing (*giluyim*) the readily expressible qualities of the essence (*giluy ha-atsmut*), it can now become the means by which the essence becomes apparent (*ha-etsem be-hitgalut*). In a manner similar to the way a person's intellect can conceive profoundly enhanced ideas as a result of speech, and a man is able to become a father through intercourse with a woman, so too, *ohr eyn sof* can express the non-binary perfection of the essence of God when in perfect alignment with *malkhut*. In a certain way, the exposure of the infinite and non-differentiated essence of God in speech, women and *malkhut* initially served to deconstruct the binary assumptions that inhered in their relationships. However, by simply maintaining this deconstruction we would be in effect constructing a new hierarchy that in many ways mimics and appropriates the earlier structure, albeit with an inversion of values. In light of this, the conclusion of the discourses seeks to reconstruct the relational infrastructure between *malkhut* and the *ohr eyn sof*, in order that the essence of God can reach beyond the binary logic of the previously hierarchical oppositional structure.

To illustrate what is at stake here and the significance of Schneersohn's approach, it might be helpful to consider the options available to him at this stage of the discourses. Once he identifies *malkhut* and the physical world as rooted in the essence of God, one approach would be to apply to it all the value and virtue previously accorded to the *ohr eyn sof and* raise up physical existence from its apparent separateness from God to a state of cleaving and attachment to God akin to the *ohr eyn sof*. This approach, while going some distance to reconsider the value of *malkhut* (and speech and women) in its binary relationship with the *ohr eyn sof*, still resorts to a privileging of one of the binary terms to the exclusion of its contrary. In this example, specifically the qualities of attachment of the *ohr eyn sof* (and intellect and the male) prevail over the apparent separateness of *malkhut*. Schneersohn took this approach in the previous discourse. An alternative approach could be the devaluing of the supra-physical order exemplified by the *ohr eyn sof*. Through the awareness of the sublime origin of *malkhut* and created existence in the essence of God, the complex supra-physical order, which entails varying degrees of attachment and cleaving to God, could be rendered redundant and no longer relevant. Schneersohn, in fact, follows this line of enquiry at the beginning of the final discourse asking quite pointedly: what is the purpose and function of the ohr *eyn sof*? With regards to the binary relationships of intellect and speech, as well as male and female, this suggestion would bring into question the importance of sensible speech and of paternity.[123]

Ultimately, Schneersohn prefers to retain the previously oppositional supra-physical infrastructure of the *ohr eyn sof* as the means to better appreciate the importance of the physical realm. In this reformed state, which Schneersohn describes as messianic, the *ohr eyn sof* is no longer a reflection of its own attachment to God that devalued the apparent separateness of creation; rather, it becomes an expression of the quality of divine autonomy that is most readily found in the apparent self-sufficiency and distinctiveness of creation. This transformation of the once hierarchically oppositional *ohr eyn sof* into a continuous

[123] Examples of this approach would include the Letterism of Isidore Isou and to some extent the maternal in the writings of Julia Kristeva. The relevance of Schneersohn's discourses of 1898 to Kristeva's theories of language and the maternal have been discussed earlier. A study of Isou's Letterism in the context of Schneersohn's theory of speech is a possible direction for future research.

complement to the essential divine quality of the physical creation is presented as the condition of a messianic era, and the achievement of a universal epoch of this order is realized by the study of the Torah and the performance of the *mitsvot*. Schneersohn explains how the Torah and *mitsvot* are themselves examples of a messianic non-oppositional binary reality, wherein the physical components of Jewish religious life elevate the reasoning and intentionality of *mitsvah* observance. This elevation removes the oppositional and hierarchical tension between intention and action and places them in a continuum that allows for their essential qualities to be revealed.

The philosophy of *mitsvot* presented here by Schneersohn can be viewed as providing the ideological underpinnings for some of the developments in *Habad* activism during the second half of the twentieth century. A key tenet in *Habad* outreach activity has been the promotion and valuing of *mitsvah* performance regardless of motivation or any long-term commitment to a religious lifestyle, on the one hand, while also considering such one-off encounters as being likely and welcome catalysts for a more sustained engagement with religious thought and practice. This approach could be understood as a double move whereby the often-entrenched oppositional binarism of religious practice that privileges intention over practice is initially deconstructed by counter-intuitively privileging the formerly subordinated physical dimension of the *mitsvah*, thereby paving the way for a future reconstructed non-oppositional relationship between intention and action in the performance of *mitsvot*. Similar to an earlier observation concerning the centrality of the person *vis-à-vis* the Torah and its commandments and how it distinguishes Schneersohn's theology from other streams of Jewish thought and practice, here again we find a distinctive theological orientation in these discourses. Unlike some traditional theologies that perceive ritual and performance as expressions of a more sublime intention and commitment, Schneersohn amplifies the centrality of the physically embedded commandments that unlock an otherwise inaccessible realm of meaning and intention.

The discourse opens with a reiteration of a key theme from the previous discourses: how even when the essential creative quality of *malkhut* is revealed, it still relies on the expressive ability of the *ohr eyn sof* to actualize creation. For even though 'the essence of the creation is from the aspect of *malkhut* alone', it is specifically through the *ohr eyn sof* 'that the creation can be actually revealed'.[124] This necessity for both the creativity of *malkhut* and the expressivity of the *ohr eyn sof* to achieve creation is compared to the necessity of both a male and a female in the creation of a child, which was discussed earlier in the second discourse. The resultant child in particular, and the world more generally, are thus configured in a manner where the substance and materiality of their existence is a product of *malkhut,* and their expression and design come from the *ohr eyn sof.*[125]

Schneersohn notes how presently, what is most appreciated and prominent is the expression and design of the component parts of creation, rather than their material substance. To quote: 'And as it is with a person below, what is appreciated in the person is that they are a dynamic existence (*metsiut be-giluy*), and the dynamism of an existence is the product of the seminal drop of the male. The primary expression of a person is in their movement and their personality (*ha-tenuah ha-hiyonit ve-ha-kohot ha-nafshiyim*) which comes from the male ... but their existential physical state (*guf etsem ha-hithavut*) is not apparent or expressed in them, there does not appear to be any appreciable advantage in the body at all.' In contrast, in the messianic era when 'the essential hiddenness of *malkhut* will be revealed',[126]

---

[124] Schneersohn (2011), 92.
[125] This presentation of reproduction is similar to Aristotle; however, the role of creating the substance and materiality is valued by Schneersohn in a manner that is not evident in Aristotle.
[126] Schneersohn (2011), 93.

then the substance and materiality of existence will be the foremost principle of reality. However, notwithstanding the prominence of *malkhut* in the messianic era, Schneersohn explains that it will still be reliant on the expressive capacity of the *ohr eyn sof* to convey its 'essential hiddenness (*he'elem ha-atsmi*)'. Similarly, the new-found appreciation of the body in the messianic era that originates in the mother will also be dependent on the expressiveness of a person's movement and personality that originates from the father. Thus, in the messianic era the body will no longer be the means and the situation, whereby the supposedly superior soulful qualities of intellect and emotions can be expressed and appreciated; rather, conversely, these soulful qualities will be the necessary tools to express and appreciate the profundity of the body.[127]

Schneersohn proceeds to broaden his thesis from the specifically located categories of the *ohr eyn sof* and *malkhut* to the more encompassing classification of *memale kol almin* and *sovev kol almin*. *Memale kol almin* (lit. fills all worlds) categorizes the expression of God (*ohr eyn sof*) that is limitable and contained within existence, in contrast to *sovev kol almin* (lit. encompasses all worlds) that while being present throughout existence, expresses, and is at times considered synonymous with, God's essential transcendence and aloofness. On these terms, Schneersohn explains that 'the entirety of a person's service in this world in the fulfilment of the Torah and the *mitsvot* is to reveal *sovev kol almin* through *memale kol almin*',[128] which will reach its perfection in the messianic era. Through using physical objects to fulfil the divine will, a person conditions the limitations and restrictions of the world which are enlivened by *memale*, to be suited to express the otherwise inexpressible *sovev*.

---

[127] See Schneersohn (2011), 92.
[128] Schneersohn (2011), 94.

To understand how it is possible for the apparently uncontainable *sovev* to be revealed and expressed through the limiting and restricting characteristics of *memale*, Schneersohn poses many of the same questions, as well as drawing similar conclusions, from the previous discourse. Schneersohn compares the revelation of *sovev* in *memale* to the grasping of an essential intellectual point after extensive intellectual analysis. When a person considers a topic thoroughly in all its details and then reaches an appreciation of the essential nature of the concept, then the entire framework of the concept in all its details is enhanced. 'The concept in general, also from the perspective of its details, becomes more wondrous and loftier, and is not so limited . . . the detail becomes united with the whole.'[129] The previously limiting and containing specifics of the concept are now infused and enlightened with the essential and unlimited core of the idea, to the point where the containing function of the details serve merely to reveal the essence of the idea and not to conceal it. In a comparable way, the varied and distinctive components of existence that originate in *memale* will become elevated in the messianic era and express the previously uncontainable aspect of *sovev*.

Kristeva's articulation of how the heterogeneity of the semiotic becomes constituted in and expressed through the symbolic can be a useful tool to understand the 'revelation of *sovev* in *memale*' discussed here. Schneersohn compares *memale* with consciousness and its ability to distinguish between things and ideas. This ability is not a function of infinite plurality and should not be mistaken as similar to the heterogeneity of the somatic in Kristeva; rather, it denotes a limiting and restricting function. In contrast, *sovev* is compared with an infinite pre-consciousness that is not limited or restricted by any specific thing or idea. Schneersohn's question,

---

[129] Schneersohn (2011), 105.

'how can *sovev* be revealed in the categories of *memale?*'[130] is akin to Kristeva's attempt to maintain the presence of the symbolic function, even once the semiotic has gained the upper hand. Schneersohn's solution values the role of *memale* as the categorical tool of expression, which is necessary for communication, and reassumes the previously constraining categories of *memale* as articulations of the infinity of the *sovev*:

> When the light of *sovev* shines through the details of *memale*, it becomes contained; however, the actual infinite light of *sovev* shines in all of them (the details of *memale*). Therefore, the details are not so limited and distinctive, because all of them, and every detail of them, is connected with the essence of *sovev* (*ha-etsem de-eyn sof ha-sovev*).[131]

Just as Kristeva maintains the importance of the symbolic as an expressive tool of the semiotic, Schneersohn preserves *memale* as the revelatory means of *sovev*. In the context of speech, the coherent categories of consciousness are necessary for the articulation of the profound origin of the letters of speech. For Schneersohn, this delicate relationship, whereby the pre-thetic letters of speech are communicated through sensible consciousness is depicted as operating within an intellectual discourse conducted in prose.[132] As I argued in the earlier chapter on language, Schneersohn's explanation is not as readily understandable as it would be if presented in the form of Kristeva's poetic language. The unsettling of the thetic function by semiotic aspects such as rhythm and intonation in poetic language is more immediately obvious than is apparent in a prose discourse. Similarly, even though Kristeva acknowledges how this unsettling is a feature of any language discourse, the reassuming of

---

[130] Schneersohn (2011), 104.
[131] Schneersohn (2011), 105.
[132] Schneersohn (2011), 105.

the symbolic thetic function in poetic language is more pronounced and recognizable. As such, Kristeva's emphasis on poetic language can help elucidate and clarify a particularly difficult section in Schneersohn's discourses.

Schneersohn explains how, while the *midrash* is ostensibly commenting on how the world was created, it is also indicating how the world could be transformed in a messianic era. According to this reading, the world was, indeed, created with the attribute of justice, which means that the *ohr eyn sof* is concealed by *malkhut*, and consciousness, men and the soul are privileged over speech, women and the body. However, in the messianic era the attribute of mercy will be combined with justice, which means the source of *malkhut* in *atsmut* will be revealed through the expressiveness of the *ohr eyn sof*. Similarly, the profundity of speech, women and the body will finally be appreciated. It might seem that Schneersohn is advocating a historical approach to the disruption of oppositional binaries and is accepting the validity of the prevailing denigration of speech, women and the body prior to the messianic era. Alternatively, by introducing an eschatological component to his exposition Schneersohn is emphasizing the extent to which human behaviour is responsible for the transformation of the world. For Schneersohn, the relationship between justice and mercy, *memale* and *sovev*, *ohr eyn sof* and *malkhut*, consciousness and speech, men and women, the soul and the body are not abstract philosophical discussions of an eternally true perspective of the world, but, rather, a constant demand to reveal the essential quality of the recipient through the provider. By placing his ideas in a historical framework, Schneersohn emphasizes the need to constantly disrupt oppositional binaries and to take on a more proactive role in preparing the world for the redemption.

Schneersohn concludes his interpretation of the *midrash* he introduced in the first discourse as follows: 'And God combined the attribute of mercy with the attribute of justice . . . so that the root and origin of *malkhut*, which is the essence of God (*eyn sof atsmut u-mehut*), should be expressed in the details of *memale*.'[133] Instead of reading the *midrash* as a final description of creation, Schneersohn interprets it to refer to a messianic future that fulfils the purpose of creation, wherein the essence of God is fully expressed in the particulars of existence. The conclusion of the discourse is focused on the path to achieving this vision, namely, the observance of the Torah and the *mitsvot*. He explains how the path to achieving this future is 'a pristine form of Torah study' (*ha-lomed Torah ke-de-ba'ei le-me-hevei*) and 'a selfless and extraordinary performance of the *mitsvot*' (*ha-oseh et ha-mitsvot bi-behinat bitul retsono le-ma'alah mi-tiv'o ve-hergelo*).[134] The Torah and the *mitsvot* are presented as examples of this anticipated messianic state, where *atsmut* is contained and revealed in the physical world through the words of the Torah and the physical components of a *mitsvah*. Notwithstanding the physicality of the words of the Torah and the materials with which the *mitsvot* are performed, they embody and express God's essential will and wisdom in the world. As already expressed in the third discourse, Schneersohn interprets the purpose of the *midrash* as informing a Jew in their observance of the Torah and *mitsvot*. Here Schneersohn goes further and explains how the Torah and *mitsvot* are themselves rooted in the essence of God and are thus the tools with which to affect the realization of God's essence being apparent and expressed in the reality of existence. The Torah and the *mitsvot* as they are revealed in the world are still identified with, and are an expression of, their source in the essence of God, such that 'in the mouth of the person who learns Torah, is the actual word of God as it is above',[135] and 'the *mitsvot* are verily the revelation

---

[133] Schneersohn (2011), 107.
[134] Schneersohn (2011), 108.
[135] Schneersohn (2011), 107.

of God's innermost will, which is truly expressed in the *mitsvah* and in the person who performs the *mitsvah*.[136] The Torah and *mitsvot* are presented as models of the intended perfection of the entirety of existence, where the differentiated categories and specifics of the physical components of the Torah and *mitsvot* reveal, rather than conceal, God's essence.

In the end, Schneersohn is asking his listeners and readers to realize how, through their own actions, they are able to transform reality. At the outset, Schneersohn explained how even in our current unredeemed state, when our present mindset privileges the provider in oppositional binary relationships, it is still possible to become aware of a hidden truth in the recipient. Even before the messianic era, a person can come to realize the essential qualities in speech, women and the body, which indicate an alternative reality other than that which is readily perceived: a reality in which the recipient originates in the most primordial origin and is the impetus for all the expressiveness of the provider. The complete revelation of this reality is the messianic promise, which is not something merely to be waited for, but will be the result of active divine service. It remains important to remember Schneersohn's conceptual and social priorities in which he sought to inspire religious piety in his followers and to anticipate the redemption. These priorities prompted him to develop a theory of language, gender, the body and existence as a whole that had hitherto not found such lucid expression in Jewish thought nor in the philosophy of his time. Schneersohn's closing words make clear his overriding intention with the entire series of discourses by stating how 'the combining of the attribute of mercy with the attribute of justice is brought about by the souls of Israel through their service of Torah and *mitsvot*.[137] The next and final chapter will conclude on

---

[136] Schneersohn (2011), 108.
[137] Schneersohn (2011), 110.

our exploration of language, gender and mysticism in Schneersohn's discourses of 1898 and consider their potential relevance for future research. As we will observe, Schneersohn's mystically infused theo-philosophical ideas have the scope to inform both a distinctive Jewish theology and a philosophical approach that resists the binary restraints of Western thought.

Conclusion

At the outset of this book, I made the seemingly implausible claim that a traditional late-nineteenth-century rabbinic thinker innovated a distinct philosophical orientation that would be mirrored in modern philosophy over half a century later. At the heart of the implausibility of this claim were a set of scholarly assumptions that work to preclude the possibility of reading a traditionalist rabbinic thinker such as Schneersohn as a contemporary philosopher, let alone as a prescient precursor to the *avant-garde* thought that emerged in France in the 1960s and 1970s. In this concluding section, I will briefly outline the contours of the argument in the previous chapters, before setting out what I consider to be the importance and the implications of treating Schneersohn as a contemporary philosopher.

In the introduction, I identified three assumptions that build upon each other to create an apparently unbridgeable distance between Schneersohn and the modern thought of Levinas, Derrida and Kristeva. Even in the academic discipline of modern Jewish philosophy, which one might consider to be the most natural site for the scholarly attention of Schneersohn, there has been hardly any serious engagement with his thought. I argued that this exclusionary practice is a legacy of an enduring binary approach to notions of tradition and modernity, where if a thinker is traditional, it is assumed they will not be attuned to modern concerns, as well as hard disciplinary boundaries between philosophical and *kabbalistic* thought, which assume a kabbalistically orientated thinker has little if any relevance for a Jewish philosophical discourse. Moreover, even if these obstacles could be overcome, and there were to be a new-found interest within the field of modern Jewish philosophy in Schneersohn as both a modern and philosophical thinker, as a *Jewish* thinker he would still likely be seen as largely outside the presumed concerns of contemporary general philosophical discourse. The situatedness of his thought within an ostensibly Jewish conceptual framework would often be seen, implicitly or explicitly, as excluding him, together with many other philosophically rich thinkers from non-Western traditions, from a canonized and entrenched philosophical chain of tradition. A certain dogmatic orthodoxy in departments of philosophy maintains a trajectory from the early Greek thought of Plato and Aristotle through to contemporary philosophy in either its continental or analytical form, all the time unwittingly ignoring, or even purposely excluding, alternative genealogies of philosophical thought. Although this exclusionary practice disregards whole swathes of alternative thought traditions, such as Indian philosophy and Chinese philosophy, it is especially ungrounded with regards to a thinker like Schneersohn, whose thought more readily approximates with the Western philosophical tradition.

Through challenging the validity of these assumptions, I endeavoured to remove some of the scholarly barriers that would discriminate against positive engagement with the intellectual project that forms the basis of this book. I showed how *kabbalistic* thought constituted a significant influence on early modern philosophy, and I echoed the arguments of other disenfranchised philosophical schools in arguing for a broadening of what is considered and treated as philosophy. I also drew heavily from the sociological theory of 'multiple modernities', and demonstrated how modernity should not be treated as synonymous with Westernization, leaving ample room for alternative models of modernization. However, while this section of my book may have successfully argued against the automatic rejection of Schneersohn as a meaningful precursor to aspects of modern thought, there remained the task of then concretely arguing for the positive assertion of Schneersohn's philosophical relevance.

In Chapters 2 and 3, I presented how notions of language and gender are examined in Schneersohn's discourses of 1898, trying as far as possible to retain the sequence and character of the original material. It became clear that notwithstanding the way in which his work is steeped within an alternative conceptual system, Schneersohn's schemas of thought readily lend themselves to concerns familiar to those who work on twentieth- and twenty-first-century philosophical thought. His extensive portrayal of speech and women as undervalued features of hierarchical oppositional structures, and his subsequent attempt at recasting them as central and primary features in their respective pairings, was shown to place him unambiguously within the interests of twentieth-century thought. Perhaps to a greater extent than the polemics in the introduction, which merely sought to remove an automatic assumption of his irrelevance to philosophical discourse, Schneersohn's sophisticated version of a linguistic turn, as well as his foray into the concerns of feminist thought, forcefully asserted the rich philosophical relevance of his thought.

Having established the philosophical significance of Schneersohn's thought, I proceeded to open up and develop a cross-cultural dialogue between Schneersohn and the modern thought of Emmanuel Levinas, Jacques Derrida and Julia Kristeva. Paying close attention to some key texts of these thinkers, I emphasized the conceptual affinity between the main ideas of the discourses of 1898 with the central theories and intellectual orientation of Levinas, Derrida and Kristeva. Considering the likelihood of a deep scepticism within a range of academic fields, of there being any like-mindedness between the traditional and *kabbalistically* orientated Schneersohn and the modern thought of Levinas, Derrida and Kristeva, these chapters go a long way to challenging the biases at the heart of this scepticism. However, the objective of this section was not only to emphasize the significance of similarities between relatively distinct systems of thought, but to also explore the possibility of how these systems of thought can inform and enhance each other. In this maiden attempt at construing a mutually beneficial dialogue between Schneersohn and modern thought, it became clear that there was both an interpretative as well as an evaluative dividend in this approach, upon which I will now elaborate.

As discussed in the introduction, there are two methodological approaches that are commonly deployed in comparative philosophy: the interpretative model which seeks to enhance the understanding of one system of thought through comparing it with another, and the evaluative model which attempts to advance a philosophical idea through the encounter and comparison of two alternate thought traditions. The methodological approach of this book, which emphasized the importance of juxtaposing Schneersohn with his modern interlocutors, developed a number of interpretative enhancements to each of the thinkers involved. Firstly, the paralleling of one set of ideas with an alternative thought tradition presents new opportunities in the communication of each tradition's ideas, and offers the prospect of articulating their philosophies in an idiom that is more readily understandable to a new audience of readers. Consequently, as a result of this book, it will now become easier for scholars familiar with modern rabbinic thought to engage with aspects of modern philosophical thought and discern possible connections with their primary area of expertise. Similarly, scholars of modern philosophy will also be able to engage with rabbinic thought and acknowledge how a different thought tradition can be informative and instructive.

A more specific interpretative benefit for our understanding of Schneersohn lies in the encounter with additional categories of recipients, such as the Other in Levinas and writing in Derrida, which can help broaden and deepen the thematic objective of the discourses.

Levinas's emphasis on the social impact of this schema of thought, and Derrida's extension of absence to the more detached form of writing, enable us to appreciate more far-reaching dimensions to Schneersohn's thought. Schneersohn's theorizing of oppositional binaries takes place primarily within the individual, in the form of speech/consciousness or body/soul, or in the intimate encounter of men and women. By showing how the same approach can be extended to broader categories outside of the self, such as in Levinas's Other and Derrida's writing, we can derive additional social implications from Schneersohn's thought. However, perhaps the most beneficial enrichment that Schneersohn can gain from this dialogue is from the emphasis on the poetic in Kristeva's thought. Schneersohn describes speech in prosaic terms, and as such it is harder for the reader to immediately appreciate how the primacy of the 'letters of speech' can remain discernible even in the spoken, sensible word. Kristeva's emphasis on the onomatopoeic qualities, which are highlighted in poetic speech, and which are more obscure in prosaic speech, offers Schneersohn a potentially more appreciable and convincing model for the point he is trying to convey.

Similarly, there have been a number of interpretative gains in our understanding of Levinas, Derrida and Kristeva. For example, the overt linking in the discourses of speech with the *kabbalistic* idea of the *tsimtsum* offers additional insight into Levinas's idea of the trace in *Otherwise than Being*, and how the latter might refer back to his discussion of a contraction in *Totality and Infinity*. Likewise, the full implication of the often unexplored 'double gesture' of Derrida, and the possibility of a reconstruction of a transformed hierarchical model, becomes clearer and more apparent in light of Schneersohn's discourses. Also, Kristeva's largely undeveloped theory of a reassumed paternal function can borrow from the more extensive deliberation in Schneersohn. The evidence of these interpretative enhancements demonstrates the potential benefits available to scholars of philosophy of engaging with Schneersohn as well as other philosophical thinkers from alternative thought traditions. Conversely, by ignoring these thinkers, many dimensions and interpretations are likely to remain undiscovered.

In addition to the interpretative value of this dialogue, there is also an important evaluative dimension that is worth emphasizing, and which brings us to consider how this book can impact and influence future research. At the outset of this book, both scholars of modern philosophy and scholars of Jewish studies might have doubted the possibility of progressively orientated thought in an otherwise socially conservative rabbi like Schneersohn. The achievement of this book in showing how a pre-twentieth-century traditionalist figure, not familiar or engaged with modern Western philosophy, prefigured many of the central themes of postmodern thought brings into question many fundamental assumptions that determine how we engage with philosophy and with traditional Jewish thinkers. Through acknowledging the possibility of a thinker, situated in a different cultural framework and discourse, posing similar questions and even coming up with similar responses to thinkers who are operating in another framework and discourse, we can begin to appreciate a far broader definition of what constitutes philosophy. Moreover, a broadened definition of philosophy, what we might call 'multiple philosophies', opens up the possibility of many interpretative and evaluative gains. Through the act of multiplying our notions of both philosophy and modernity, we might be able to discover hitherto ignored and overlooked dimensions of contemporary thought and culture.

Additionally, this book presents a challenge to a prevailing culture in the academic study of traditional Jewish thinkers in the modern period. In contrast to scholarship on medieval Jewish thought, which accentuates the philosophical acumen of thinkers such as Saadia, Maimonides and Gersonides albeit within a prism of their affinity with Greek thought, there is a distinct lack of emphasis by scholars of modern Jewish thought on the philosophical dimension of traditional rabbinic thinkers. As discussed at length in the introduction, there are institutionalized reasons for the exclusion of these thinkers; however, the discovery of Schneersohn's philosophically prescient thought should encourage a reappraisal of scholarly priorities when studying these figures. Meaning to say that in addition to the importance of historical, sociological and theological studies, there is a necessity to also consider the philosophical aspect of their work.[1] For while these other scholarly enquiries are, of course, important and relevant, the emergence of Schneersohn's meaningful philosophical contribution opens up a new direction and approach for the study of traditional Jewish thinkers of the modern period. In the first instance, this new direction would accept and respect the possibility that any given thinker may have the capacity of innovative philosophical thought, and then proceed to place particular emphasis on appreciating the philosophical contours of their work. Furthermore, in contrast to an approach that uses the historical and sociological to explain the nature of a thinker's ideas, this new direction would, instead, consider the philosophical orientation of a thinker as critical in our understanding of the historical and sociological aspects of their life.

In the modern period, scholars have been attracted mainly to Jewish religious philosophers who have themselves engaged with the wider philosophical tradition. The loosening of disciplinary boundaries in both the academic fields of philosophy and Jewish studies, as suggested earlier, presents a new opportunity for scholars of religious and traditional philosophy. Unlike the study of philosophy of religion, which might be characterized as using Western philosophical

---

[1] See Wolfson (2016, 45–6), where he makes a similar argument.

categories to analyse religious thought and religious concerns, 'religious philosophies' could be described as the philosophical ideas that are innovated as a result of religious texts, culture and experiences. In this way, this book's portrayal of Schneersohn's thought and its fruitful engagement with modern philosophy can provide a helpful paradigm for future research and overcome the historical suppression of other traditional religious philosophers.

Bibliography

Aarsleff, H. (1982), *From Locke to Saussure: Essays on the Study of Language and Intellectual History*, Chicago, IL: University of Minnesota Press.

Aeschylus. (1952), *The Complete Plays of Aeschylus*, trans. G. Murray, London: George Allen & Unwin Ltd.

Ajzenstat, O. (2001), *Driven Back to the Text: The Premodern Sources of Levinas's Postmodernism*, Pittsburgh, PA: Duquesne University Press.

Altein, Y. L., ed. (2006), *Heikhal ha-Besht* 16, Brooklyn, NY: Heikhal Menahem.

Alter, R. (1981), *The Art of Biblical Narrative*, New York, NY: Basic Books.

Altmann, A. (2016), 'Moses Narboni's "Epistle on *Shiur Qoma*"', in A. Altmann (ed.), *Jewish Medieval and Renaissance Studies*, 180–209, London: Routledge.

Arens, H. (1984), *Aristotle's Theory of Language and its Tradition*, Amsterdam: Benjamins.

Aristotle (1984), *The Complete Works of Aristotle v. 1–2*, ed. J. Barnes, Princeton, NJ: Princeton University Press.

Bahye ibn Asher (2007), *Midrash Rabbeinu Bahye al ha-Torah v.2*, Jerusalem: Mekor ha-Sefarim.

Baker, G. and Morris, K. J. (1996), *Descartes' Dualism*, New York, NY: Routledge.

Bakhtin, M. (1981), *The Dialogic Imagination,* trans. M. Holquist and C. Emerson, Austin, TX: University of Texas Press.

Baldwin, T., ed. (2003), *The Cambridge History of Philosophy 1870–1945*, Cambridge: Cambridge University Press.

Barlow, L. (2009), 'A Theology of Meaning: Hasidism and Deconstruction in Elie Wiesel's Souls on Fire', *Studies in American Jewish Literature*, 28: 41–5.

Barth, R. (1972), 'To Write: An Intransitive Verb?' in R. Macksey and E Donato (eds), *The Structuralist Controversy: The Languages of Criticism and the Sciences of Man*, 134–44, Baltimore, MD: John Hopkins University Press.

Belmonte, N. (2002), 'Evolving Negativity: From Hegel to Derrida',
  Philosophy & Social Criticism, 28 (1): 18–58.
Beltran, M. (2016), *The Influence of Abraham Cohen de Herrera's Kabbalah
  on Spinoza's Metaphysics*, Boston, MA: Brill.
Berlin, I. (2000), *Three Critics of the Enlightenment: Vico, Hamann, Herder*,
  London: Pimlico.
Biale, D. (1979), *Gershom Scholem: Kabbalah and Counter-History*,
  Cambridge, MA: Harvard University Press.
Bielik-Robson, A. (2018), 'The Marrano God: Abstraction, Messianicity,
  and Retreat in Derrida's "Faith and Knowledge"', *Religions*, 10 (1): 22–45.
Bielik-Robson, A. (2021), 'Derrida Denudata: Tsimtsum and the Derridean
  Metaphysics of Non-Presence', in A. Bielik-Robson and D. H Weiss (eds),
  *Tsimtsum and Modernity: Lurianic Heritage in Modern Philosophy and
  Theology*, 389–418, Berlin: De Gruyter.
Bielik-Robson, A. and Weiss, D. H., eds. (2021), *Tsimtsum and Modernity:
  Lurianic Heritage in Modern Philosophy and Theology*, Berlin: De Gruyter.
Boyarin, D. (1990), *Intertextuality and the Reading of Midrash*,
  Bloomington, IN: Indiana University Press.
Boyarin, D. (1993), *Carnal Israel: Reading Sex in Talmudic Culture*, Berkeley,
  CA: University of California Press.
Boyarin, D. (2003), *Sparks of the Logos: Essays in Rabbinic Hermeneutics*,
  Leiden: Brill.
Braine, D. (2014), *Language and Human Understanding: The Roots of
  Creativity in Speech and Thought*, Washington, DC: The Catholic
  University of America Press.
Brawer, N. (2000), *Resistance and Response to Change: The Leadership of
  Rabbi Shalom Dovber Schneersohn (1860–1920)*, PhD. diss., University
  College London.
Brody, D. (2001), 'Levinas's Maternal Method from "Time and the Other"
  Through Otherwise Than Being: No Woman's Land?', in T. Chanter
  (ed.), *Feminist Interpretations of Emmanuel Levinas*, 53–77, University
  Park, PA: Pennsylvania State University Press.
Brown, K. (2006), *Nietzsche and Embodiment: Discerning Bodies and Non-
  dualism*, Albany, NY: SUNY Press.

Buber, M. and Rosenzweig, F. (1994), *Scripture and Translation*, Bloomington, IN: Indiana University Press.

Candler, P. (2006), *Theology, Rhetoric, Manuduction, or Reading Scripture Together on the Path to God*, Grand Rapids, MI: William B. Eerdmans Publishing Company.

Carpenter, A. D. (2008), 'Embodying Intelligence: Animals and Us in Plato's *Timaeus*', in Zovko, M. (ed.), *Platonism and Forms of Intelligence*, 39–56, Berlin: Akademie Verlag.

Carpenter, A. D. (2010), 'Embodied (intelligent?) Souls: Plants in Plato's *Timaeus*', *Phronesis*, 55: 281–303.

Cassirer, E. (1946), *Language and Myth*, trans. S. K. Langer, New York, NY: Dover Publications.

Chalier, C. (1982), *Figures du féminin*, Paris: Surveillèe.

Chalier, C. (2002), *La Trace de l'infini: Emmanuel Levinas et la Source Hébraïque*, Paris: Éditions du Cerf.

Chanter, T., ed. (2001), *Feminist Interpretations of Emmanuel*, University Park, PA: Pennsylvania State University Press.

Cherniss, J. L. and Smith, S. B., eds. (2018), *The Cambridge Companion to Isaiah Berlin*, Cambridge: Cambridge University Press.

Chomsky, N. (2006), *Language and Mind*, Cambridge: Cambridge University Press.

Cline, E. M. (2013), *Confucius, Rawls, and the Sense of Justice*, New York, NY: Fordham University Press.

Cohen, A. A. (1969), 'The Myth of the Judeo-Christian Tradition', in *Commentary Magazine*. Available online: https://www.commentarymagazine.com/articles/the-myth-of-the-judeo-christian-tradition (accessed 18 July 2018).

Cohen de Hererra, A. (2002), *Gate of Heaven,* trans. K. Krabbenhoft, Leiden: Brill.

Cohen, R. A. (1994), *Elevations: The Height of the Good in Rosenzweig and Levinas*, Chicago, IL: University of Chicago Press.

Connell, S. M. (2000), 'Aristotle and Galen on Sex Difference and Reproduction: A New Approach to an Ancient Rivalry', *Studies in the History and Philosophy of Science*, 31 (3): 405–27.

Connell, S. M. (2016), *Aristotle on Female Animals: A Study of the Generation of Animals*, Cambridge: Cambridge University Press.

Connolly, T. (2015), *Doing Philosophy Comparatively*, London: Bloomsbury.

Coudert, A. (1995), *Leibniz and the Kabbalah*, London: Kluwer Academic.

Curtay, J. P. (1985), *Letterism and Hypergraphics: The Unknown Avant-Garde 1945–1985*, New York, NY: Franklin Furnace.

Dahl, N. and Segal, A. (1978), 'Philo and the Rabbis on the Names of God', *Journal for the Study of Judaism*, 9 (2): 1–28.

Dan, J. (1997), 'Gershom Scholem: Between Mysticism and Scholarship', *The Germanic Review: Literature, Culture, Theory*, 72 (1): 4–22.

Davidson, H. A. (1974), 'The Study of Philosophy as a Religious Obligation', in S. D. Goltein (ed.), *Religion in a Religious Age*, 53–68, Cambridge, MA: Association for Jewish Studies.

Davis, C. (2007), *Levinas: An Introduction*, Cambridge: Polity Press.

De Beauvoir, S. (1997), *The Second Sex*, London: Vintage Books.

Derrida, J. (1973), *Speech and Phenomena: And Other Essays on Husserl's Theory of Signs*, trans. D. B. Allison, Evanston, IL: Northwestern University Press.

Derrida, J. (1981), *Dissemination*, trans. B. Johnson London: Athlone.

Derrida, J. (1982), *Positions*, trans. A. Bass, Chicago, IL: University of Chicago Press.

Derrida, J. (1988), *The Ear of the Other: Otobiography, Transference, Translation*, ed. C. McDonald, Lincoln, NE: University of Nebraska Press.

Derrida, J. (1994), *Specters of Marx: The State of Debt, the Work of Mourning, and the New International*, trans. P. Kamuf, London: Routledge.

Derrida, J. (1995), *On the Name*, ed. T. Dutoit, Stanford, CA: Stanford University Press.

Derrida, J. (2001), *Writing and Difference*, trans. A. Bass, London: Routledge.

Derrida, J. (2002), *Acts of Religion*, London: Routledge.

Dinstag, Y. (1964), 'ha-Moreh Nevuchim ve-Sefer ha-Mada be-Sifrut ha-Hasidut', in S. Belkin (ed.), *Sefer ha-Yovel li-khvod Avraham Weiss*, 307–30, New York, NY: Shulzinger Press.

Ehrlich, A. M. (2000), *Leadership in the HaBaD Movement: A Critical Evaluation of HaBaD Leadership, History, and Succession*, Northvale, NJ: Aaronson Press.

Eisenstadt, S. N. (1973), *Tradition, Change, and Modernity*, New York, NY: John Wiley & Sons.

Eisenstadt, S. N. (2000), 'Multiple Modernities', *Daedalus*, 129 (1): 1–30.

Eisenstadt, S. N. (2003), *Comparative Civilizations & Multiple Modernities*, Leiden: Brill.

Eliach, D. (2002), *Sefer ha-Gaon*, Jerusalem: Makhon Moreshet ha-Yeshivot.

Elior, R. (1993), *The Paradoxical Ascent to God: The Kabbalistic Theosophy of Habad Hasidism*, New York, NY: SUNY Press.

Fagan, M. (2013), *Ethics and Politics after Poststructuralism: Levinas, Derrida and Nancy*, Edinburgh: Edinburgh University Press.

Fagenblat, M. (2010), *A Covenant of Creatures: Levinas's Philosophy of Judaism*, Stanford, CA: Stanford University Press.

Faubion, J. D. (1993), *Modern Greek Lessons: A Primer in Historical Constructivism*, Princeton, NJ: Princeton University Press.

Faur, J. (1986), *Golden Doves with Silver Dots: Semiotics and Textuality in Rabbinic Tradition*, Bloomington, IN: Indiana University Press.

Feder, E. K., Rawlinson, M. C. and Zakin, E. , eds. (1997), *Derrida and Feminism: Recasting the Question of Woman*, London: Routledge.

Feder, E. K. and Zakin, E. (1997), 'Flirting with the Truth: Derrida's Discourse with "Woman" and Wenches' in E. K. Feder, M. C. Rawlinson and E. Zakin, (eds), *Derrida and Feminism: Recasting the Question of Woman*, 21–52, London: Routledge.

Fishkoff, S. (2003), *The Rebbe's Army: Inside the World of Chabad-Lubavitch*, New York, NY: Schocken Books.

Foxbrunner, R. (1993), *Habad: The Hasidism of R. Shneur Zalman of Lyady*, Northvale, NJ: Aronson Press.

Frank, D. (1997), 'The New Rhetoric, Judaism, and Post-Enlightenment Thought: The Cultural Origins of Perelmanian Philosophy', *Quarterly Journal of Speech*, 83 (3): 311–31.

Frank, D., Leaman, O. and Manekin, C. H., eds. (2000), *The Jewish Philosophy Reader*, London: Routledge.

Frankel, Z. (1851), *Ueber den Einflus der Palestinensichen Exegese auf die Alexandrinische Hermeneutik*, Leipzig: J. A. Barth.

Franks, P. (2006), 'Everyday Speech and Revelatory Speech in Rosenzweig and Wittgenstein', *Philosophy Today*, 50 (1): 24–39.

Gadamer, H. (1975), *Truth and Method*, London: Sheed & Ward.

Garfield, J. L. (2002), *Empty Words: Buddhist Philosophy and Cross-Cultural Interpretation*, Oxford: Oxford University Press.

Garfield, J. L. (2015), 'Two Truths and Method', in K. Tanaka, Y. Deguchi, J. L. Garfield and G. Priest (eds), *The Moon Points Back*, 245–62, New York, NY: Oxford University Press.

Glizenstein, H. (1969), *Tomkhei Temimim*, Brooklyn, NY: Kehot Publication Society.

Golomb, M. H. (1994), *Sha'arei Limud ha-Hasidut*, Brooklyn, NY: Kehot Publication Society.

Goodman, L., ed. (1992), *Neoplatonism and Jewish Thought*, Albany, NY: SUNY Press.

Goodman-Thau, E., Mattenklott, G. and Schulte, C., eds. (1994), *Kabbala und Romantik*, Tübingen: Niemeyer.

Gotlieb, J. (2009), *Rationalism in Hasidic Attire: Habad's Harmonistic Approach to Maimonides*, Ramat Gan: Bar-Ilan University Press.

Gottlieb, J. (2009), *Sekhaltanut biLevush Hasidi: Demuto shel ha-Rambam be-Hasidut Habad*, Ramat-Gan, Israel: University of Bar-Ilan Press.

Gribetz, S., Grossberg, D. M., Himmelfarb, M. and Schäfer, P., eds. (2016), *Genesis Rabbah in Text and Context*, Tübingen: Mohr Siebeck.

Halbertal, M. (2002), 'Jacob Katz on Halakhah, Orthodoxy and History', in J. M. Harris (ed.), *Pride of Jacob: Essays on Jacob Katz and His Work*, 163–72, Cambridge, MA: Harvard University Center for Jewish Studies.

Hallamish, M. (1980), 'The Theoretical System of Rabbi Shneur Zalman of Liady', PhD. Diss., The Hebrew University of Jerusalem.

Hamann, J. (2007), *Writings on Philosophy and Language*, trans. K. Haynes, Cambridge: Cambridge University Press.

Handelman, S. A. (1982), *The Slayers of Moses: The Emergence of Rabbinic Interpretation in Modern Literary Theory*, Albany, NY: SUNY Press.

Handelman, S. A. (1985), 'Fragments of the Rock: Contemporary Literary Theory and the Study of Rabbinic Texts – A Response to David Stern', *Prooftexts*, 5 (1): 75–95.

Handelman, S. A. (1991), *Fragments of Redemption: Jewish Thought and Literary Theory in Benjamin, Scholem, and Levinas*, Bloomington, IN: Indiana University Press.

Harris, J., ed. (2007), *Maimonides After 800 Years: Essays on Maimonides and His Influence*, Cambridge, MA: Harvard University Center for Jewish Studies.

Hegel, G. (1931), *The Phenomenology of Mind*, trans. J. Baillie, London: Allen & Unwin.

Heilman, S. and Friedman, M. (2010), *The Rebbe: The Life and Afterlife of Menachem Mendel Schneerson*, Princeton, NJ: Princeton University Press.

Hertzberg, A. (1968), *The French Enlightenment and the Jews*, New York, NY: Columbia University Press.

Holquist, M. (1990), *Dialogism: Bakhtin and his World*, London: Routledge.

Humboldt, W., Buck, G. C. and Raven, F. A. (1971), *Linguistic Variability and Intellectual Development*, Coral Gables, FL: University of Miami Press.

Husik, I. (1966), *A History of Medieval Jewish Philosophy*, New York, NY: Harper & Row.

Hutton, S. (1999), 'Henry More, Anne Conway and the Kabbalah: A Cure for the Kabbalist Nightmare?' in A. P. Coudert, S. Hutton, R. H. Popkin and G. M. Weiner (eds), *Judaeo-Christian Intellectual Culture in the Seventeenth Century*, 27–42, Dordrecht: Kluwer.

Ibn Aderet, S. (1657), *Teshuvot ha-Rashba*, Livorno: Yedidyah Kaf Nahat.

Idel, M. (1988), *Kabbalah: New Perspectives*, New Haven, CT: Yale University Press.

Idel, M. (1998), 'Abulafia's Secrets of the Guide: A Linguistic Turn', *Revue De Metaphysique et De Morale*, 4 (Octobre–Decembre): 495–528.

Idel, M. (2019), *The Privileged Divine Feminine in Kabbalah*, Berlin: De Gruyter.

Isou, I. (1947), *Introduction à une Nouvelle Poésie et une Nouvelle Musique*, Paris: Gallimard.

Jackson, F. and Smith, M., eds. (2008), *The Oxford Handbook of Contemporary Philosophy*, Oxford: Oxford University Press.

Jacobs, L. (2006), *Seeker of Unity*, London: Vallentine Mitchell.

Jacobson, I. (1996), *Zikaron le-Beit Yisrael*, ed. S. D. Levine, Brooklyn, NY: Kehot Publication Society.

Johnson, M. (1987), *The Body in the Mind*, Chicago, IL: University of Chicago Press.

Kahn, Y. and Lipskier, S. D., eds. (1975), *Sefer ha-Erkhin v. 3*, Brooklyn, NY: Kehot Publication Society.

Kahn, Y. and Lipskier, S. D., eds. (1976), *Sefer ha-Erkhin v. 4*, Brooklyn, NY: Kehot Publication Society.

Kant, I. (1998), *Religion Within the Boundaries of Mere Reason,* trans. A. Wood and G. Di Giovanni, Cambridge: Cambridge University Press.

Katz, C. E. (2003), *Levinas, Judaism, and the Feminine: The Silent Footsteps of Rebecca*, Bloomington, IN: Indiana University Press.

Katz, J. (1986), 'Orthodoxy in Historical Perspective', in P. Y. Meddling (ed.), *Studies in Contemporary Jewry II*, 3–17, Bloomington, IN: Indiana University Press.

Katz, M. (2011), 'A Rabbi, a Priest, and a Psychoanalyst: Religion in the Early Psychoanalytic Case History', *Contemporary Jewry*, 31 (1): 3–24.

Katz, S. (1995), 'The Epistemology of the Kabbalah: Toward a Jewish Philosophy of Rhetoric', *Rhetoric Society Quarterly*, 25 (1–4): 107–22.

Kellner, M. (1986), *Dogma in Medieval Jewish Thought: From Maimonides to Abravanel*, Oxford: Oxford University Press.

Kellner, M. (1987), 'Is Contemporary Jewish Philosophy Possible? – No', in N. Samuelson (ed.), *Studies in Jewish Philosophy*, 17–28, Lanham, MD: University Press of America.

Koch, K. (2006), *Franz Joseph Molitor und die Jüdische Tradition: Studien zu den Kabbalistischen Quellen der "Philosophie der Geschichte"*, Berlin: De Gruyter.

Kristeva, J. (1975), 'D'une identité l'autre: Le suject du langage poétique', *Tel Quel*, 62: 10–27.

Kristeva, J. (1977), *Polylogue*, Paris: Èditions du Seuil.

Kristeva, J. (1980), *Desire in Language: A Semiotic Approach to Literature and Art*, ed. L. S. Roudiez, New York, NY: Columbia University Press.

Kristeva, J. (1984), *Revolution in Poetic Language*, trans. M. Waller, New York, NY: Columbia University Press.

Kristeva, J. (1986), *The Kristeva Reader*, ed. T. Moi, New York, NY: Columbia University Press.

Lakoff, G. and Johnson, M. (1980), *Metaphors We Live By*, Chicago, IL: University of Chicago Press.

Lakoff, G. and Johnson, M. (1999), *Philosophy in the Flesh: The Embodied Mind and Its Challenge to Western Thought*, New York, NY: Basic Books.

Larson, G. J. and Deutsch, E., eds. (1988), *Interpreting Across Boundaries: New Essays in Comparative Philosophy*, Princeton, NJ: Princeton University Press.

Last-Stone, S. (1996), 'Justice, Mercy, and Gender in Rabbinic Thought', *Cardozo Studies in Law and Literature*, 8 (1): 139–77.

Leaman, O. and Nyman, C. (1998), 'Anti-Semitism', in *The Routledge Encyclopedia of Philosophy* v. 1, 311–4, London: Routledge.

Lechte, J. (1990), *Julia Kristeva*, London: Routledge.

Leigh, R. (2021), 'Hasidic Thought and Tsimtsum's Linguistic Turn', in A. Bielik- Robson and D. H. Weiss (eds), *Tsimtsum and Modernity: Lurianic Heritage in Modern Philosophy and Theology*, 83–103, Berlin: De Gruyter.

Levinas, E. (2006), *Entre Nous: Thinking-of-the-other*, trans. M. B. Smith and B. Harshav, London: Continuum.

Levinas, E. (2007), *Beyond the Verse: Talmudic Readings and Lectures*, trans. G. D. Mole, London: Continuum.

Levinas, E. (2008a), *Totality and Infinity: An Essay on Exteriority,* trans. A. Lingis, Pittsburgh, PA: Duquesne University Press.

Levinas, E. (2008b), *Otherwise than Being: Or Beyond Essence,* trans. A. Lingis, Pittsburgh, PA: Duquesne University Press.

Levine, L. I. (1998), *Judaism & Hellenism in Antiquity: Conflict or Confluence*, Seattle, WA: University of Washington Press.

Levine, S. D. (2001), *Lubavitch*, Brooklyn, NY: Chabad-Lubavitch Central Library.

Levine, S. D. (2010), 'Admur ha-Rashab al ha-Bikur Etsel Freud'. Available online: http://col.org.il/show_news.rtx?artID=55582 (accessed 3 February 2017).

Levine, S. W. (2004), *Mystics, Mavericks, and Merrymakers: An Intimate Journey among Hasidic Girls*, New York, NY: NYU Press.

Levy, G. (2011), 'Rabbinic Language from an Integrationist Perspective', *Language Sciences*, 33 (4): 695–707.

Lieberman, H. (1980), *Ohel Rahel* v. 2, Brooklyn, NY: Empire Press.

Liebes, Y. (2000), 'Midotav shel ha-Elohim', *Tarbiz*, 70 (1): 51–74.

Lloyd, G. E. R. (1966), *Polarity and Analogy: Two Types of Argumentation in Early Greek Thought*, Cambridge: Cambridge University Press.

Lloyd, G. (1984), *The Man of Reason: 'Male' and 'Female' in Western Philosophy*, Minneapolis, MN: University of Minnesota Press.

Lodge, D. (1985), 'Deconstruction for the Masses'. Available online: https://www.nytimes.com/1985/05/12/books/deconstruction-for-the-masses.html (accessed 25 October 2018).

Loewenthal, N. (1990), *Communicating the Infinite: The Emergence of the Habad School*, Chicago, IL: University of Chicago Press.

Loewenthal, N. (2000), '"Daughter/Wife of Hasid" – Or: "Hasidic Woman"?', *Jewish Studies*, 40: 21–8.

Loewenthal, N. (2013), 'Midrash in Habad Hasidism', in M. Fishbane and J. Weinberg (eds), *Midrash Unbound: Transformations and Innovations*, 439–56, London: The Littman Library of Jewish Civilization.

Mahmood, S. (2012), *Politics of Piety: The Islamic Revival and the Feminist Subject*, Princeton, NJ: Princeton University Press.

Mannheim, K. (1971), *Karl Mannheim*, New York, NY: Oxford University Press.

Marmorstein, A. (1927), *The Old Rabbinic Doctrine of God*, London: Oxford University Press.

Marmorstein, A. (1932), 'Philo and the Names of God', *Jewish Quarterly Review*, 22: 295–306.

Mazzeo, J. (1962), 'St. Augustine's Rhetoric of Silence', *Journal of The History of Ideas*, 23 (2): 175–96.

Meir, J. and Sagiv, G., eds. (2016), *Ḥabad: Historyah, Hagut ye-Dimui*, Jerusalem: Zalman Shazar Press.

Mendes-Flohr, P. R. and Reinharz, J., eds. (1995), *The Jew in the Modern World: A Documentary History*, New York, NY: Oxford University Press.

Meskin, J. (2000), 'Toward a New Understanding of the Work of Emmanuel Levinas', *Modern Judaism*, 20 (1): 78–102.

Meskin, J. (2007), 'The Role of Lurianic Kabbalah in the Early Philosophy of Emmanuel Levinas', *Levinas Studies*, 2: 49–77.

Meyer, M. (1967), *The Origins of the Modern Jew: Jewish Identity and European Culture in Germany 1749–1824*, Detroit, MI: Wayne State University Press.

Mindel, N. (1973), *The Philosophy of Chabad*, Brooklyn, NY: Kehot Publication Society.

Molitor, F. (1834), *Philosophie der Geschichte oder über die Tradition*, Münster: Theissing.

Mondshine, Y., ed. (1987), *Kerem Habad 3*, Kfar Habad: Makhon Oholei Shem-Lubavitch.

Mopsik, C. (1991), 'La Pensée d'Emmanuel Levinas et la Cabale', in C. Chalier and M. Abensour (eds), *Emmanuel Levinas: Ce Cahier de l'herne*, 428–41, Paris: Editions de l'Herne.

Morgan, M. (2007), *Discovering Levinas*, Cambridge: Cambridge University Press.

Morgan, M. and Gordon, P., eds. (2007), *The Cambridge Companion to Modern Jewish Philosophy*, Cambridge: Cambridge University Press.

Morris, B. J. (1998), *Lubavitcher Women in America: Identity and Activism in the Postwar Era*, Albany, NY: SUNY Press.

Nadler, A. (2007), 'The Rambam Revival in Early Modern Jewish Thought: Maskilim, Mithnagdim, and Hasidim on Maimonides Guide of the Perplexed', in J. M. Harris (ed.), *Maimonides After 800 Years: Essays on Maimonides and His Influence*, 231–56, Cambridge, MA: Harvard University Press.

Naeh, S. (1997), 'Poterion en cheiri kyriou: Philo and the Rabbis on the Powers of God and the Mixture in the Cup', *Scripta Classica Israelica*, 16: 91–101.

Niehoff, M. (1995), 'What's in a Name? Philo's Mystical Philosophy of Language', *Jewish Studies Quarterly*, 2 (3): 220–52.

Ochs, P. (1985), 'Torah, Language and Philosophy: A Jewish Critique', *International Journal of Philosophical Religion*, 18 (3): 115–22.

Oetinger, F. (1979), *Theologia ex Idea Vitae Deducta*, ed. K. Ohly, Berlin: De Gruyter.

Ofrat, G. (2001), *The Jewish Derrida*, Syracuse, NY: Syracuse University Press.

Oliver, K. (1988), 'The Maternal Operation: Circumscribing the Alliance', in E. K. Feder, M. C. Rawlinson, and E. Zakin (eds), *Derrida and Feminism: Recasting the Question of Woman*, 53–68, London: Routledge.

Oliver, K., ed. (1993), *Ethics, Politics, and Difference in Julia Kristeva's Writing*, London: Routledge.

Olson, C. (2002), *Indian Philosophers and Postmodern Thinkers: Dialogues on the Margins of Culture*, Oxford: Oxford University Press.

Outlaw, L. T. (2007), 'What is Africana Philosophy?', in G. Yancy (ed.), *Philosophy in Multiple Voices*, 109–44, Lanham, MD: Rowman & Littlefield Publishers.

Paltiel Y. Y. (2010), 'Classes on Ranat'. Available online: http://insidechassidus.org/media/Classes/MM/Ranat/RN%2005b.mp3 (accessed 4 August 2016).

Perlow, H. (1992), *Likutei Sippurim*, Brooklyn, NY.

Perpich, D. (2001), 'From the Caress to the Word: Transcendence and the Feminine in the Philosophy of Emmanuel Levinas', in T. Chanter (ed.), *Feminist Interpretations of Emmanuel Levinas*, 28–52, University Park, PA: Pennsylvania State University Press.

Philip, F., ed. (2014), *Philosophical Works of Etienne Bonnot, Abbe De Condillac*, Hoboken, NY: Taylor and Francis.

Philo (1930), *Philo v. 3*, trans. F. H. Colson and G. H. Whitaker, Cambridge, MA: Harvard University Press.

Pickstock, C. (1998), *After Writing: On the Liturgical Consummation of Philosophy*, Oxford: Blackwell Publishers.

Pickstock, C. (2011), 'The Late Arrival of Language: Word, Nature and the Divine in Plato's Cratylus', *Modern Theology*, 27 (2): 238–62.

Plato (1953), *The Dialogues of Plato v. 3*, trans. B. Jowett, Oxford: Clarendon Press.

Plato (1997), *Plato: Complete Works*, ed. J. M. Cooper, Indianapolis, IN: Hackett Publishing Company.

Purcell, M. (2006), *Levinas and Theology*, Cambridge: Cambridge University Press.

Rapoport, A. (1988), 'Hagiography with Footnotes: Edifying Tales and the Writing of History in Hasidism', *History and Theory*, 27 (4): 119–59.

Ravitzky, A. (2007), 'Dimensions and Varieties of Orthodox Judaism', in A. Gotzmann and C. Wiese (eds), *Modern Judaism and Historical Consciousness: Identities, Encounters, Perspectives*, 391–416, Leiden: Brill.

Reddy, M. J. (1979), 'The Conduit Metaphor: A Case of Frame Conflict in Our Language about Language', in A. Ortony (ed.), *Metaphor and Thought*, 284–97, Cambridge: Cambridge University Press.

Rickert, T. (2007), 'Toward the Chōra: Kristeva, Derrida, and Ulmer on Emplaced Invention', *Philosophy & Rhetoric*, 40 (3): 251–73.

Rorty, R. (1992), *The Linguistic Turn*, Chicago, IL: University of Chicago Press.

Rosati, M. and Stoeckl, K., eds. (2012), *Multiple Modernities and Postsecular Societies*, Farnham: Ashgate.

Rosato, J. (2012), 'Woman as Vulnerable Self: The Trope of Maternity in Levinas's Otherwise than Being', *Hypatia*, 27 (2): 348–65.

Rotenstreich, N. (1963), *The Recurring Pattern: Studies in Anti-Judaism in Modern Thought*, London: Weidenfeld & Nicolson.

Roth, A. (2013), 'Reshimu: Mahloket Hasidut Lubavitch ve-Kopoust', *Kabbalah*, 30: 221–52.

Rötzer, F. (1995), *Conversations with French Philosophers*, trans. G. E. Aylesworth, Atlantic Heights, NJ: Humanities Press.

Rousseau, J. (1998), *Essay on the Origin of Languages and Writings Related to Music*, ed. J. Scott, Hanover, NH: University Press of New England.

Rubin, E. (2015), 'Intimacy in the Place of Otherness: How Rationalism and Mysticism Collaboratively Communicate the Midrashic Core of Cosmic Purpose'. Available online: http://www.chabad.org/2893106 (accessed 17 May 2015).

Sagi, A. (2006), 'Orthodoxy as a Problem', in S. Salmon, A. Ravitzky and A. S. Ferziger (eds), *Orthodox Judaism: New Perspectives*, 21–54, Jerusalem: The Hebrew University Magnes Press.

Satlow, M. (1996), '"Texts of Terror": Rabbinic Texts, Speech Acts, and the Control of Mores', *AJS Review*, 21 (2): 273–98.

Saussure, F. (2013), *Course in General Linguistics*, trans. R. Harris, London: Bloomsbury.

Schatz-Uffenheimer, R. (1993), *Hasidism as Mysticism: Quietistic Elements in Eighteenth-Century Hasidic Thought*, Princeton, NJ: Princeton University Press.

Schleiermacher, F. (1996), *On Religion: Speeches to Its Cultured Despisers*, ed. R. Crouter, Cambridge: Cambridge University Press.

Schneersohn, M. M. (1968), *Ohr ha-Torah Shemot* v. 6, Brooklyn, NY: Kehot Publication Society.

Schneersohn, M. M. (1975), *Ohr ha-Torah Shir ha-Shirim* v. 2, Brooklyn, NY: Kehot Publication Society.

Schneersohn, M. M. (1977), *Ohr ha-Torah Devarim* v. 5, Brooklyn, NY: Kehot Publication Society.

Schneersohn, M. M. (1985), *Ohr ha-Torah Devarim* v. 6, Brooklyn, NY: Kehot Publication Society.

Schneersohn, M. M. (1989), *Kitsurim ve-Ha'arot le-Sefer Likutei Amarim*, Brooklyn, NY: Kehot Publication Society.

Schneersohn, S. (1988), *Sefer ha-Ma'amarim 5634* [1873–4], Brooklyn, NY: Kehot Publication Society.

Schneersohn, S. (2000), *Sefer ha-Ma'amarim 5627* [1866–7], Brooklyn, NY: Kehot Publication Society.

Schneersohn, S. (2004), *Sefer ha-Ma'amarim 5631* v. 1 [1870–1], Brooklyn, NY: Kehot Publication Society.

Schneersohn, S. B. (1978), *Samah Tesamah 5657* [1897], Brooklyn, NY: Kehot Publication Society.

Schneersohn, S. B. (1980), *Hagahot le-Dibbur ha-Mathil Patah Eliyahu 5658* [1898], Brooklyn, NY: Kehot Publication Society.

Schneersohn, S. B. (1984a), *Sefer ha-Ma'amarim 5658* [1897–8], Brooklyn, NY: Kehot Publication Society.

Schneersohn, S. B. (1984b), *Sefer ha-Ma'amarim 5678* [1917–18], Brooklyn, NY: Kehot Publication Society.

Schneersohn, S. B. (1986a), *Sefer ha-Ma'amarim 5646–50* [1885–90], Brooklyn, NY: Kehot Publication Society.

Schneersohn, S. B. (1986b), *Igrot Kodesh* v. 3, Brooklyn, NY: Kehot Publication Society.

Schneersohn, S. B. (1987), *Sefer ha-Ma'amarim 5652–5653* [1891–3], Brooklyn, NY: Kehot Publication Society.

Schneersohn, S. B. (1988), *Sefer ha-Ma'amarim 5679* [1918–19], Brooklyn, NY: Kehot Publication Society.

Schneersohn, S. B. (1989), *Sefer ha-Maamarim 5668* [1907–8], Brooklyn, NY: Kehot Publication Society.

Schneersohn, S. B. (1991), *be-Shaah she-Hikdimu 5672* v. 1–3 [1912–16], Brooklyn, NY: Kehot Publication Society.

Schneersohn, S. B. (1992), *Sefer ha-Maamarim Likut 2*, Brooklyn, NY: Kehot Publication Society.

Schneersohn, S. B. (1993), *Sefer ha-Maamarim 5664* [1903–4], Brooklyn, NY: Kehot Publication Society.

Schneersohn, S. B. (1998), *Sefer ha-Maamarim 5670* [1909–10], Brooklyn, NY: Kehot Publication Society.

Schneersohn, S. B. (2000a), *Hanokh le-Naar*, Brooklyn, NY: Kehot Publication Society.

Schneersohn, S. B (2000b), *Yom Tov Shel Rosh Hashanah 5659* [1898], trans. Y. Marcus, Brooklyn, NY: Kehot Publication Society.

Schneersohn, S. B. (2003a), *Forces in Creation*, trans. M. Miller, Brooklyn, NY: Kehot Publication Society.

Schneersohn, S. B. (2003b), *Sefer ha-Sihot: Torat Shalom*, Brooklyn, NY: Kehot Publication Society.

Schneersohn, S. B. (2005), *The Power of Return,* trans. Y. Danzinger, A. Vaisfiche and A. Sollish, Brooklyn, NY: Kehot Publication Society.

Schneersohn, S. B. (2010), *Yom Tov Shel Rosh Hashanah 5666* [1906–8], Brooklyn, NY: Kehot Publication Society.

Schneersohn, S. B. (2011), *Sefer ha-Ma'amarim 5659* [1898–9], Brooklyn, NY: Kehot Publication Society.

Schneersohn, S. B. (2013), *Torat Shalom: Sha'alot u-Teshuvot*, Brooklyn, NY: Kehot Publication Society.

Schneersohn, S. Z. A. (2008), *va-Yisharnah ha-Parot*, Brooklyn, NY: Kehot Publication Society.

Schneersohn, Y. Y. (1982), *Igrot Kodesh* v. 1, Brooklyn, NY: Kehot Publication Society.

Schneersohn, Y. Y. (1985), *Igrot Kodesh* v. 3, Brooklyn, NY: Kehot Publication Society.

Schneersohn, Y. Y. (1986a), *Sefer ha-Maamarim 5687–8* [1926–8], Brooklyn, NY: Kehot Publication Society.

Schneersohn, Y. Y. (1986b), *Sefer ha-Maʾamarim 5699–700* [1938–40], Brooklyn, NY: Kehot Publication Society.

Schneersohn, Y. Y. (1986c), *Sefer ha-Maʾamarim 5701–03* [1940–3], Brooklyn, NY: Kehot Publication Society.

Schneersohn, Y. Y. (1986d), *Sefer ha-Sihot 5700–02* [1939–42], Brooklyn, NY: Kehot Publication Society.

Schneersohn, Y. Y. (1992), *Likkutei Diburim* 1–4, Brooklyn, NY: Kehot Publication Society.

Schneersohn, Y. Y. (2004), *Sefer ha-Sihot 5620–7* [1920–7], Brooklyn, NY: Kehot Publication Society.

Schneerson, M. M. (1991), *Sefer ha-Maʾamarim Melukat* v. 2, Brooklyn, NY: Kehot Publication Society.

Schneerson, M. M. (1995), *ha-Yom Yom*, Brooklyn, NY: Kehot Publication Society.

Schneerson, M. M. (1997), *Sefer ha-Toldot Admur Maharash*, Brooklyn, NY: Kehot Publication Society.

Schneerson, M. M. (1998), *Likutei Sihot* v. 2, Brooklyn, NY: Kehot Publication Society.

Schneerson, M. M. (1999), *Likutei Sihot* v. 20, Brooklyn, NY: Kehot Publication Society.

Schneerson, M. M. (2000), *Likutei Sihot* v. 10, Brooklyn, NY: Kehot Publication Society.

Schneerson, M. M. (2003a), *Reshimot* 1–5, Brooklyn, NY: Kehot Publication Society.

Schneerson, M. M. (2003b), *On the Essence of Chassidus*, trans. Y. Greenberg and S. Handelman, Brooklyn, NY: Kehot Publication Society.

Schneerson, M. M. (2006), *Likkutei Sihot* v. 15, Brooklyn, NY: Kehot Publication Society.

Schneuri, D. B. (1991), *Maamarei Admur Hoemtzai - Kuntreisim*, Brooklyn, NY: Kehot Publication Society.

Schochet, I. (1995), *Chassidic Dimensions*, Brooklyn, NY: Kehot Publication Society.

Scholem, G. (1954), *Major Trends in Jewish Mysticism*, New York, NY: Schocken Books.

Scholem, G. (1972), 'The Name of God and the Linguistic Theory of the Kabbala: (Part 2)', *Diogenes*, 20 (80): 164–94.

Scholem, G. (1974), *The Messianic Idea in Judaism and Other Essays on Jewish Spirituality*, New York, NY: Schocken Books.

Scholem, G. and S. Pleasance (1972), 'The Name of God and the Linguistic Theory of the Kabbala', *Diogenes*, 20 (79): 59–80.

Schrift, A. (1995), *Nietzsche's French Legacy: A Genealogy of Poststructuralism*, New York, NY: Routledge.

Schulte, C. (1992), 'Zimzum in the Works of Schelling', *Iyyun*, 41: 21–40.

Schulte, C. (2014), *Zimzum: Gott und Weltursprung*, Berlin: Judischer Verlag im Suhrkamp Verlag.

Schwartz, D. (2010), *Mahshevet Habad: mi-Reishit ad Aharit*, Ramat Gan: Bar Ilan University Press.

Schwarzschild, S. (1985), 'An Introduction to the Thought of R. Isaac Hutner', *Modern Judaism* 5 (3): 235–77.

Schwarzschild, S. (1987), 'An Agenda for Jewish Philosophy in the 1980s', in N. Samuelson (ed.), *Studies in Jewish Philosophy*, 101–25, Lanham, MD: University Press of America.

Seeskin, K. (1990), *Jewish Philosophy in a Secular Age*, Albany, NY: SUNY Press.

Seidler, M., ed. (2013), *Rabbinic Theology and Jewish Intellectual History: The Great Rabbi Loew of Prague*, London: Routledge.

Sefer Yetzirah (1965), Jerusalem: Levin Epstein.

Shneur Zalman of Liady (1958), *Ma'amarei Admur ha-Zaken: Ithalekh Liozna*, Brooklyn, NY: Kehot Publication Society.

Shneur Zalman of Liady (1975), *Ma'amarei Admur ha-Zaken 5562* v. 1. [1801–2], Brooklyn, NY: Kehot Publication Society.

Shneur Zalman of Liady (1978), *Likutei Amarim Tanya*, Brooklyn, NY: Kehot Publication Society.

Shneur Zalman of Liady (1987*), Igrot Kodesh Admur ha-Zaken, Admur ha-Emotzai, Admur ha-Tsemah Tsedek*, Brooklyn, NY: Kehot Publication Society.

Shneur Zalman of Liady (1998), *Likutei Amarim Tanya: Bi-Lingual Edition*, trans. N. Mindel, N. Mangel, Z. Posner and J. I. Schochet, Brooklyn, NY: Kehot Publication Society.

Shneur Zalman of Liady (2001), *Torah Ohr*, Brooklyn, NY: Kehot
Publication Society.

Shneur Zalman of Liady (2002a), *Likutei Torah*, Brooklyn, NY: Kehot
Publication Society.

Shneur Zalman of Liady (2002b), *Shulhan Arukh* v. 2, Brooklyn, NY: Kehot
Publication Society.

Shneur Zalman of Liady (2005), *Shulhan Arukh* v. 5, Brooklyn, NY: Kehot
Publication Society.

Shneur Zalman of Liady (2006), *Ma'amarei Admur ha-Zaken 5572* [1811–
12], Brooklyn, NY: Kehot Publication Society.

Shneuri, D. (1989), *Ma'amarei Admur ha-Emtsai Shemot* v. 2, Brooklyn, NY:
Kehot Publication Society.

Shneuri, D. (2006), *Tract on Ecstasy*, trans. L. Jacobs, London: Vallentine
Mitchell.

Sikka, S. (2001), 'The Delightful Other: Portraits of the Feminine in
Kierkegaard, Nietzsche, and Levinas', in T. Chanter (ed.), *Feminist
Interpretations of Emmanuel Levinas*, 96–118, University Park, PA:
Pennsylvania State University Press.

Silber, M. (1992), 'The Emergence of Ultra-Orthodoxy: The Invention
of a Tradition', in J. Wertheimer (ed.), *The Uses of Tradition*, 23–82,
Cambridge, MA: Harvard University Press.

Silver, D. J. (1965), *Maimonidean Criticism and the Maimonidean
Controversy 1180–1240*, Leiden: Brill.

Smelik, W. (2013), *Rabbis, Language and Translation in Late Antiquity*,
Cambridge: Cambridge University Press.

Smith, D. (1998), 'Philosopher Gamely in Defense of His Ideas?' Available
online: https://www.nytimes.com/1998/05/30/arts/philosopher-gamely
-in-defense-of-his-ideas.html (accessed 25 October 2018).

Spinoza, B. (2007), *Theological-Political Treatise*, ed. J. Israel, Cambridge:
Cambridge University Press.

Sprinker, M., ed. (1999), *Ghostly Demarcations: A Symposium on Jacques
Derrida's Specters of Marx*, London: Verso.

Srajek, M. C. (1998), *In the Margins of Deconstruction: Jewish Conceptions
of Ethics in Emmanuel Levinas and Jacques Derrida*, Dordrecht: Kluwer
Academic.

Stahmer, H. (1968), *'Speak That I May See Thee'!*, New York, NY: Macmillan.

Stanford, S. (2000), *The Metaphysics of Love: Gender and Transcendence in Levinas*, London: Bloomsbury.

Steinsaltz, A. (1988), *The Long Shorter Way: Discourses on Chasidic Thought*, Northvale, NJ: Aronson Press.

Steinsaltz, A. (2016), *The Sustaining Utterance: Discourses on Chasidic Thought*, New Milford, CT: Maggid Books.

Stern, D. (1981), 'Rhetoric and Midrash: The Case of the Mashal', *Prooftexts*, 1: 261–91.

Stiver, D. (1996), *The Philosophy of Religious Language*, Cambridge, MA: Blackwell Publishers.

Taylor, C. (2011), 'Understanding the Other: A Gadamerian View on Conceptual Schemes', in C. Taylor, *Dilemmas and Connections: Selected Essays*, 24–38, Cambridge, MA: Harvard University Press.

Taylor, M. C. (1993), *Nots*, Chicago, IL: University of Chicago Press.

Telushkin, J. (2014), *Rebbe: The Life and Teachings of Menachem M. Schneerson, The Most Influential Rabbi in Modern History*, New York, NY: Harper Wave.

Tirosh-Samuelson, H. (2003), 'Philosophy and Kabbalah: 1200–1600', in D. H. Frank and O. Leaman (eds), *The Cambridge Companion to Medieval Jewish Philosophy*, 218–57, Cambridge: Cambridge University Press.

Tuana, N. (2007), 'What is Feminist Philosophy?', in G. Yancy (ed.), *Philosophy in Multiple Voices*, 21–48, Lanham, MD: Rowman & Littlefield Publishers.

Ushpal, I. B. (1975), *Likut Darkhei Hesed*, Brooklyn, NY: Chevra Kadisha of Aguch.

Walton, D. (2012), *Doing Cultural Theory*, London: SAGE Publications.

Weber, M. (1964), *The Theory of Social and Economic Organization*, trans. A. M. Henderson and T. Parsons, New York, NY: Free Press.

Weiss, D. H. (2013), 'Embodied Cognition in Classical Rabbinic Literature', *Zygon: Journal of Religion and Science*, 48 (3): 788–807.

Weiss, J. G. (1985), 'Contemplative Mysticism and "Faith" in Hasidic Piety', in J. G. Weiss, *Studies in East European Jewish Mysticism and Hasidism*, 43–55, Oxford: Oxford University Press.

Wittrock, B. (2000), 'Modernity: One, None, or Many?: European Origins and Modernity as a Global Condition', *Daedalus*, 129 (1): 31–60.

Wolfson, E. R. (1995), *Circle in the Square: Studies in the Use of Gender in Kabbalistic Symbolism*, Albany, NY: SUNY Press.

Wolfson, E. R. (2000), *Abraham Abulafia – Kabbalist and Prophet: Hermeneutics, Theosophy and Theurgy*, Los Angeles, CA: Cherub Press.

Wolfson, E. R. (2002), 'Assaulting the Border: Kabbalistic Traces in the Margins of Derrida', *Journal of the American Academy of Religion*, 70 (3): 475–514.

Wolfson, E. R. (2006), 'Secrecy, Modesty, and the Feminine: Kabbalistic Traces in the Thought of Levinas', *Journal of Jewish Thought and Philosophy*, 14 (1–2): 193–224.

Wolfson, E. R. (2009a), *Language, Eros, Being: Kabbalistic Hermeneutics and Poetic Imagination*, New York, NY: Fordham University Press.

Wolfson, E. R. (2009b), *Open Secret: Postmessianic Messianism and the Mystical Revision of Menaḥem Mendel Schneerson*, New York, NY: Columbia University Press.

Wolfson, E. R. (2013), 'Nequddat ha-Reshimu – The Trace of Transcendence and the Transcendence of the Trace', *Kabbalah: Journal for the Study of Jewish Mystical Texts*, 30: 75–120.

Wolfson, E. R. (2014), *Giving Beyond the Gift: Apophasis and Overcoming Theomania*, New York, NY: Fordham University Press.

Wolfson, E. R. (2016), 'Achronic Time, Messianic Expectation, and the Secret of the Leap in Habad', in J. Meir and G Sagiv (eds), *Habad Hasidism: History, Theology and Image*, 45–89, Jerusalem: Zalman Shazar Press.

Wolfson, E. R. (2021), 'Tsimtsum, Lichtung, and the Leap of Bestowing Refusal: Kabbalistic and Heideggerian Metaontology in Dialogue', in A. Bielik- Robson and D. H. Weiss (eds), *Tsimtsum and Modernity: Lurianic Heritage in Modern Philosophy and Theology*, 141–89, Berlin: De Gruyter.

Wyschogrod, E. (1989), 'Interview with Emmanuel Levinas: December 31, 1982', *Philosophy and Theology*, 4 (2): 105–18.

Yancy, G., ed. (2007), *Philosophy in Multiple Voices*, Lanham, MD: Rowman & Littlefield Publishers.

Yu, J. and Bunnin, N. (2001), 'Saving the Phenomena: An Aristotelian Method in Comparative Philosophy', in B. Mou (ed.), *Two Roads to Wisdom? Chinese and Analytic Philosophical Traditions*, 293–312, La Salle, IL: Open Court.

Zank, M. (2000), *The Idea of Atonement in the Philosophy of Hermann Cohen*, Providence, RI: Brown Judaic Studies.

Zevin, S. Y. (1997), 'Hokhmot Hitsoniyot', in S. Y. Zevin (ed.), *Encyclopedia Talmudit* v. 15, 55–80, Jerusalem: Talmudic Encyclopedia Publications.

Index

Page numbers followed with "n" refer to footnotes.

Abulafia, Abraham 29
Alter, Robert 62
Aristotle 26, 73, 74, 121–3, 206
atheism 180
atsmut (essence of God) 79,
    81, 86, 87, 97, 143–4,
    166–8, 171, 175–7, 187,
    192–3, 201–2
   letters of 97, 176–7
avodah (service) 157

Bakhtin, Mikhail 17
binah (understanding) 116–17,
    145, 185–6
Boyarin, Daniel 62, 123
Buber, Martin 13, 21

Chein, Avraham Yehudah x
chōra 135
Cohen, Hermann 11, 19
comparative philosophy 10–14,
    208
Connell, Sophia M. 123
consciousness 3, 6, 9, 50, 51, 55,
    78, 81, 82, 90–1, 93–6,
    106–10, 200, 201
   emotional 83, 84, 87, 107,
     169, 170, 172
   intellectual 51, 55, 87, 107,
     169, 170, 172
   speech and 78–9, 83, 84,
     86, 94, 170
creation 60–1, 63–6, 148–50, 158,
    163, 172–4, 182–4, 186,
    189, 191, 197

da'at (knowledge) 145, 146, 185
deconstruction 5–6, 87–9, 94, 98,
    107, 131, 132
delineation of philosophy 26
Derrida, Jacques 1, 5–6, 8, 12,
    15, 18, 21, 53, 87–91,
    95, 96, 98, 100–3, 107,
    130–4, 140–2,
    177–82, 207–9
   critique of gender identities 132
   deconstruction 5–6, 87–9, 94,
    98, 107, 131, 132
   Dissemination 178, 181
   double gesture 89–91,
    95, 102, 209
   logocentrism 89, 131
   material-physical speech 93
   messianicity 181–2
   notion of writing 89–91, 93–5,
    97–8, 101–2
   phallogocentrism 6, 130–2
   primordial nonpresence 96
   proto-writing 97, 98
   reactionary feminism 131
   revelation and revealability
    181
   sexual difference 130–3
   speech 87, 91–4
   trace 96–7, 102
   transparency of speech 92, 93
   tsimtsum 178–9
Dissemination (Derrida) 178, 181
divine sovereignty 167
double gesture of Derrida 89–91,
    95, 102, 209

Eisenstadt, Shmuel Noah 24–5
Elior, Rachel 32–3
emotional consciousness 83, 84, 87,
    107, 169, 170, 172
emotional traits 145–6
epistemological pluralism 155
erotic encounter 118, 120, 126,
    138
  patriarchal supremacy in 129
eser sephirot (ten attributes) 145
evil 184–6
exclusion of Jews and Jewish
    thought 7–8, 18–36
existence, substance and
    materiality of 197–8

female role in reproduction 119–26
feminine 126–8
femininity 126, 134
finiteness 97, 144–6. *See also*
    infiniteness
Freud, Sigmund 15, 43, 45–7, 49

Gadamer, Hans-Georg 18, 74
garments of soul (*levushim*) 66–7
Garver, Newton 73
gender
  differences 121–4, 134
  kabbalistic thought of 124–5
  language and 133–4,
    137, 139, 140
Greek culture and philosophy 27

Habad viii, ix, x, xiii, 2, 2 n.4, 7 n.9,
    9, 12, 14–16, 31–6, 38–41,
    42 n.14, 45, 47, 64, 65 n.23,
    83, 117, 117 n.14, 125, 140,
    142–3, 146, 148, 151, 153,
    155, 157, 159, 160, 165–7,
    170, 189, 196
Hallamish, Moshe 33–4
Hamann, Johann Georg 73
Handelman, Susan 14–15, 141
Hareidi communities 153

hasidism ix, 7 n.9, 29 n.68,
    30–3, 37–41, 43, 43 n.20,
    45–8, 56–7, 174
hasidut 34nn91, 39, 157
haskalah 157
Hegel's Judaism 19
hemshekh 41, 48, 56 n.46, 180
hokhmah (wisdom) 67 n.31, 70,
    117, 148, 185
  sephirah of 145, 146, 149, 185
Husserl, Edmund 21, 104–6,
    108, 135

Idel, Moshe 30
immanence 25–6
infiniteness 143–6, 144 n.10,
    168, 174–7
intellectual consciousness 51,
    55, 83, 84, 87, 107,
    169, 170, 172
Israel and Torah 152–3

Jacobs, Louis 15
Jewish
  mysticism 16, 30, 32, 141–2,
    178, 182
  philosophy exclusion 18–36
  rationalist philosophy 28–9
Jews, discrimination against 21
Judaism 11, 19, 22–3, 26, 30,
    41, 123, 154
Judeo-Christian tradition 11
justice 60–1, 63, 65, 154–60, 163–4,
    173–4, 182, 184–6, 188–93,
    201–3. *See also* mercy

kabbalah 12, 16, 26, 28–32, 34, 34
    n.91, 38, 124, 140–1, 147,
    165, 173, 174, 178–80, 188,
    205–6. *See also tsimtsum*
  gender imagery of 124–5
  negative critiques 30
  texts 30–1
Kant's Judaism 19

khora   140, 178–9
Kristeva, Julia   1, 5, 6, 8, 12, 18,
        53, 103–10, 134–8, 140,
        199–200, 207, 209
    idea of a *chōra*   135
    motherhood and
        femininity   134–5
    paternal symbolic
        function   135–7
    poetic language   106, 108–10,
        136, 138, 200, 201
    semiotic functions of
        language   103–10,
        135, 199–200
    structural linguistics   104–5
    symbolic functions of
        language   103–10,
        135, 199–201

language
    critique   75
    and gender   133–4, 137, 139, 140
    onomatopoeic theory of   106
    ontological primacy
        of   70, 169, 176
    philosophy of   73, 75
    poetic   106, 108–10
    semiotic function   103–10,
        135, 176
    speech and   72–5, 176
    symbolic function
        of   103–10, 176
    of thought   92–3
Last-Stone, Suzanne   156
letters
    of *atsmut*   97, 176–7
    of *malkhut*   177, 183–4,
        188, 190, 191
    of speech   70, 76, 83, 86, 94, 96,
        101, 106, 169–72, 200, 209
    of the trace   87 n.98, 97
Levinas, Emmanuel   ix, 1, 5, 7, 8, 11,
        12, 15, 18, 21, 53, 76–80,
        102, 126–30, 134, 140, 141,
        173–7, 207–9

androcentric approach   126
    concept of saying and said   84–6
    feminine   126–8
    idea of infinity   76, 78–81,
        83, 174–5
    phenomenology of eros   128
    postmodern critique of
        oppositional binaries   76
    theory of speech   177
    tsimtsum   173–5, 177
Liebes, Yehudah   156
linguistic turn   68, 177
Lloyd, Genevieve   122
Loewenthal, Naftali   33
logocentrism   89, 131, 153–4
love of God   160–2
Luria, Isaac   166
Lurianic *kabbalah*   165
Lurianic *tsimtsum*   165, 166, 179

Mahmoud, Saba   35
Maimonides   33, 34, 39
male role in reproduction
        119, 125, 170
malkhut   52, 63–6, 63 n.16, 117,
        134, 148–52, 165 n.62,
        187–92, 194–8, 201, 202
    comparison with speech   64–5
    letters of   177, 183–4,
        188, 190, 191
    sephirah of   113, 118, 145, 146,
        149, 150, 192
Mannheim, Karl   23
mashal (the parable)   62
materiality   107
    of existence, substance
        and   94, 197–8
maternal body   133–5
maternity   120, 123, 126, 128,
        129, 133, 134
memale kol almin   193, 198–200
Mendelssohn, Moses   11
mercy   60–1, 63, 65, 154–6,
        163, 173, 183, 185–6,
        188–93, 201–3

messianicity 181–2, 195, 202, 203
midrash 38, 59–65, 60 n.5, 99, 117,
139, 154, 155, 157, 158,
162, 163, 166, 183 n.110,
185–90, 201, 202
midrashim 49–50, 63, 155
Mindel, Nissan 34
mitsvah 196, 202, 203
mitsvot 77, 130, 152, 154, 185, 196,
198, 202, 203
modernity/modernization 23–6
traditional Judaism of 24
motherhood 133–5
multiple modernities 24
mysticism
Habad 34, 140
Jewish 16, 30, 32, 141–2,
178, 182
kabbalistic 16

Narboni, Moses 29
Nothnagel, Hermann 45

ohr eyn sof (light of infinitude) 97,
143–4, 144 n.10, 146,
166–8, 170–2, 175, 180–4,
187–98, 201
onomatopoeic theory of
language 75 n.58, 106
ontological primacy
of language 70, 169, 176
of recipient 4, 52, 53, 99
oppositional binaries 3–4, 7,
8, 50–5, 88–9, 93, 98,
99, 201, 203
*Otherwise than Being: Or Beyond
Essence* (Levinas) 77, 79,
84–7, 128, 175, 177, 209
otiyot ha-reshimu 171, 172

paradox of creation 175
paternal role in reproduction 121
paternal symbolic function 135–7
patriarchal 120, 126, 127, 129
penitence 162

phallogocentrism 6, 130–2
phenomenology of eros 128
Philo 123, 155, 156, 156 n.32
Plato 20, 73, 74, 121, 122, 135,
206
Plutarch 156, 157
poetic language 106, 108–10, 136,
138, 200, 201
postmodernism 4, 53, 54
criticism of 5
pre-thetic letters of speech 106, 200
primordial nonpresence 95, 96
primordial trace 98–9, 101–2
proto-writing 97, 98

rabbinic thought 14–15, 17, 18
rationalist philosophy, Jewish 28–9
reactionary feminism 131
receptivity 51, 116, 117,
132, 137, 148
reproduction 114, 116–18,
122, 128
female roles in 119–26
male roles in 119, 125, 170
revealability 181
revelation 181
of *ohr eyn sof* 184
Rosenzweig, Franz 13, 14, 177

Sabbateanism 30
said concept 84–6, 175, 177
Saussure, Ferdinand de 68, 104
saying concept 5, 84–6, 175, 177
Schatz-Uffenheimer, Rivkah 32
Schleiermacher, Friedrich 14
Schneersohn, Shalom Ber 2
analysis of speech 66–71
body/soul relationship 71–2
childhood 37–8
and Derrida, Jacques 87–8
discourses of 1898 1, 5, 6, 9, 12,
13, 35–6, 45, 49, 58, 59
editing the draft of 56–8
oppositional binaries in 2–4,
7, 8, 50–5

erotic encounter of female
    118, 120, 129
family   37
female/mother roles in reproduc-
    tion   119–20, 126
Habad thought   39, 41
hemshekh   41, 48
idea of speech   66–72, 77–9,
    82–4, 87, 90–2, 94, 98,
    169, 175–7
language of thought   92–3
leadership of Habad-
    Lubavitch   40
letters of speech   70, 76,
    83, 86, 96, 106, 169–70,
    200
linguistic theory   175
male roles in
    reproduction   119–20
marriage   39
messianicity   181, 195
midrashim   49–50
modern philosophical
    thought   11–12
ohr eyn sof   180
overview of main themes   49–55
paralysis   44, 45
postmodernism   4–5, 53, 54
reproduction   116–18
sexual intercourse   114–15, 118
symbolic function of
    language   110
trace (*reshimu*)   97–8
tsimtsum   175–7, 180
verbal intercourse   114–15
Vienna medical trip
    of 1903   43–7
visit to Freud   43, 45–7, 49
Schneersohn, Shmuel   37–9,
    44, 56 n.46
Schneersohn, Shterna Sarah   39
Schneersohn, Yosef Yitshak   40,
    43 n.20, 45–6
Schneersohn, Zalman Aharon   39

Schneersohn, Menachem Mendel
    37–8, 57
Schneerson, Menachem Mendel
    2 n.4, 41 n.14, 58, 130 n.51
Scholem, Gershom   15, 28, 30–2
Schrift, Alan D.   88
sefirot   32
semen   114–20
semiotic functions of language
    103–10, 135, 199–200
sephirah   64
    of *hokhmah*   145, 185
    of *malkhut*   113, 118, 145–6,
        149, 150, 192
sephirot   52, 63–5, 65 n.23, 145, 146,
    146 n.13, 148–51, 165, 185
sephirotic female   124, 134
sexual difference   130–3
sexual intercourse   114,
    115, 117, 118
Shneur Zalman of Liady   ix, 32–4,
    125, 166–8
Sofer, Shmuel   58
Soloveitchik, Joseph   21
soul   50, 52, 55, 66, 67, 70
    and body   71–2
    garments (*levushim*) of   65 n.23,
        66–7
sovev kol almin   193, 198–201
speech   66–71, 77–8, 82–3, 87,
    90–2, 94, 95, 150, 169,
    175–7, 200, 201
    comparison with *malkhut*   64–5
    and consciousness   78–9, 83, 84,
        86, 94, 96, 170
    and language   72–5, 176
    letters of   70, 76, 83, 86, 94, 96,
        101, 106, 169–71
    transparency of   92, 93
    and women   2–4, 8–9, 50–5,
        109, 139, 153, 194, 195,
        201, 203, 207
Spinoza, Barukh   11, 22
structural linguistics   104–5

substance and materiality of
     existence   94, 197–8
symbolic functions of language
     103–10, 135, 199–201

Talmud   39, 117, 124
Tanya   7 n.9, 32, 34, 125
teshuvah (return/repentance)   157,
     160 n.51, 162–3, 183
theion   180
Theologico-Political Treatise
     (Spinoza)   22
Tomkhei Temimim   40, 41
     n.14, 42 n.14
Torah   52, 55, 118, 130, 140, 152–4,
     161, 185, 196, 198, 202, 203
Totality and Infinity (Levinas)   76–7,
     126, 128, 174–7, 209
trace (*reshimu*)   5, 16, 85, 90, 91,
     96–9, 101–2, 168, 171,
     172, 175–7
traditional Judaism,
     modernization of   22
transcendental ego   105–7
transcendental ideal   25–6

translation   13–14
tsimtsum   5, 30 n.73, 32, 97, 140,
     144–5, 165–8, 170–81,
     190, 191, 209

van Helmont, Francis Mercury   31
verbal intercourse   114

Weber, Max   23
Wittrock, Bjorn   23
Wolfson, Elliot   15–16, 124–5
women
     in reproduction   119–26
     speech and   2–4, 8, 9, 50–5,
          109, 139, 153, 194, 195,
          201, 203, 207
The World of Emanation (*olam ha-
     atsilut*)   148–50

Yancy, George   20
yeshivah (rabbinical school)   viii, ix,
     40–2, 42 n.14, 46, 48, 56, 56
     n.45, 57, 160 n.51

Zohar   63, 63 n.16, 151, 168